THE OXFORD Practical ATLAS

Acknowledgements

The publishers would like to thank the
Telegraph Colour Library
for permission to reproduce
the photograph on page 8.

Cover image:
Tom Van Sant / Geosphere Project, Santa Monica,
Science Photo Library.

The illustrations are by Chapman Bounford,
Hard Lines, and Gary Hinks.

The page design is by Adrian Smith.

Oil spillage data is from
*Oil Pollution Survey around the Coast
of the United Kingdom, 1995*
by kind permission of the publishers,
ACOPS (Advisory Committee on Protection of the Sea).

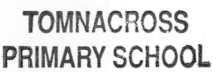

OXFORD
UNIVERSITY PRESS

Great Clarendon Street, Oxford OX2 6DP

Oxford University Press is a department of the University of Oxford.
It furthers the University's objective of excellence in research, scholarship,
and education by publishing worldwide in

Oxford New York

Auckland Bangkok Buenos Aires Cape Town Chennai
Dar es Salaam Delhi Hong Kong Istanbul Karachi Kolkata
Kuala Lumpur Madrid Melbourne Mexico City Mumbai Nairobi
São Paulo Shanghai Taipei Tokyo Toronto

Oxford is a registered trade mark of Oxford University Press
in the UK and in certain other countries

© Oxford University Press 2003

First published 2003

Reprinted with corrections 2004

© Maps copyright Oxford University Press

ISBN 0 19 832067 1 (hardback)

ISBN 0 19 832066 3 (paperback)

3 5 7 9 10 8 6 4 2

Printed in Italy

Editorial Adviser

Patrick Wiegand

Oxford University Press

2 **Contents** The World, The British Isles

The World

Countries	4–5
Land and Water	6–7
Climate and Ecosystems	8–9
Earthquakes and Volcanoes	10–11
Population	12–13
Development and Interdependence	14–15
Environment and Pollution	16–17

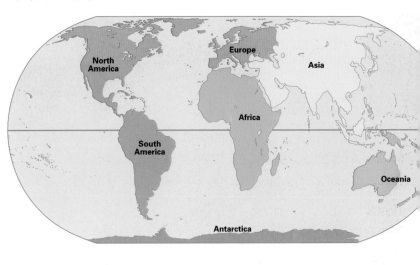

The British Isles

Countries	18
Land and Water	19
Climate	20–21
Population	22
Farming and Industry	23
Energy	24
Communications	25
Pollution	26
Scenery and Conservation	27
Topographic map	28
Orkney and Shetland Islands	29
Scottish Highlands and Islands	30–31
Northern Ireland	32
Southern Scotland	33
Northern England	34–35
Wales	36
English West Midlands	37
South East England	38–39
South West England	40–41

Maps that show general features of regions, countries or continents are called **topographic maps.** These maps are shown with a light band of colour in the contents list.

For example:

South West England

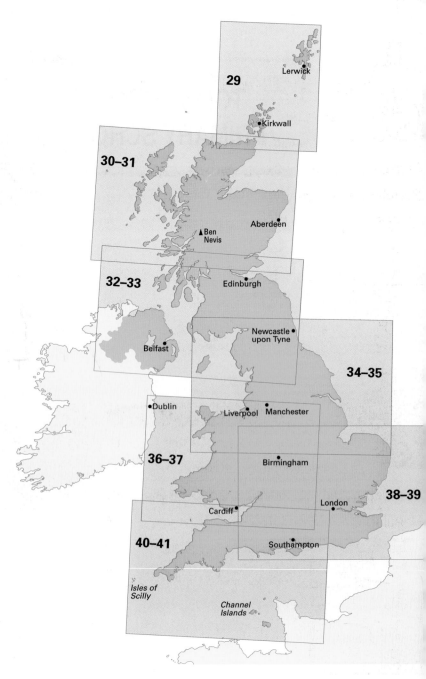

Contents Continents and Poles 3

Europe

Topographic map	42–43
European Union	43
Wealth	43
Climate and Ecosystems	44
Farming, Energy, and Minerals	45
Industry and Environmental issues	46
Population	47
France	48
Benelux, Germany, Alps	49
Spain and Portugal	50
Italy	51

56–57
48 49
50 51

Asia

Countries, Land and Water	52
Climate and Ecosystems	53
Farming, Energy, Minerals, and Industry	54
Population and Environmental issues	55
Northern Eurasia	56–57
Southern Asia	58
China and Japan	59
South East Asia	60
The Middle East and North Africa	61

56–57
59
59
58
60

Africa

Countries, Land and Water	62
Climate and Ecosystems	63
Farming, Energy, Minerals, and Industry	64
Population and Environmental issues	65
North and West Africa	66
South and East Africa	67

61
66
67

Oceania

Countries, Land and Water	68
Climate and Ecosystems	69
Farming, Energy, Minerals, and Industry	70
Population and Environmental issues	71
Australia	72
New Zealand	73

72
73

North America

Countries, Land and Water	74
Climate and Ecosystems	75
Farming, Energy, Minerals, and Industry	76
Population and Environmental issues	77
Canada, Greenland, USA, Mexico and the Caribbean	78–79

78–79

South America

Countries, Land and Water	80
Climate and Ecosystems	81
Farming, Energy, Minerals, and Industry	82
Population and Environmental issues	83
South America	84–85

84–85

The Poles

The Arctic Ocean	86
Antarctica	86

Index

Index	87-96

Key

CANADA	Country name
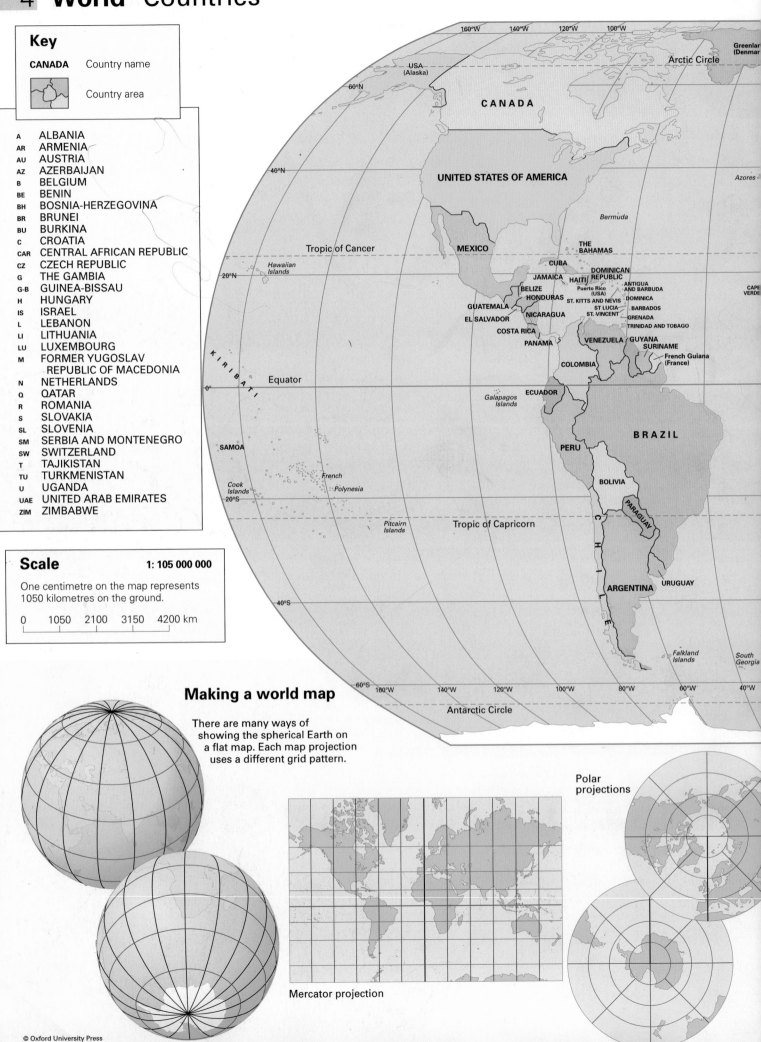	Country area

A	ALBANIA
AR	ARMENIA
AU	AUSTRIA
AZ	AZERBAIJAN
B	BELGIUM
BE	BENIN
BH	BOSNIA-HERZEGOVINA
BR	BRUNEI
BU	BURKINA
C	CROATIA
CAR	CENTRAL AFRICAN REPUBLIC
CZ	CZECH REPUBLIC
G	THE GAMBIA
G-B	GUINEA-BISSAU
H	HUNGARY
IS	ISRAEL
L	LEBANON
LI	LITHUANIA
LU	LUXEMBOURG
M	FORMER YUGOSLAV REPUBLIC OF MACEDONIA
N	NETHERLANDS
Q	QATAR
R	ROMANIA
S	SLOVAKIA
SL	SLOVENIA
SM	SERBIA AND MONTENEGRO
SW	SWITZERLAND
T	TAJIKISTAN
TU	TURKMENISTAN
U	UGANDA
UAE	UNITED ARAB EMIRATES
ZIM	ZIMBABWE

Scale

1: 105 000 000

One centimetre on the map represents 1050 kilometres on the ground.

0	1050	2100	3150	4200 km

Making a world map

There are many ways of showing the spherical Earth on a flat map. Each map projection uses a different grid pattern.

Mercator projection

Polar projections

Arctic Circle

RUSSIAN FEDERATION
(RUSSIA)

NORWAY SWEDEN FINLAND
ESTONIA
LATVIA
DENMARK BELARUS
UNITED KINGDOM
POLAND
GERMANY UKRAINE
FRANCE MOLDOVA
MONACO ITALY
ANDORRA
SPAIN BULGARIA
GEORGIA
GREECE TURKEY
MOROCCO MALTA
TUNISIA CYPRUS SYRIA
ALGERIA LIBYA EGYPT IRAQ IRAN
JORDAN KUWAIT
SAUDI BAHRAIN
ARABIA UAE OMAN
MALI NIGER CHAD SUDAN YEMEN REPUBLIC
ERITREA DJIBOUTI
NIGERIA ETHIOPIA
TOGO CAR SOMALIA
GHANA CAMEROON
EQUATORIAL GUINEA KENYA
GABON CONGO RWANDA BURUNDI
Cabinda (Angola) DEMOCRATIC REPUBLIC OF CONGO TANZANIA
ANGOLA ZAMBIA MALAWI COMOROS
NAMIBIA ZIM MOZAMBIQUE MADAGASCAR MAURITIUS Réunion
BOTSWANA SWAZILAND
REPUBLIC OF SOUTH AFRICA LESOTHO

KAZAKHSTAN
MONGOLIA
UZBEKISTAN KYRGYZSTAN
Jammu and Kashmir
AFGHANISTAN CHINA
PAKISTAN NEPAL BHUTAN
NORTH KOREA
SOUTH KOREA JAPAN
Tropic of Cancer
INDIA
MYANMAR
BANGLADESH LAOS
THAILAND VIETNAM
CAMBODIA
SRI LANKA
MALDIVES
Socotra
Chagos Archipelago
SEYCHELLES

TAIWAN
PHILIPPINES
Northern Marianas (USA)
Guam (USA)
FEDERATED STATES OF MICRONESIA
MARSHALL ISLANDS

MALAYSIA
SINGAPORE
Equator
NAURU
KIRIBATI

INDONESIA
PAPUA NEW GUINEA
SOLOMON ISLANDS
TUVALU
EAST TIMOR
VANUATU
SAMOA
FIJI
New Caledonia
Tropic of Capricorn
TONGA
AUSTRALIA

NEW ZEALAND

Kerguelen

Eckert IV Projection

Antarctic Circle

Prime Meridian

Transverse Mollweide projection

Eckert IV projection (Atlantic centred, as main map)

Eckert IV projection (Pacific centred)

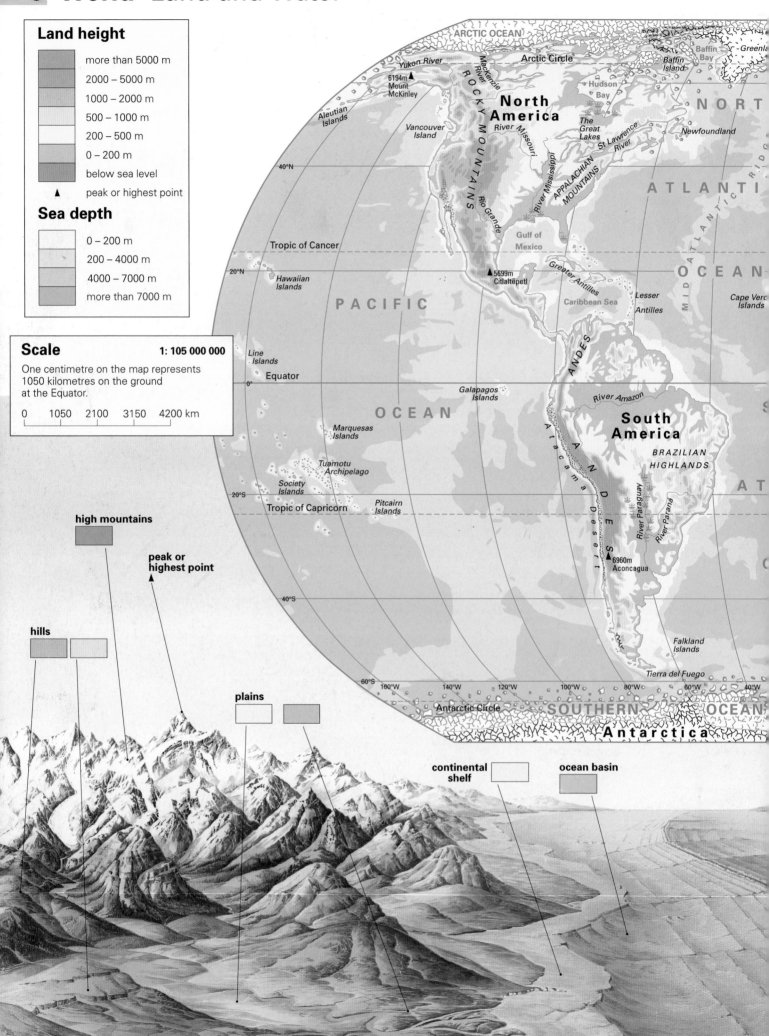

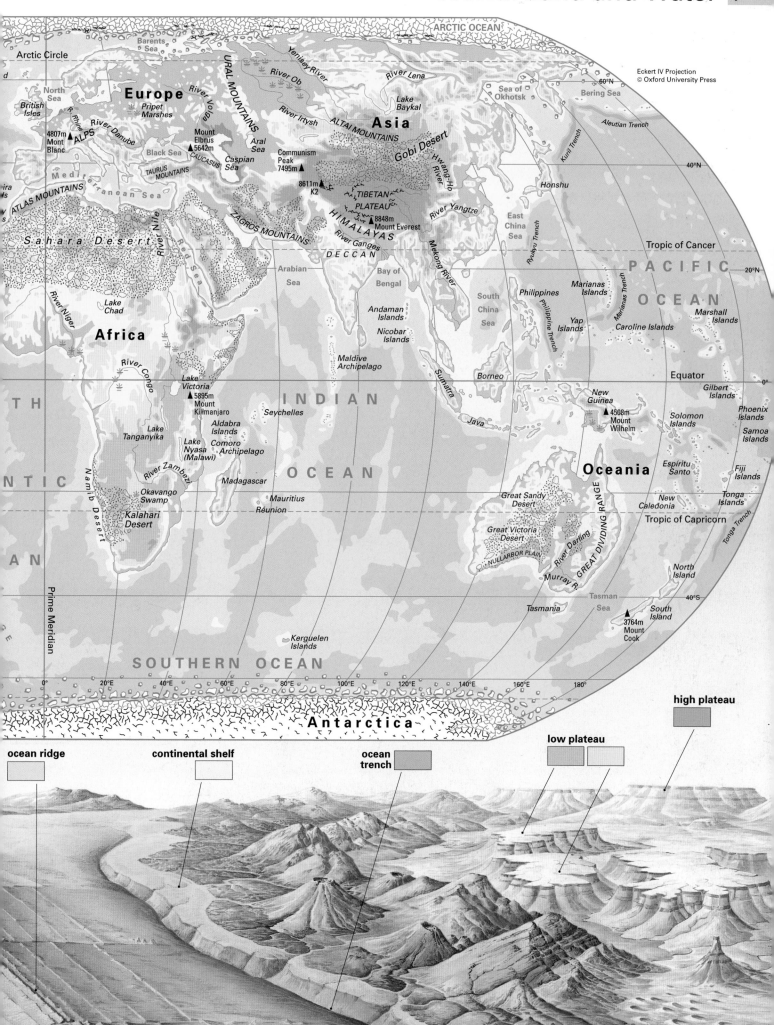

ARCTIC OCEAN

Eckert IV Projection
© Oxford University Press

Arctic Circle

Barents Sea

60°N

Europe

North Sea

British Isles

R. Rhine

4807m Mont Blanc

ALPS

River Volga

Pripet Marshes

URAL MOUNTAINS

Yenisey River

River Ob

River Irtysh

River Lena

Sea of Okhotsk

Bering Sea

Aral Sea

Mount Elbrus 5642m

CAUCASUS

Communism Peak 7495m

ALTAI MOUNTAINS

Lake Baykal

Asia

40°N

Black Sea

TAURUS MOUNTAINS

Caspian Sea

8611m K2

Gobi Desert

Honshu

River Danube

ira

Mediterranean Sea

ZAGROS MOUNTAINS

TIBETAN PLATEAU

Hwang-Ho

Aleutian Trench

Kuril Trench

ls

ATLAS MOUNTAINS

HIMALAYAS

8848m Mount Everest

River Yangtze

East China Sea

Ryukyu Trench

Sahara Desert

River Nile

Red Sea

River Ganges

DECCAN

Mekong River

Tropic of Cancer

River Niger

Lake Chad

Arabian Sea

Bay of Bengal

South China Sea

Philippines

Marianas Islands

Marianas Trench

20°N

P A C I F I C   O C E A N

Africa

Andaman Islands

Nicobar Islands

Philippine Trench

Yap Islands

Caroline Islands

Marshall Islands

River Congo

Lake Victoria

5895m Mount Kilimanjaro

Seychelles

Maldive Archipelago

Sunatra

Borneo

Equator

Gilbert Islands

0°

T H

Aldabra Islands

I N D I A N

Java

New Guinea

4508m Mount Wilhelm

Solomon Islands

Phoenix Islands

Lake Tanganyika

Comoro Archipelago

O C E A N

Samoa Islands

N T I C

Lake Nyasa (Malawi)

River Zambezi

Madagascar

Oceania

Espíritu Santo

Fiji Islands

Namib Desert

Okavango Swamp

Mauritius

Réunion

Great Sandy Desert

New Caledonia

Tonga Islands

A N

Kalahari Desert

Great Victoria Desert

GREAT DIVIDING RANGE

Tropic of Capricorn

NULLARBOR PLAIN

River Darling

North Island

Prime Meridian

Murray R.

Tasman Sea

40°S

Tonga Trench

Kerguelen Islands

Tasmania

3764m Mount Cook

South Island

GE

S O U T H E R N   O C E A N

0°   20°E   40°E   60°E   80°E   100°E   120°E   140°E   160°E   180°

Antarctica

high plateau

low plateau

ocean ridge

continental shelf

ocean trench

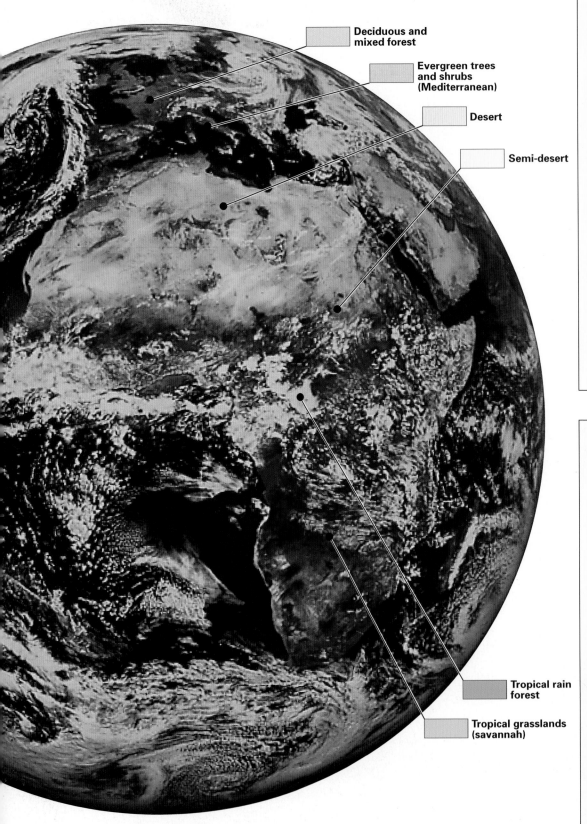

Deciduous and mixed forest

Evergreen trees and shrubs (Mediterranean)

Desert

Semi-desert

Tropical rain forest

Tropical grasslands (savannah)

Climatic regions

Hot tropical rainy

rain all year

monsoon

dry in winter

Very dry

with no reliable rain

with a little rain

Influenced by the sea: warm summers, mild winters

with dry summers (Mediterranean type)

with dry winters

with no dry season

Cool

with dry winters

rain all year

Cold polar

no warm season and fairly dry

Mountain

height of the land strongly affects the climate

Ecosystems

Vegetation types are those which would occur naturally without interference by people

Coniferous forest

cone bearing trees

Deciduous and mixed forest

leaf shedding and coniferous tress

Tropical rain forest

many species of lush, tall trees

Tropical grasslands (savannah)

tall grass parkland with scattered trees

Thorn forest

low trees and shrubs with spines or thorns

Evergreen trees and shrubs

plants and small trees with leathery leaves

Temperate grasslands

prairies, steppes, pampas and veld

Semi-desert

short grasses and drought-resistant scrub

Desert

sand and stones, very little vegetation

Tundra

moss and lichen, with few trees

Ice

no vegetation

Mountains

thin soils, steep slopes and high altitude affects type of vegetation

A Meteosat view of the Earth recorded by a geostationary satellite positioned 36 000 km above the intersection of the Prime Meridian and the Equator

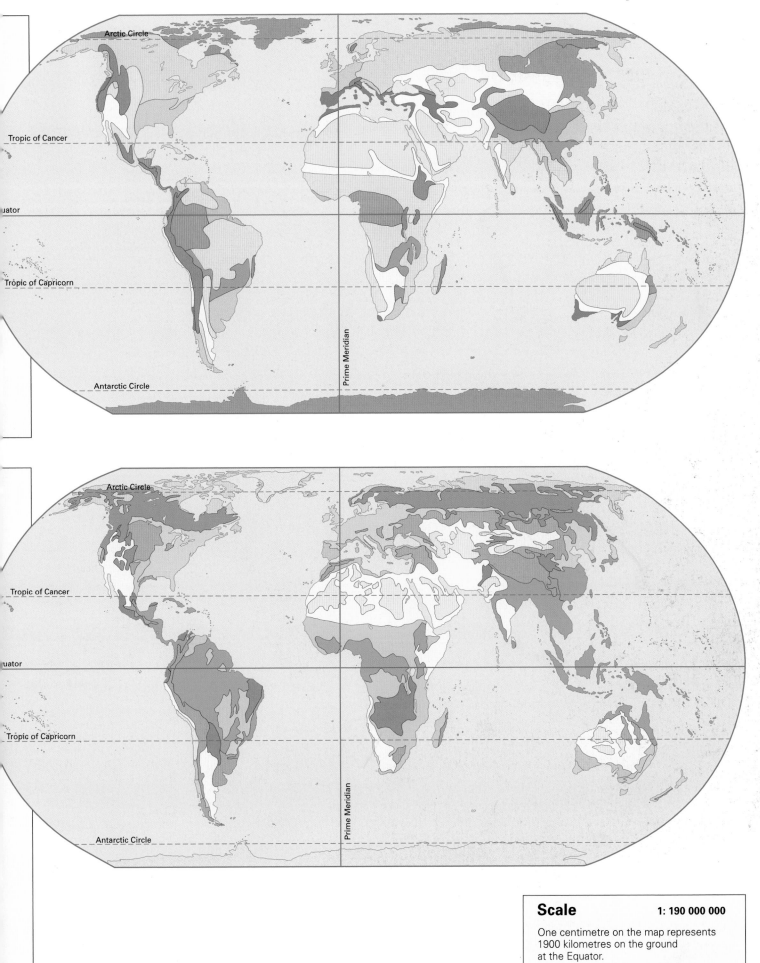

Arctic Circle

Tropic of Cancer

Equator

Tropic of Capricorn

Prime Meridian

Antarctic Circle

Arctic Circle

Tropic of Cancer

Equator

Tropic of Capricorn

Prime Meridian

Antarctic Circle

Scale   1: 190 000 000

One centimetre on the map represents
1900 kilometres on the ground
at the Equator.

| 0 | 1900 | 3800 | 5700 km |

Eckert IV Projection   © Oxford University Press

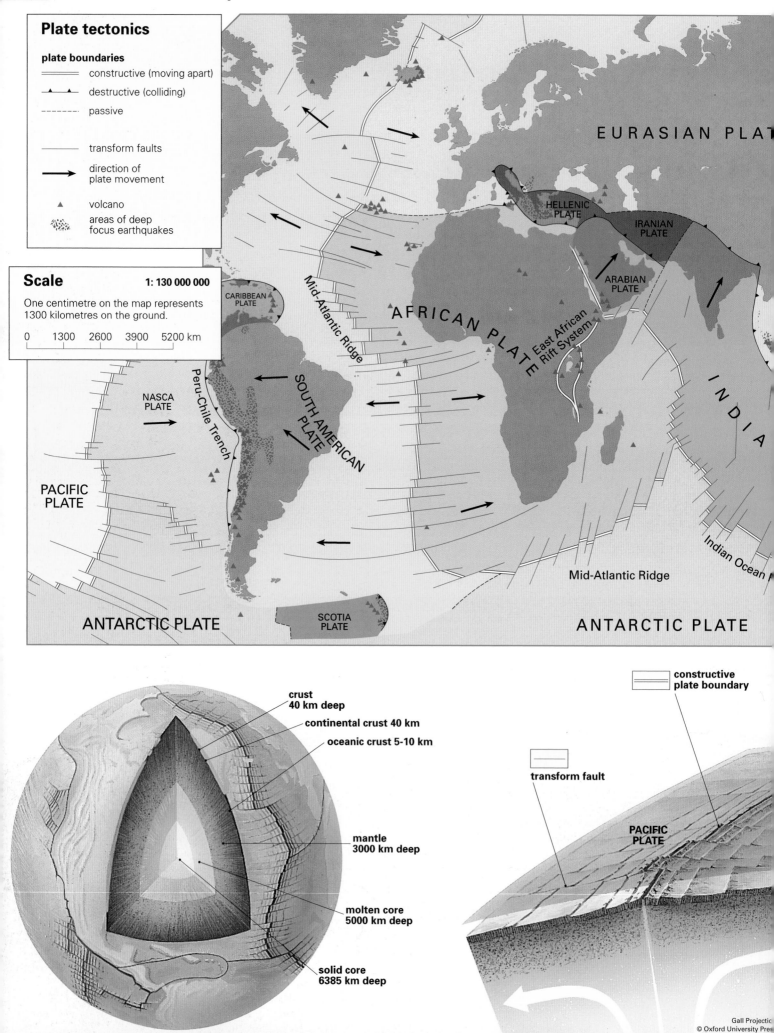

Plate tectonics

plate boundaries

- constructive (moving apart)
- destructive (colliding)
- passive

transform faults

direction of plate movement

▲ volcano

areas of deep focus earthquakes

Scale

1: 130 000 000

One centimetre on the map represents 1300 kilometres on the ground.

0   1300   2600   3900   5200 km

EURASIAN PLATE

HELLENIC PLATE

IRANIAN PLATE

ARABIAN PLATE

CARIBBEAN PLATE

AFRICAN PLATE

East African Rift System

Mid-Atlantic Ridge

NASCA PLATE

Peru-Chile Trench

SOUTH AMERICAN PLATE

INDIA

PACIFIC PLATE

Indian Ocean

Mid-Atlantic Ridge

ANTARCTIC PLATE

SCOTIA PLATE

ANTARCTIC PLATE

crust
40 km deep

continental crust 40 km

oceanic crust 5-10 km

mantle
3000 km deep

molten core
5000 km deep

solid core
6385 km deep

constructive
plate boundary

transform fault

PACIFIC PLATE

Gall Projection
© Oxford University Press

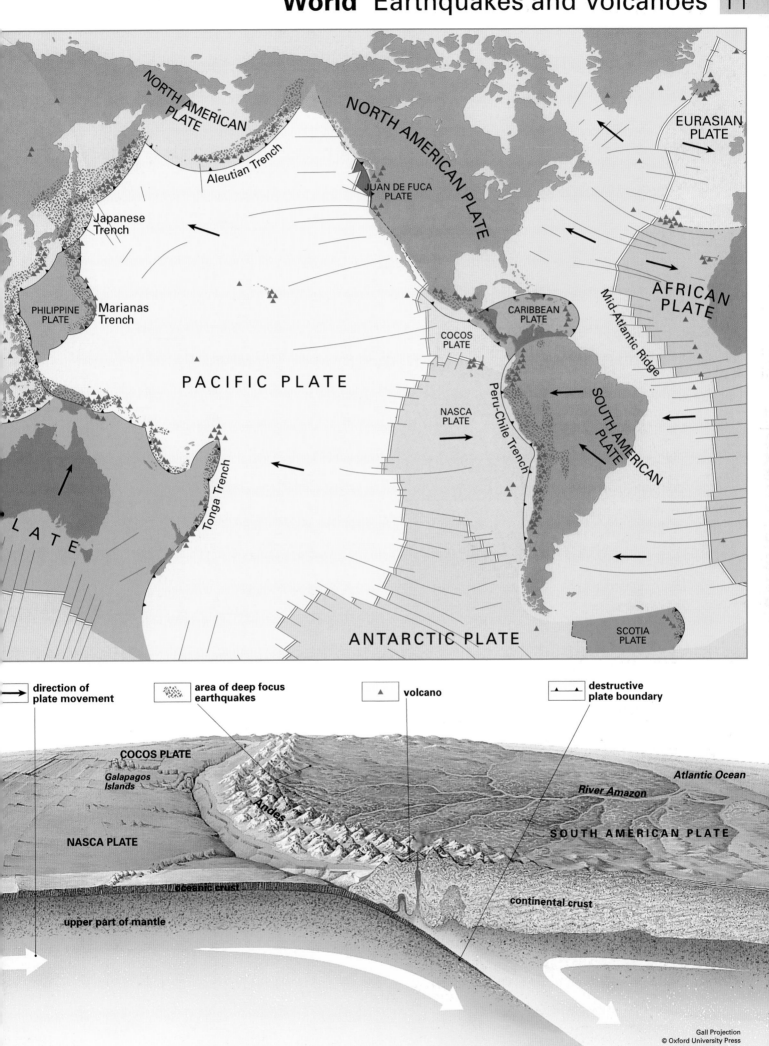

NORTH AMERICAN PLATE

NORTH AMERICAN PLATE

EURASIAN PLATE

Aleutian Trench

JUAN DE FUCA PLATE

Japanese Trench

AFRICAN PLATE

Mid-Atlantic Ridge

PHILIPPINE PLATE

Marianas Trench

CARIBBEAN PLATE

COCOS PLATE

PACIFIC PLATE

NASCA PLATE

Peru-Chile Trench

SOUTH AMERICAN PLATE

Tonga Trench

PLATE

ANTARCTIC PLATE

SCOTIA PLATE

direction of plate movement

area of deep focus earthquakes

▲ volcano

destructive plate boundary

COCOS PLATE

Galapagos Islands

Andes

Atlantic Ocean

River Amazon

SOUTH AMERICAN PLATE

NASCA PLATE

oceanic crust

continental crust

upper part of mantle

Gall Projection
© Oxford University Press

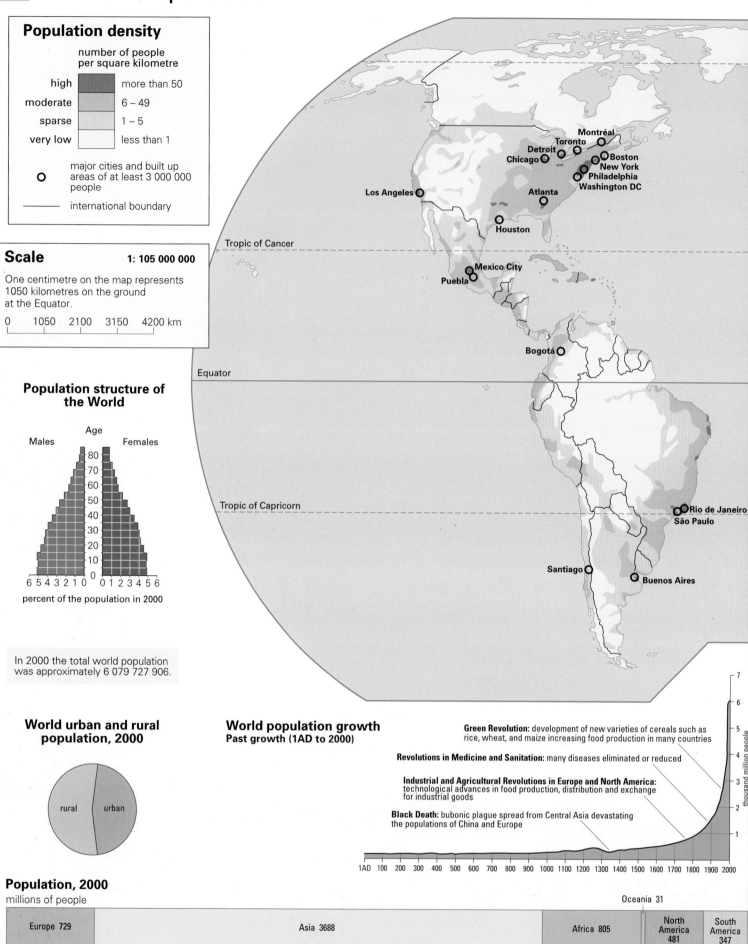

Population density

number of people
per square kilometre

high		more than 50
moderate		6 – 49
sparse		1 – 5
very low		less than 1

○ major cities and built up areas of at least 3 000 000 people

— international boundary

Scale
1: 105 000 000

One centimetre on the map represents 1050 kilometres on the ground at the Equator.

0   1050   2100   3150   4200 km

Population structure of the World

Age

Males — Females

80
70
60
50
40
30
20
10
0

6 5 4 3 2 1 0   0 1 2 3 4 5 6

percent of the population in 2000

In 2000 the total world population was approximately 6 079 727 906.

Tropic of Cancer

Equator

Tropic of Capricorn

Montréal
Toronto
Detroit
Chicago
Boston
New York
Philadelphia
Washington DC
Los Angeles
Atlanta
Houston
Mexico City
Puebla
Bogotá
Rio de Janeiro
São Paulo
Santiago
Buenos Aires

World urban and rural population, 2000

rural | urban

World population growth
Past growth (1AD to 2000)

Green Revolution: development of new varieties of cereals such as rice, wheat, and maize increasing food production in many countries

Revolutions in Medicine and Sanitation: many diseases eliminated or reduced

Industrial and Agricultural Revolutions in Europe and North America: technological advances in food production, distribution and exchange for industrial goods

Black Death: bubonic plague spread from Central Asia devastating the populations of China and Europe

1AD 100 200 300 400 500 600 700 800 900 1000 1100 1200 1300 1400 1500 1600 1700 1800 1900 2000

thousand million people
7
6
5
4
3
2
1

Population, 2000
millions of people

Oceania 31

Europe 729	Asia 3688	Africa 805	North America 481	South America 347

Land areas
thousands of square kilometres

Europe 10 498	Asia 44 387	Africa 30 335	Oceania 8503	North America 24 241	South America 17 832	Antarctica 13 340

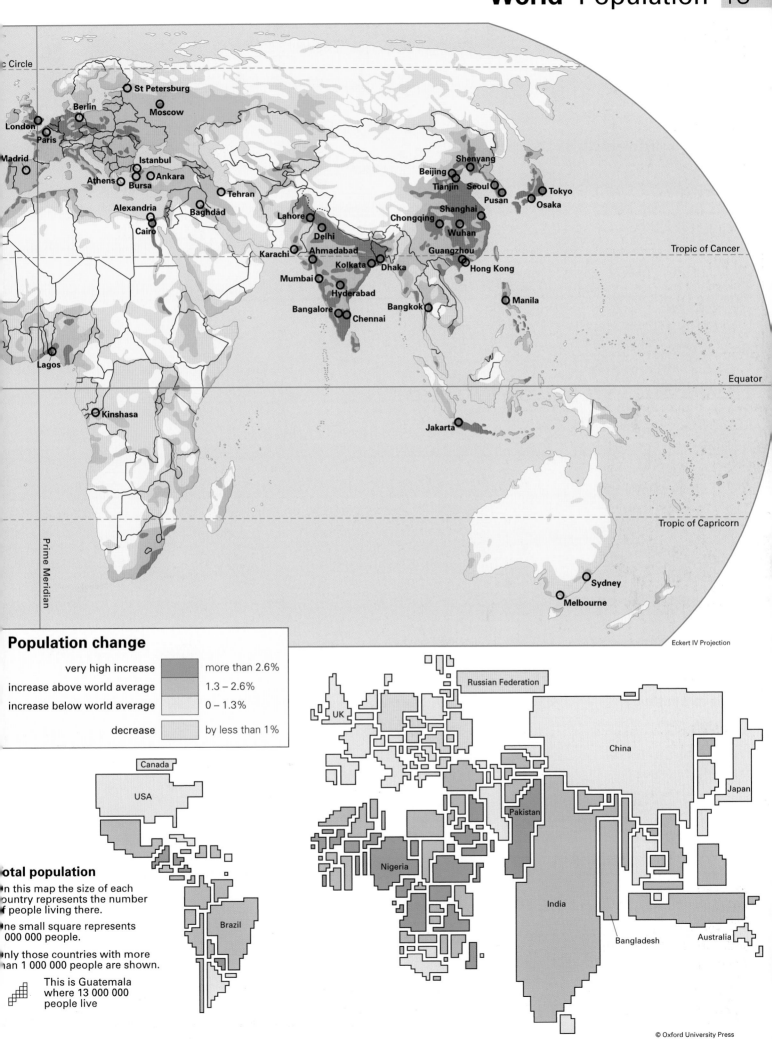

St Petersburg
Berlin
Moscow
London
Paris
Madrid
Istanbul
Athens Ankara
Bursa
Tehran
Alexandria
Baghdād
Cairo
Lahore
Delhi
Karachi
Ahmadabad
Kolkata Dhaka
Mumbai
Hyderabad
Bangalore Chennai
Bangkok
Shenyang
Beijing
Tianjin Seoul
Pusan
Shanghai
Chongqing
Wuhan
Guangzhou
Hong Kong
Tokyo
Osaka
Manila
Lagos
Kinshasa
Jakarta
Sydney
Melbourne

c Circle

Tropic of Cancer

Equator

Tropic of Capricorn

Prime Meridian

Eckert IV Projection

Population change

very high increase		more than 2.6%
increase above world average		1.3 – 2.6%
increase below world average		0 – 1.3%
decrease		by less than 1%

otal population

n this map the size of each
ountry represents the number
f people living there.

ne small square represents
000 000 people.

nly those countries with more
han 1 000 000 people are shown.

This is Guatemala
where 13 000 000
people live

Russian Federation

UK

China

Japan

Canada

USA

Pakistan

Nigeria

India

Brazil

Bangladesh

Australia

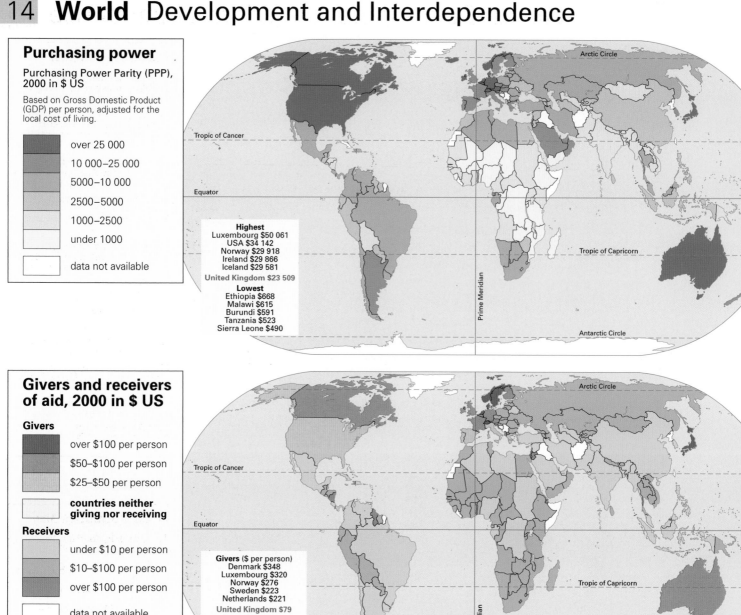

Purchasing power

Purchasing Power Parity (PPP),
2000 in $ US

Based on Gross Domestic Product
(GDP) per person, adjusted for the
local cost of living.

- over 25 000
- 10 000–25 000
- 5000–10 000
- 2500–5000
- 1000–2500
- under 1000
- data not available

Highest
Luxembourg $50 061
USA $34 142
Norway $29 918
Ireland $29 866
Iceland $29 581
United Kingdom $23 509

Lowest
Ethiopia $668
Malawi $615
Burundi $591
Tanzania $523
Sierra Leone $490

Givers and receivers of aid, 2000 in $ US

Givers
- over $100 per person
- $50–$100 per person
- $25–$50 per person
- **countries neither giving nor receiving**

Receivers
- under $10 per person
- $10–$100 per person
- over $100 per person
- data not available

Givers ($ per person)
Denmark $348
Luxembourg $320
Norway $276
Sweden $223
Netherlands $221
United Kingdom $79

Receivers ($ per person)
Dominica $219.4
Cape Verde $220.3
Seychelles $227.3
Vanuatu $232.7
São Tomé & Principe $253.9

Life expectancy

Average number of years a baby
born in 2000 can expect to live

- over 70 years
- 65–70 years
- 60–65 years
- 55–60 years
- under 55 years
- data not available

Highest
Japan 81 years
San Marino 80 years
Sweden 80 years
Switzerland 80 years
United Kingdom 77 years

Lowest
Malawi 39 years
Rwanda 39 years
Angola 38 years
Zambia 37 years

Scale   1: 240 000 000

One centimetre on the map
represents 2400 kilometres
on the ground at the Equator.

0   2400   4800   7200 km

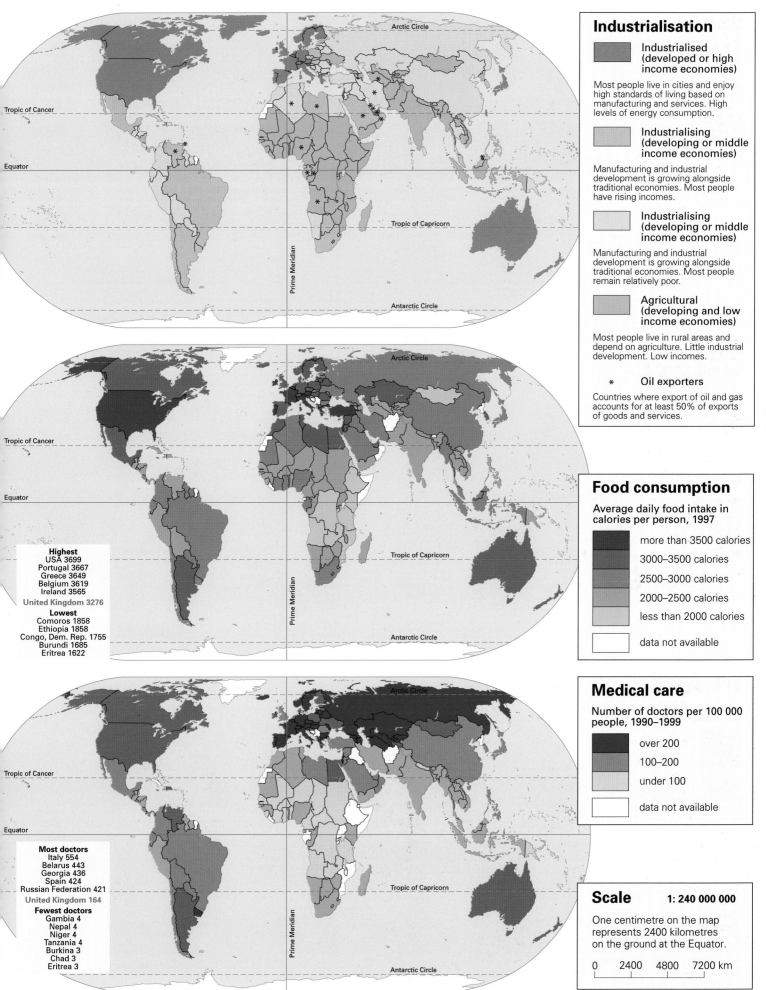

Industrialisation

Industrialised (developed or high income economies)

Most people live in cities and enjoy high standards of living based on manufacturing and services. High levels of energy consumption.

Industrialising (developing or middle income economies)

Manufacturing and industrial development is growing alongside traditional economies. Most people have rising incomes.

Industrialising (developing or middle income economies)

Manufacturing and industrial development is growing alongside traditional economies. Most people remain relatively poor.

Agricultural (developing and low income economies)

Most people live in rural areas and depend on agriculture. Little industrial development. Low incomes.

* Oil exporters

Countries where export of oil and gas accounts for at least 50% of exports of goods and services.

Food consumption

Average daily food intake in calories per person, 1997

more than 3500 calories

3000–3500 calories

2500–3000 calories

2000–2500 calories

less than 2000 calories

data not available

Highest
USA 3699
Portugal 3667
Greece 3649
Belgium 3619
Ireland 3565
United Kingdom 3276
Lowest
Comoros 1858
Ethiopia 1858
Congo, Dem. Rep. 1755
Burundi 1685
Eritrea 1622

Medical care

Number of doctors per 100 000 people, 1990–1999

over 200

100–200

under 100

data not available

Most doctors
Italy 554
Belarus 443
Georgia 436
Spain 424
Russian Federation 421
United Kingdom 164
Fewest doctors
Gambia 4
Nepal 4
Niger 4
Tanzania 4
Burkina 3
Chad 3
Eritrea 3

Scale   1: 240 000 000

One centimetre on the map represents 2400 kilometres on the ground at the Equator.

0   2400   4800   7200 km

Eckert IV Projection   © Oxford University Press

Water

Surplus

Enough water to support vegetation and crops without irrigation.

large surplus

surplus

Deficiency

Not enough water to support vegetation and crops without irrigation. After long periods of deficiency, these areas may lose their natural vegetation.

deficiency

chronic deficiency

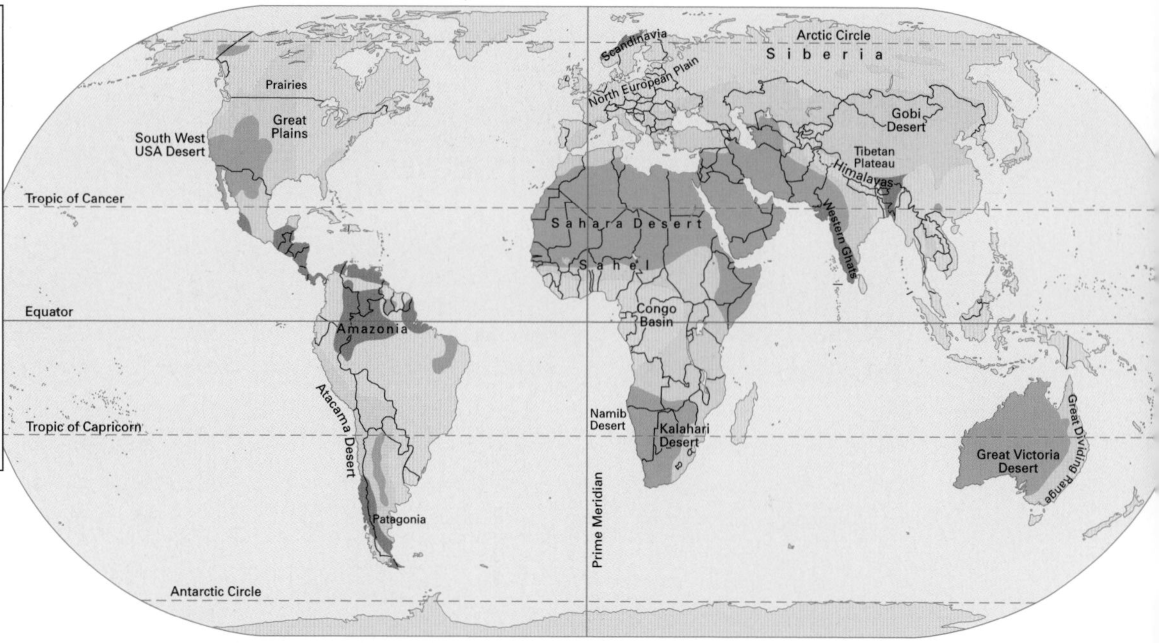

Map labels (Water): Scandinavia · North European Plain · Arctic Circle · S i b e r i a · Prairies · Great Plains · South West USA Desert · Gobi Desert · Tibetan Plateau · Himalayas · Tropic of Cancer · Sahara Desert · Sahel · Western Ghats · Equator · Congo Basin · Amazonia · Atacama Desert · Namib Desert · Kalahari Desert · Tropic of Capricorn · Great Victoria Desert · Great Dividing Range · Patagonia · Prime Meridian · Antarctic Circle

Desertification

existing areas of desert

areas with a high risk of desertification

areas with a moderate risk of desertification

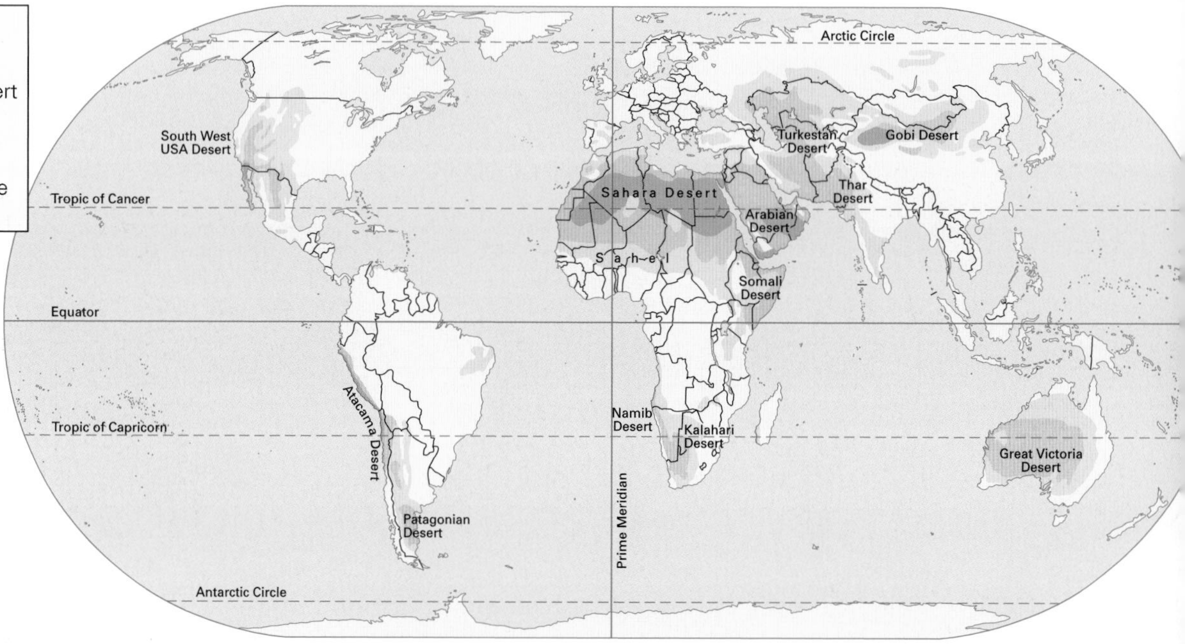

Map labels (Desertification): Arctic Circle · South West USA Desert · Turkestan Desert · Gobi Desert · Tropic of Cancer · Sahara Desert · Arabian Desert · Thar Desert · Sahel · Somali Desert · Equator · Atacama Desert · Namib Desert · Kalahari Desert · Tropic of Capricorn · Great Victoria Desert · Patagonian Desert · Prime Meridian · Antarctic Circle

Tropical deforestation

existing areas of rainforest

former areas of rainforest

Countries losing greatest areas of forest (000 hectares per year)
Brazil 2554
Indonesia 1084
Congo, Democratic Republic 740
Bolivia 581
Mexico 508

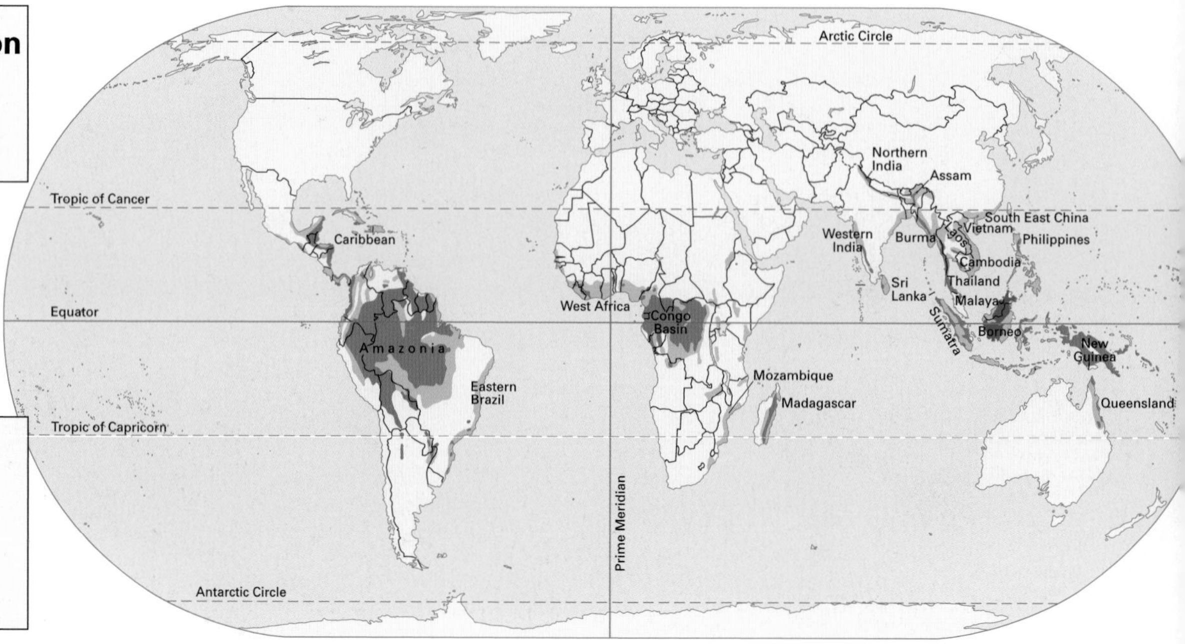

Map labels (Tropical deforestation): Arctic Circle · Tropic of Cancer · Caribbean · Northern India · Assam · South East China · Western India · Burma · Vietnam · Philippines · Sri Lanka · Cambodia · Thailand · Malaya · Equator · West Africa · Congo Basin · Amazonia · Sumatra · Borneo · New Guinea · Eastern Brazil · Mozambique · Madagascar · Queensland · Tropic of Capricorn · Prime Meridian · Antarctic Circle

Scale   1: 240 000 000

One centimetre on the map represents 2400 kilometres on the ground at the Equator.

0   2400   4800   7200 km

Eckert IV Projection

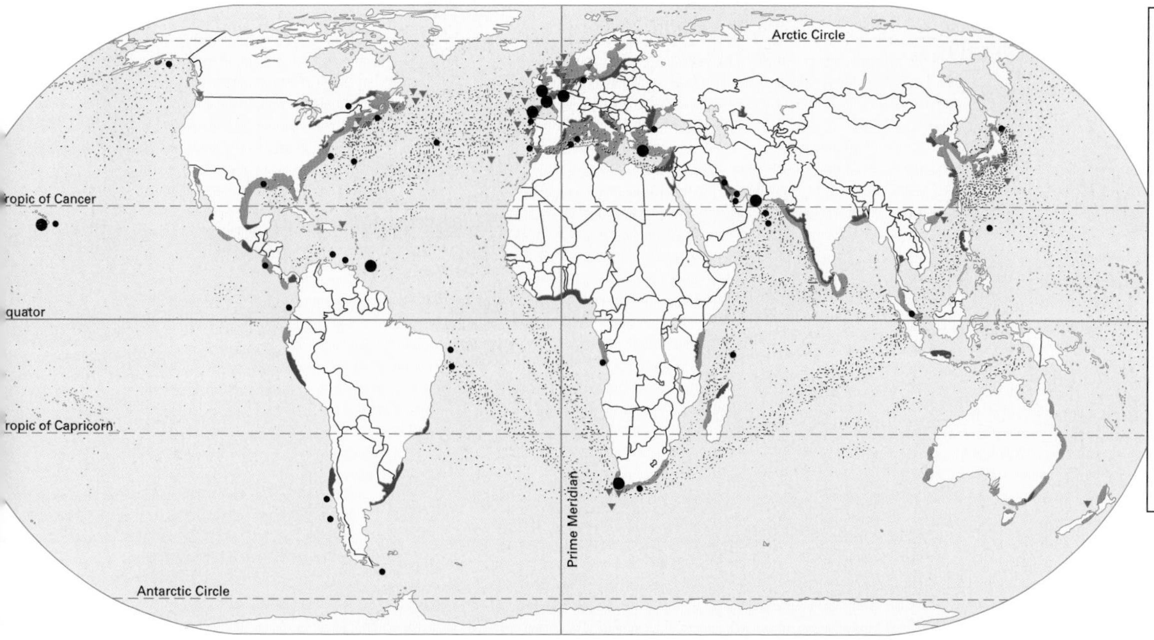

Sea pollution

Oil spills

●   over 100 000 tonnes

•   under 100 000 tonnes

Oil slicks

pollution from routine tanker and other shipping operations

Other sea pollution

areas severely polluted for all or part of the year

areas persistently affected by pollution

▼   deep sea dump sites

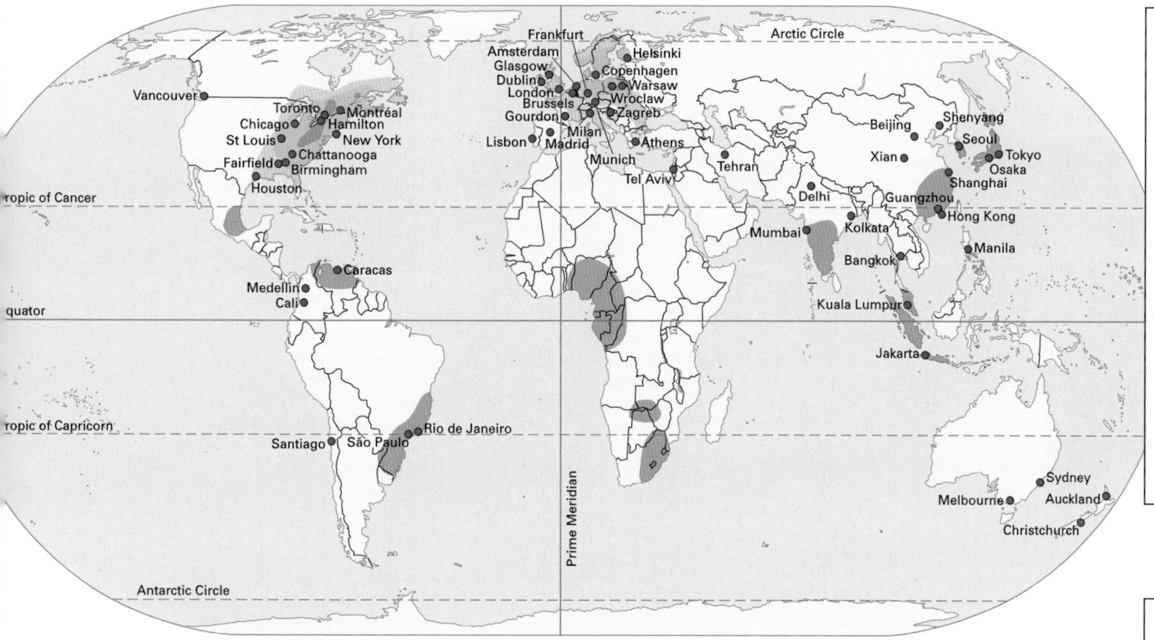

(Map 1 — Sea pollution. Labels: Arctic Circle, Tropic of Cancer, Equator, Tropic of Capricorn, Antarctic Circle, Prime Meridian)

Acid rain

Areas of acid rain deposition

A pH scale measures acidity. 'Clean' rain water is slightly acidic with a pH of 5.6

pH less than 4.2 (most acidic)

pH 4.2 – 4.6

pH 4.6 – 5.0

other areas where acid rain is becoming a problem

Air pollution

•   cities where sulphur dioxide emissions are recorded and exceed recommended levels

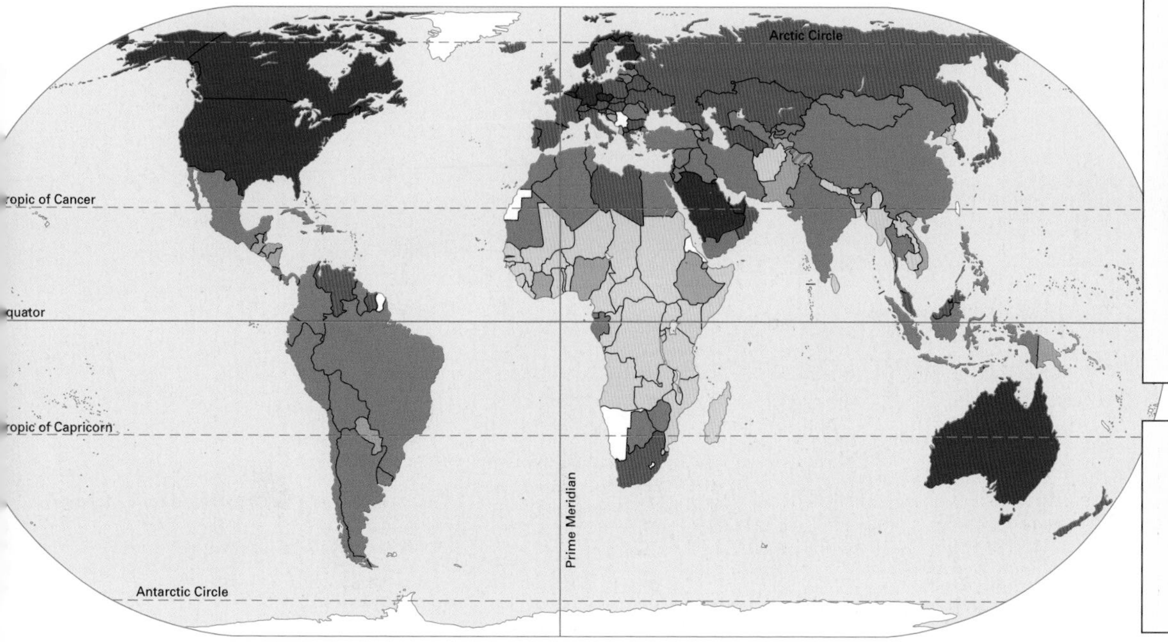

(Map 2 — Acid rain. City labels: Vancouver, Toronto, Montréal, Hamilton, Chicago, St Louis, New York, Chattanooga, Fairfield, Birmingham, Houston, Caracas, Medellín, Cali, Santiago, São Paulo, Rio de Janeiro, Frankfurt, Amsterdam, Glasgow, Dublin, London, Brussels, Gourdon, Lisbon, Madrid, Munich, Milan, Zagreb, Warsaw, Wroclaw, Copenhagen, Helsinki, Athens, Tel Aviv, Tehran, Beijing, Xian, Shenyang, Seoul, Tokyo, Osaka, Shanghai, Delhi, Guangzhou, Hong Kong, Kolkata, Mumbai, Bangkok, Manila, Kuala Lumpur, Jakarta, Sydney, Melbourne, Auckland, Christchurch. Latitude labels: Arctic Circle, Tropic of Cancer, Equator, Tropic of Capricorn, Antarctic Circle, Prime Meridian)

Global warming

Carbon dioxide emissions in tonnes per person, 1997

Global warming is caused by adding 'greenhouse gases' (carbon dioxide, methane, CFCs) to the atmosphere

over 10.0

5.0–10.0

1.0–5.0

0.5–1.0

under 0.5

data not available

(Map 3 — Global warming. Latitude labels: Arctic Circle, Tropic of Cancer, Equator, Tropic of Capricorn, Antarctic Circle, Prime Meridian)

Scale   1: 240 000 000

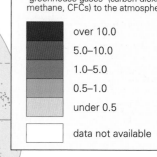

One centimetre on the map represents 2400 kilometres on the ground at the Equator.

0   2400   4800   7200 km

Eckert IV Projection

© Oxford University Press

Key

—·—·— international boundary

— — — national boundary

Scale

1: 4 500 000

One centimetre on the map represents
45 kilometres on the ground.

| 0 | 45 | 90 | 135 | 180 km |

Key to unitary authorities in Scotland

1	West Dunbartonshire	9	Falkirk
2	East Dunbartonshire	10	West Lothian
3	North Lanarkshire	11	City of Edinburgh
4	Glasgow City	12	Midlothian
5	East Renfrewshire	13	East Lothian
6	Renfrewshire	14	North Ayrshire
7	Inverclyde	15	East Ayrshire
8	Clackmannanshire	16	Dundee City

Key to districts in Northern Ireland

1	Belfast	14	Fermanagh
2	Newtownabbey	15	Omagh
3	Carrickfergus	16	Cookstown
4	Castlereagh	17	Magherafelt
5	North Down	18	Strabane
6	Ards	19	Londonderry
7	Down	20	Limavady
8	Newry & Mourne	21	Coleraine
9	Banbridge	22	Ballymoney
10	Lisburn	23	Moyle
11	Craigavon	24	Ballymena
12	Armagh	25	Larne
13	Dungannon	26	Antrim

United Kingdom

Republic of Ireland

England is divided into counties and some new unitary authorities. Wales and Scotland are divided into unitary authorities. Northern Ireland is divided into districts.

The Republic of Ireland is divided into counties.

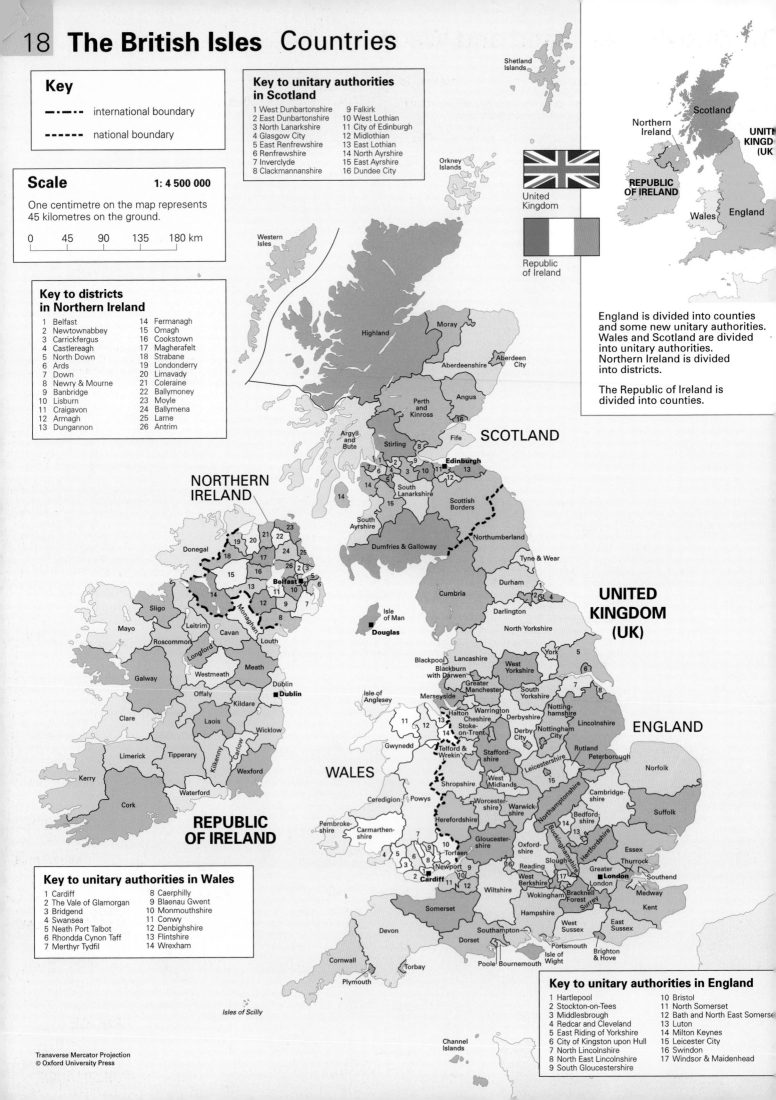

Key to unitary authorities in Wales

1	Cardiff	8	Caerphilly
2	The Vale of Glamorgan	9	Blaenau Gwent
3	Bridgend	10	Monmouthshire
4	Swansea	11	Conwy
5	Neath Port Talbot	12	Denbighshire
6	Rhondda Cynon Taff	13	Flintshire
7	Merthyr Tydfil	14	Wrexham

Key to unitary authorities in England

1	Hartlepool	10	Bristol
2	Stockton-on-Tees	11	North Somerset
3	Middlesbrough	12	Bath and North East Somerset
4	Redcar and Cleveland	13	Luton
5	East Riding of Yorkshire	14	Milton Keynes
6	City of Kingston upon Hull	15	Leicester City
7	North Lincolnshire	16	Swindon
8	North East Lincolnshire	17	Windsor & Maidenhead
9	South Gloucestershire		

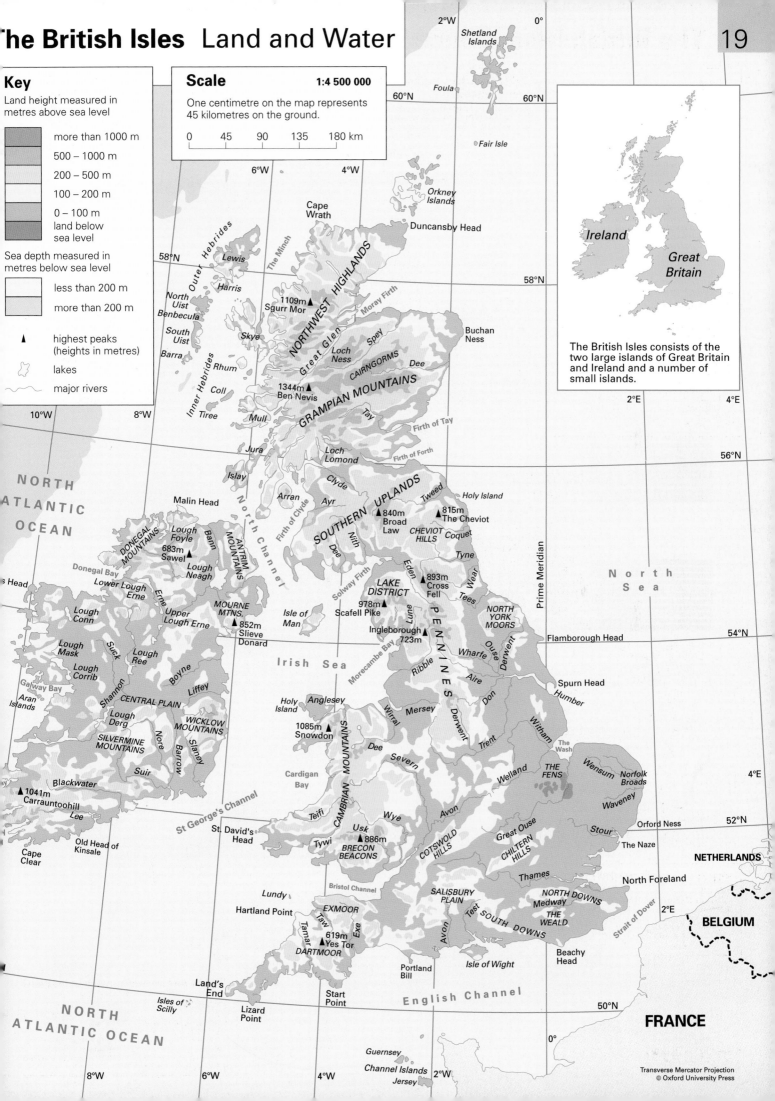

Key

Land height measured in metres above sea level

- more than 1000 m
- 500 – 1000 m
- 200 – 500 m
- 100 – 200 m
- 0 – 100 m
- land below sea level

Sea depth measured in metres below sea level

- less than 200 m
- more than 200 m

▲ highest peaks (heights in metres)

lakes

major rivers

Scale

1:4 500 000

One centimetre on the map represents 45 kilometres on the ground.

0   45   90   135   180 km

The British Isles consists of the two large islands of Great Britain and Ireland and a number of small islands.

Transverse Mercator Projection
© Oxford University Press

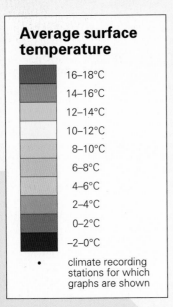

Average surface temperature

	16–18°C
	14–16°C
	12–14°C
	10–12°C
	8–10°C
	6–8°C
	4–6°C
	2–4°C
	0–2°C
	–2–0°C

• climate recording stations for which graphs are shown

Scale

1: 8 000 000

One centimetre on the map represents 80 kilometres on the ground.

0   80   160   240 km

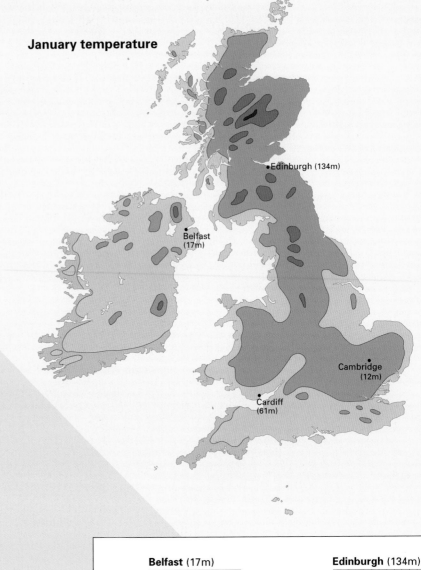

January temperature

Edinburgh (134m)

Belfast (17m)

Cambridge (12m)

Cardiff (61m)

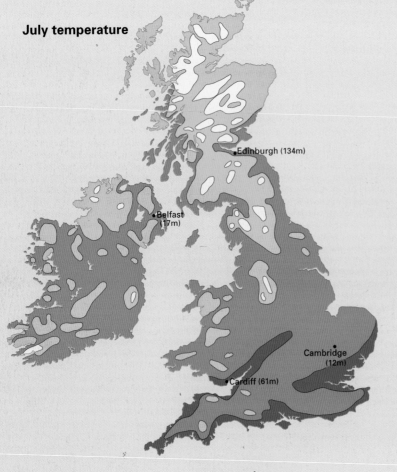

July temperature

Edinburgh (134m)

Belfast (17m)

Cambridge (12m)

Cardiff (61m)

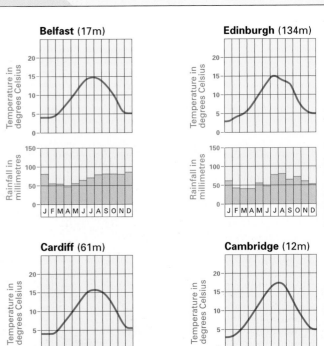

Belfast (17m)

Temperature in degrees Celsius

Rainfall in millimetres

J F M A M J J A S O N D

Edinburgh (134m)

Temperature in degrees Celsius

Rainfall in millimetres

J F M A M J J A S O N D

Cardiff (61m)

Temperature in degrees Celsius

Rainfall in millimetres

J F M A M J J A S O N D

Cambridge (12m)

Temperature in degrees Celsius

Rainfall in millimetres

J F M A M J J A S O N D

Transverse Mercator Projection
© Oxford University Press

Average annual rainfall

- more than 2400 millimetres
- 1200 – 2400 millimetres
- 800 – 1200 millimetres
- less than 800 millimetres
- • climate recording stations for which graphs are shown

Scale   1: 8 000 000

One centimetre on the map measures 80 kilometres on the ground.

0   80   160   240 km

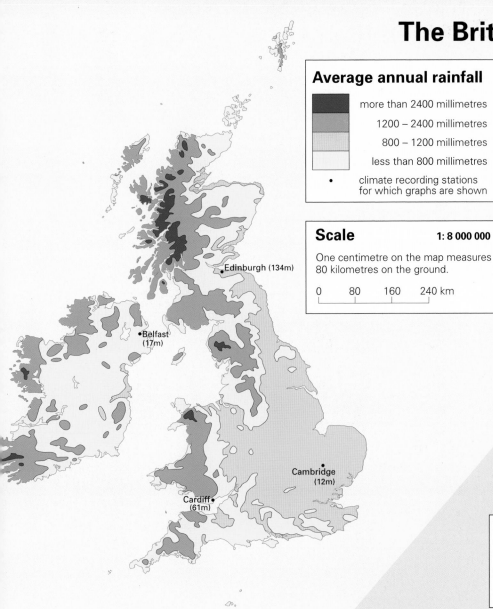

Edinburgh (134m)

Belfast (17m)

Cambridge (12m)

Cardiff (61m)

Drought and flood

- inland areas in regular danger of flooding
- coastal areas in regular danger of flooding
- areas in regular danger of drought

Scale   1: 16 000 000

One centimetre on the map represents 160 kilometres on the ground.

0   160   320   480 km

water cycle

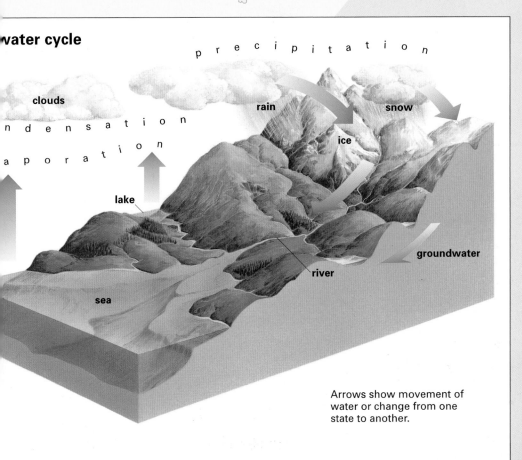

precipitation

clouds

rain

snow

condensation

ice

evaporation

lake

groundwater

river

sea

Arrows show movement of water or change from one state to another.

Cold winters, cool summers

Mild winters, cool summers

Cool winters, warm summers

Mild winters, warm summers

Climate regions

- - - - - average January temperature (4°C)
- ———— average July temperature (16°C)

Transverse Mercator Projection
© Oxford University Press

Population structure of the United Kingdom

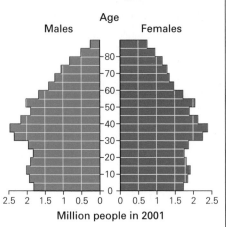

Age
Males | Females

2.5 1.5 0.5 0 0 0.5 1 1.5 2 2.5
  2   1   0.5
Million people in 2001

Population density

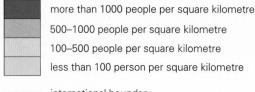

	more than 1000 people per square kilometre
	500–1000 people per square kilometre
	100–500 people per square kilometre
	less than 100 person per square kilometre

- - - - international boundary

——— national boundary

——— county, unitary authority, or district boundary

Major cities

● with more than 6 million people

● with 1 million people

● with between 400 000 and 1 million people

· with between 100 000 and 400 000 people

Scale   1: 8 000 000

One centimetre on the map represents
80 kilometres on the ground.

0   80   160   240 km

British Isles population data

United Kingdom	Overall population density 243 people per square kilometre
Republic of Ireland	Overall population density 54 people per square kilometre

Total population 2001
England	50.0 million people
Wales	2.9 million people
Scotland	5.1 million people
Northern Ireland	1.7 million people
United Kingdom	**59.7 million people**
Republic of Ireland	3.8 million people

Population change

Change in population in each county,
region or district, 1981 – 1999

very large increase	(more than 20%)
large increase	(10–20%)
small increase	(less than 10%)
small decrease	(less than 10%)
large decrease	(more than 10%)

- - - - international boundary

——— national boundary

——— county, unitary authority, or district boundar

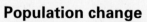

Farming, forestry and fishing

mostly livestock farms (cattle are kept for meat)

mostly hill farms (sheep are kept for meat and wool)

mostly dairy farms (cows are kept for milk)

mostly arable farms (crops are grown)

**Many farms in Britain are mixed farms.
Farmers grow crops and keep animals.**

forestry (trees are planted for wood)

market gardening (fruit and vegetables are grown)

no farming (built-up areas)

fishing port

main fishing grounds

- - - - - international boundary

Scale   1: 8 000 000

One centimetre on the map represents
80 kilometres on the ground.

0   80   160   240 km

United Kingdom employment structure

The number of people employed in each activity , 2001

Primary activity
agriculture, farming, fishing,
mining, and quarrying

Secondary activity
manufacturing industry

Tertiary activity
energy and water supply,
construction, transport
and other services

Quaternary activity
information services

0 1 2 3 4 5 6 7 8 9 10 11 12 13
million people

Industry and business

major industrial area

· office and business centre

- - - - - international boundary

——— national boundary

Central
Lowlands
Glasgow ·Edinburgh

Newcastle
Tyneside

Belfast

Dublin

*Greater
Manchester*   Leeds
Merseyside *West Yorkshire*
Manchester
South Yorkshire

*East
Midlands*

·Birmingham
*West
Midlands*

*South
Wales*   *Greater
London* City of London
Cardiff Bristol   Croydon

Southampton

verse Mercator Projection
ford University Press

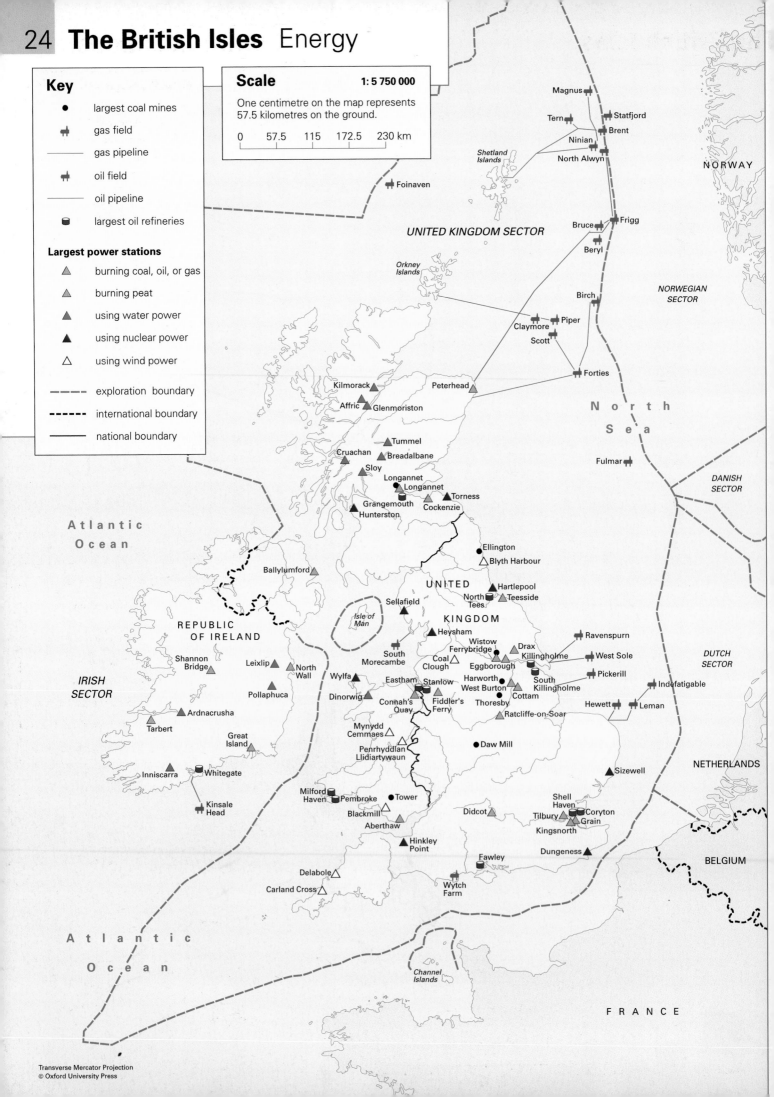

Key

- ● largest coal mines
- ⛏ gas field
- — gas pipeline
- ⛏ oil field
- — oil pipeline
- ⬛ largest oil refineries

Largest power stations

- ▲ burning coal, oil, or gas
- ▲ burning peat
- ▲ using water power
- ▲ using nuclear power
- △ using wind power

- – – – exploration boundary
- ▪▪▪▪ international boundary
- —— national boundary

Scale

1: 5 750 000

One centimetre on the map represents 57.5 kilometres on the ground.

0   57.5   115   172.5   230 km

Transverse Mercator Projection
© Oxford University Press

Map labels:

Magnus, Tern, Statfjord, Brent, Ninian, North Alwyn, Shetland Islands, Foinaven, UNITED KINGDOM SECTOR, Bruce, Frigg, Beryl, NORWAY, NORWEGIAN SECTOR, Orkney Islands, Birch, Piper, Claymore, Scott, Kilmorack, Peterhead, Forties, North Sea, Affric, Glenmoriston, Fulmar, DANISH SECTOR, Tummel, Cruachan, Breadalbane, Sloy, Longannet, Longannet, Torness, Grangemouth, Cockenzie, Hunterston, Atlantic Ocean, Ellington, Blyth Harbour, UNITED, Ballylumford, Sellafield, Isle of Man, Hartlepool, North Tees, Teesside, KINGDOM, REPUBLIC OF IRELAND, Heysham, Ravenspurn, Shannon Bridge, Leixlip, North Wall, Wylfa, South Morecambe, Coal Clough, Wistow, Ferrybridge, Drax, Killingholme, West Sole, DUTCH SECTOR, IRISH SECTOR, Pollaphuca, Dinorwig, Eastham, Stanlow, Eggborough, Harworth, West Burton, South Killingholme, Pickerill, Indefatigable, Ardnacrusha, Connah's Quay, Fiddler's Ferry, Thoresby, Cottam, Hewett, Leman, Tarbert, Great Island, Mynydd Cemmaes, Ratcliffe-on-Soar, Inniscarra, Whitegate, Penrhyddlan Llidiartywaun, Daw Mill, Sizewell, NETHERLANDS, Kinsale Head, Milford Haven, Pembroke, Tower, Shell Haven, Blackmill, Didcot, Tilbury, Coryton, Grain, Aberthaw, Kingsnorth, Hinkley Point, Dungeness, BELGIUM, Fawley, Delabole, Wytch Farm, Carland Cross, Channel Islands, Atlantic Ocean, FRANCE

the British Isles

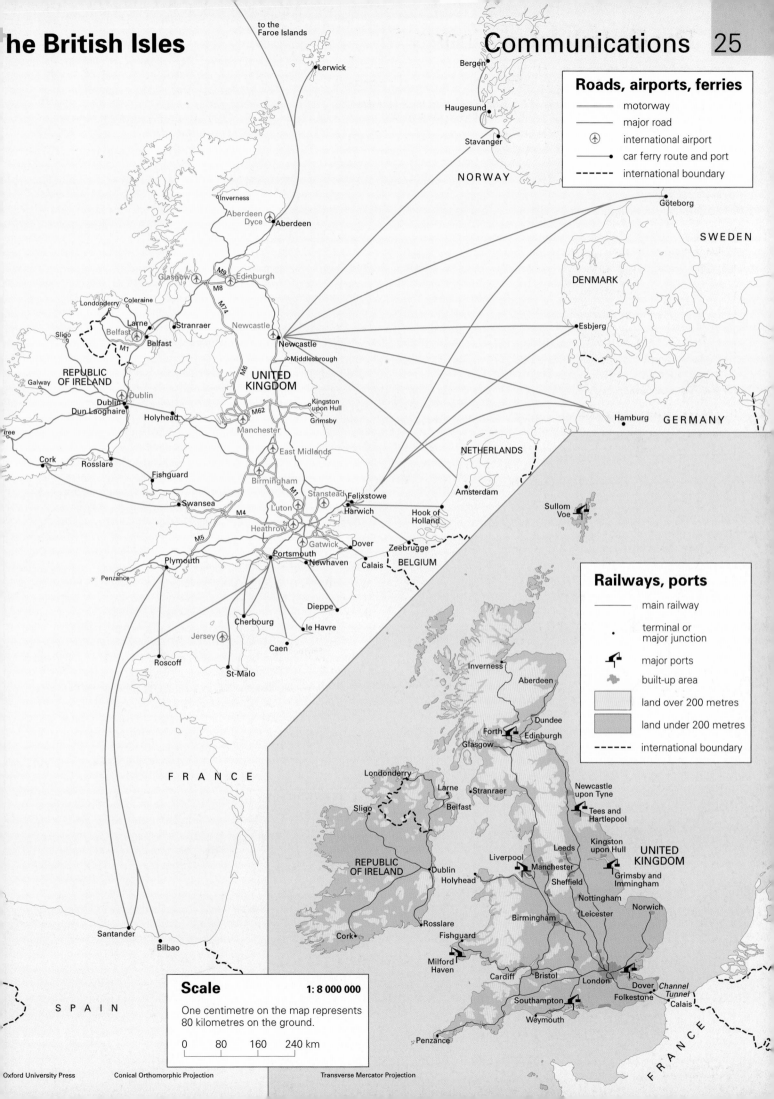

Key

- built-up areas
- most polluted rivers and estuaries
- most polluted beaches and coastline
- ▼ sea dumping sites for sewage waste
- ▽ sea dumping sites for industrial waste
- ● sₒ accidental oil spills, 1989–1998

Areas worst affected by acid rain

- very heavy pollution
- heavy pollution
- moderate pollution
- light pollution
- very light pollution
- - - - international boundary
- national boundary

Scale   1: 4 500 000

One centimetre on the map represents 45 kilometres on the ground.

0   45   90   135   180 km

Sulphur emissions

Industrial sites in the United Kingdom emitting the largest amounts of sulphur, in 1995–97.

thousand tonnes of sulphur

- ● over 100
- ● 50–100
- ● 20–50

Source: The Swedish NGO Secretariat on Acid Rain

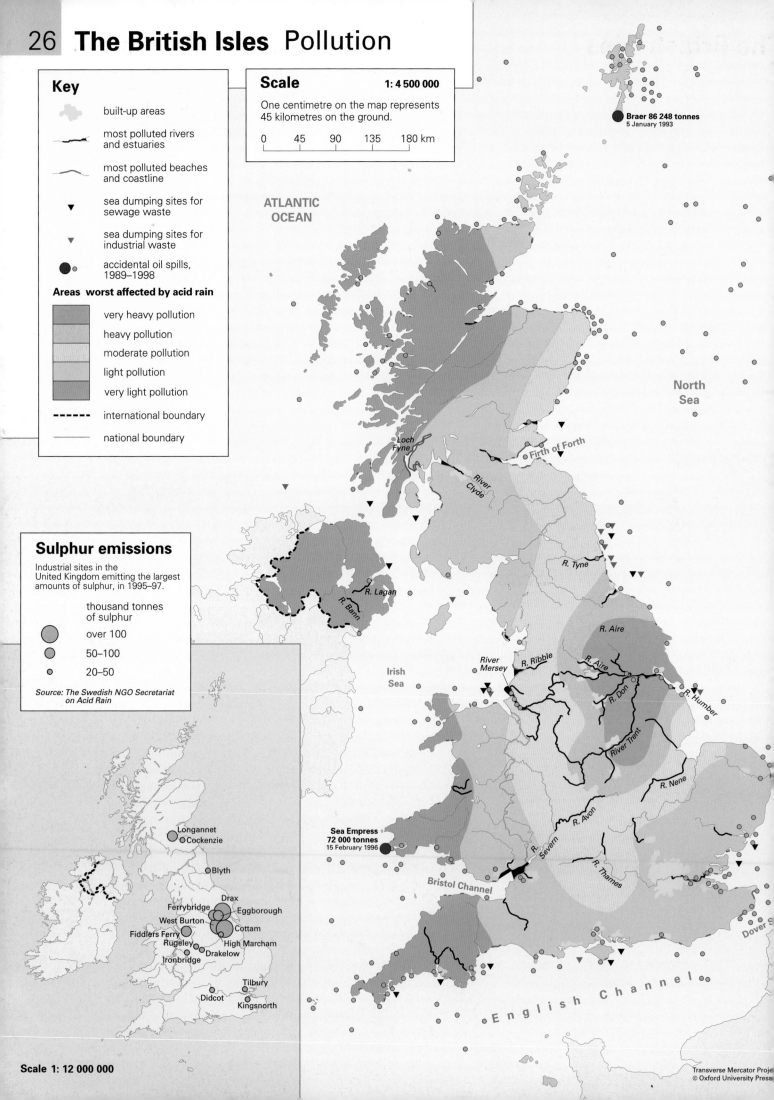

Braer 86 248 tonnes 5 January 1993

ATLANTIC OCEAN

North Sea

Loch Fyne

Firth of Forth

River Clyde

R. Lagan

R. Bann

R. Tyne

R. Aire

River Mersey

R. Ribble

R. Aire

R. Don

R. Humber

River Trent

R. Nene

R. Avon

R. Severn

R. Thames

Irish Sea

Sea Empress 72 000 tonnes 15 February 1996

Bristol Channel

Dover S

English Channel

Longannet
Cockenzie
Blyth
Drax
Ferrybridge
Eggborough
West Burton
Cottam
Fiddlers Ferry
Rugeley
High Marcham
Drakelow
Ironbridge
Tilbury
Didcot
Kingsnorth

Scale 1: 12 000 000

Transverse Mercator Proje
© Oxford University Press

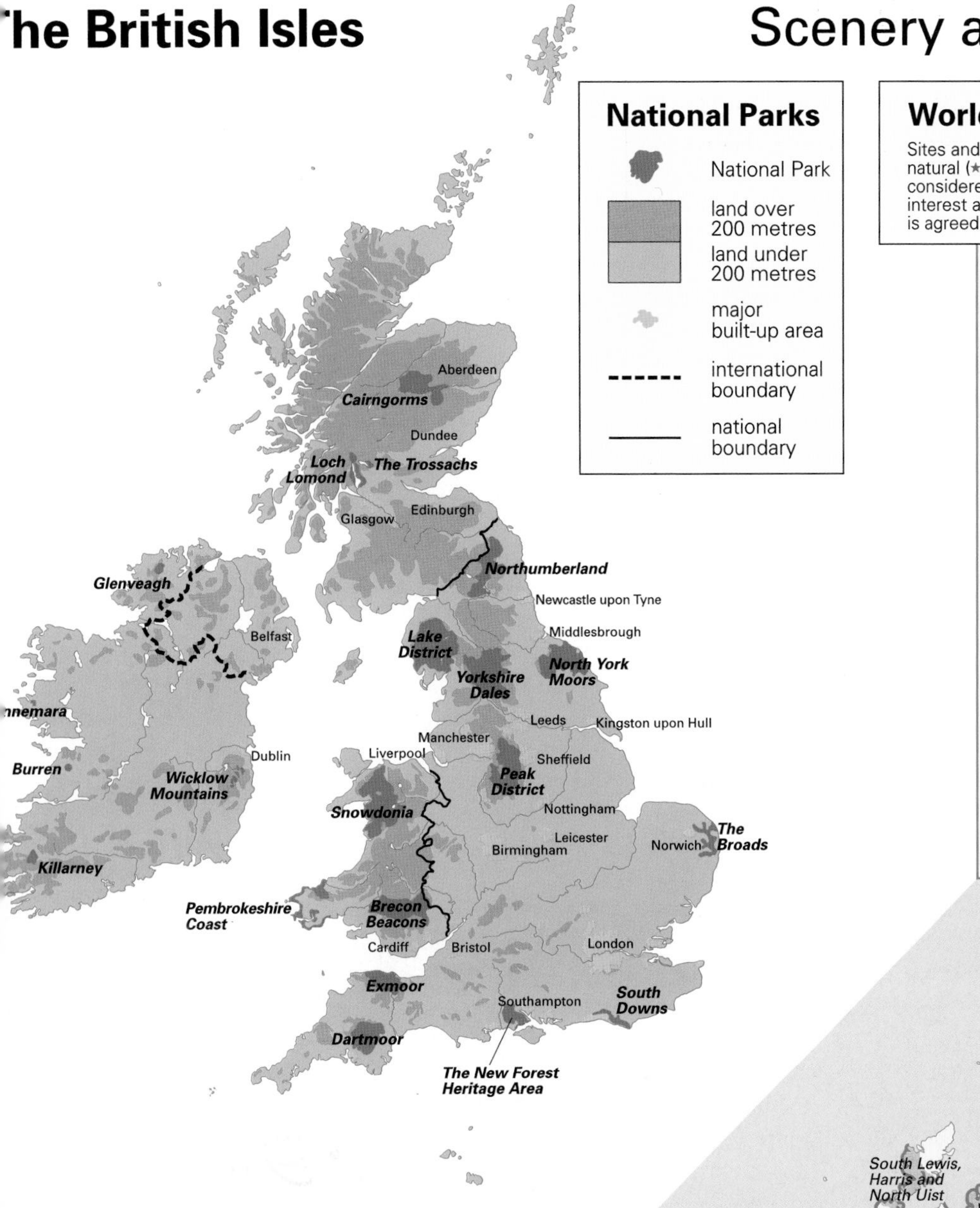

National Parks

- National Park
- land over 200 metres
- land under 200 metres
- major built-up area
- ---- international boundary
- —— national boundary

World Heritage Sites

Sites and monuments of world-wide natural (∗) and cultural heritage (∗), considered to be of such exceptional interest and value that their protection is agreed by international cooperation.

Map labels — National Parks / relief map

Aberdeen
Cairngorms
Dundee
Loch Lomond
The Trossachs
Glasgow
Edinburgh
Glenveagh
Belfast
Northumberland
Newcastle upon Tyne
Middlesbrough
Lake District
nnemara
Dublin
Wicklow Mountains
Yorkshire Dales
North York Moors
Leeds
Kingston upon Hull
Burren
Manchester
Liverpool
Sheffield
Peak District
Snowdonia
Nottingham
Leicester
Birmingham
Norwich
The Broads
Killarney
Pembrokeshire Coast
Brecon Beacons
Cardiff
Bristol
London
Exmoor
Southampton
South Downs
Dartmoor
The New Forest Heritage Area

Map labels — World Heritage Sites

The Heart of Neolithic Orkney
St Kilda
Giant's Causeway
New Lanark
Old and New Towns of Edinburgh
Hadrian's Wall
Durham Castle/ Cathedral
Archaeological Ensemble of the Bend of the Boyne
Fountain's Abbey/ Studley Royal Park
Saltaire
Castles/Town Walls of King Edward
Derwent valley Mills
Ironbridge Gorge
Blenheim Palace
Blaenavon
Westminster Palace/Abbey
Bath
Stonehenge/ Avebury
Canterbury Cathedral
Dorset and East Devon Coast

Scale

1: 8 000 000

One centimetre on the map represents 80 kilometres on the ground.

0   80   160   240 km

Other protected areas

- Areas of Outstanding Natural Beauty (England, Wales, Northern Ireland); National Scenic Areas (Scotland)
- Heritage Coast (England and Wales); Coastal Conservation Zones (Scotland); Conservation designated coast (Northern Ireland);
- major built-up area
- ---- international boundary
- —— national boundary

Map labels — Other protected areas

South Lewis, Harris and North Uist
Wester Ross
Ben Nevis and Glen Coe
Jura
Antrim Coast and Glens
Sperrin
Mourne
Upper Tweeddale
North Pennines
Nidderdale
Forest of Bowland
Anglesey
Lincolnshire Wolds
Norfolk Coast
Clwydian Range
Lleyn
Shropshire Hills
Suffolk Coast and Heaths
Wye Valley
Cotswolds
Gower
North Wessex Downs
Chilterns
Surrey Hills
Kent Downs
Cranbourne Chase
High Weald
Blackdown Hills
Dorset
Sussex Downs
Bodmin Moor
Isle of Wight

sverse Mercator Projection
ford University Press

Key

- – – – – international boundary
- ———— national boundary
- ═════ motorway and main road
- ——— railway
- ✈ main airport
- 〰 river
- �',lake
- ▲ peak or highest point

towns

- ⬡ built-up areas
- ■ largest towns
- ● large towns
- • other towns

Land height

measured in metres above sea level

- more than 1000 m
- 500 – 1000 m
- 200 – 500 m
- 100 – 200 m
- less than 100 m
- land below sea level

Scale   1 : 4 500 000

One centimetre on the map represents
45 kilometres on the ground.

0   45   90   135   180 km

© Oxford University Press
Transverse Mercator Projection

Map labels

Shetland Islands
Orkney Islands
Cape Wrath
NORTHWEST HIGHLANDS
Outer Hebrides
Lewis
Skye
Mull
Islay
Inverness
Loch Ness
Great Glen
River Spey
CAIRNGORMS
River Dee
Aberdeen
1344m ▲ Ben Nevis
GRAMPIAN MOUNTAINS
R. Tay
SCOTLAND
Dundee
Loch Lomond
Glasgow
Edinburgh
Firth of Forth
River Clyde
Ayr
SOUTHERN UPLANDS
R. Tweed
Stranraer
CHEVIOT HILLS
UNITED KINGDOM
Firth of Clyde
North Channel
NORTHERN IRELAND
Coleraine
Londonderry
R. Bann
ANTRIM MOUNTAINS
Larne
Lough Neagh
Belfast
River Erne
Sligo
REPUBLIC OF IRELAND
852m ▲ Slieve Donard
Isle of Man
Newcastle upon Tyne
River Tyne
Sunderland
Carlisle
River Eden
LAKE DISTRICT
978m ▲ Scafell Pike
River Tees
Middlesbrough
NORTH YORK MOORS
PENNINES
River Ouse
Bradford
Leeds
Kingston upon Hull
River Aire
Sheffield
River Humber
NORTH SEA
Irish Sea
Lough Corrib
Galway
R. Boyne
R. Liffey
Dublin
WICKLOW MOUNTAINS
Holyhead
Anglesey
Manchester
Liverpool
River Mersey
ENGLAND
Nottingham
The Wash
Tiree
River Shannon
River Blackwater
River Suir
River Barrow
Rosslare
1041m ▲ Carrauntoohill
Cork
Fishguard
St George's Channel
1085m ▲ Snowdon
CAMBRIAN MOUNTAINS
R. Dee
Cardigan Bay
River Teifi
River Tywi
WALES
BRECON BEACONS
River Usk
Swansea
Cardiff
Newport
Bristol Channel
Bristol
R. Wye
R. Severn
Wolverhampton
Birmingham
COTSWOLD HILLS
River Avon
Leicester
THE FENS
Northampton
R. Trent
Norwich
R. Wensum
R. Great Ouse
R. Stour
Oxford
CHILTERN HILLS
Luton
R. Thames
Reading
London
Southend-on-Sea
NORTH DOWNS
Dover
Strait of
EXMOOR
R. Exe
SALISBURY PLAIN
SOUTH DOWNS
Southampton
Bournemouth
Portsmouth
Brighton
Weymouth
Isle of Wight
DARTMOOR
Exeter
Plymouth
Land's End
Penzance
Isles of Scilly
English Channel
NORTH ATLANTIC OCEAN
Channel Islands
Cherbourg
Le Havre
FRANCE
R. Seine
Rouen
Prime Meridian

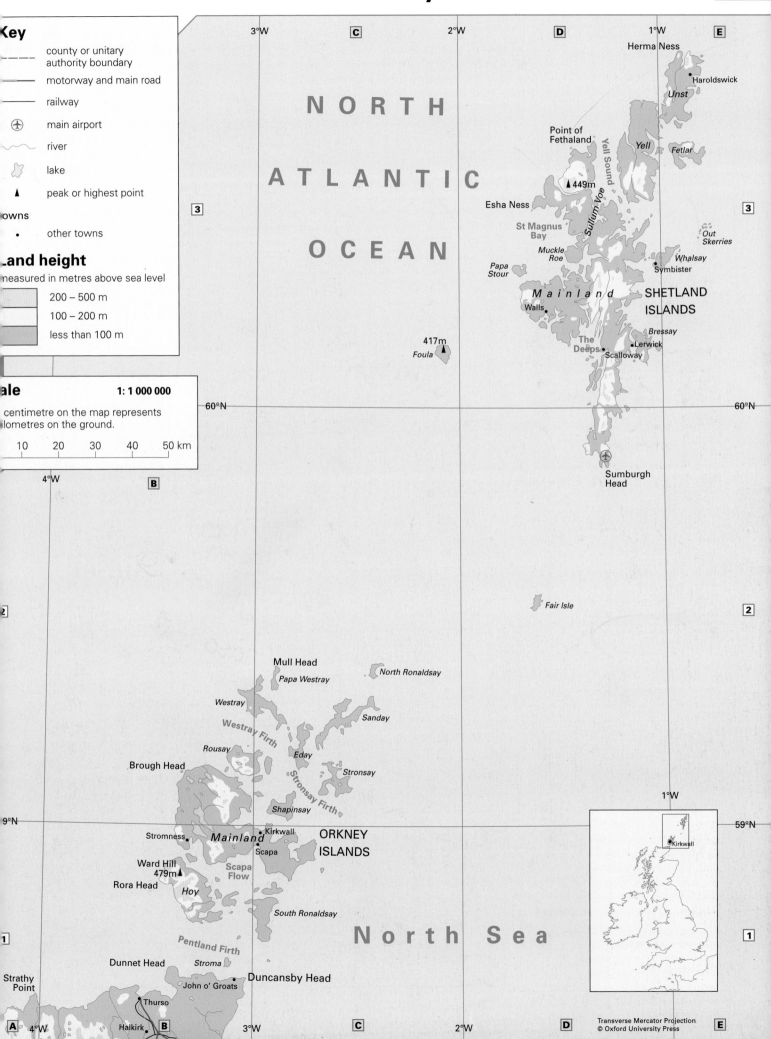

Key

- – – – county or unitary authority boundary
- ═══ motorway and main road
- ─┼─ railway
- ✈ main airport
- ∿ river
- lake
- ▲ peak or highest point

owns
- • other towns

Land height
measured in metres above sea level

- 200 – 500 m
- 100 – 200 m
- less than 100 m

ale
1: 1 000 000

centimetre on the map represents
ilometres on the ground.

| 10 | 20 | 30 | 40 | 50 km |

4°W   B

NORTH
ATLANTIC
OCEAN

Herma Ness
Haroldswick
Unst
Point of
Fethaland
Yell Sound
Yell
Fetlar
▲449m
Esha Ness
St Magnus Bay
Out Skerries
Muckle Roe
Whalsay
Papa Stour
Symbister
Mainland   SHETLAND ISLANDS
Walls
Bressay
The Deeps
Lerwick
Scalloway

417m
Foula ▲

60°N   60°N

Sumburgh Head

Fair Isle

2   2

Mull Head
Papa Westray
North Ronaldsay
Westray
Sanday
Westray Firth
Rousay
Eday
Brough Head
Stronsay
Stronsay Firth
Shapinsay
Stromness
Kirkwall   ORKNEY ISLANDS
Mainland
Scapa
1°W
9°N   Ward Hill 479m▲   59°N
Rora Head
Hoy   Scapa Flow
Kirkwall
South Ronaldsay

North Sea

Pentland Firth
Dunnet Head   Stroma
Strathy Point   Duncansby Head
John o' Groats
Thurso
A 4°W   B   Halkirk   C   2°W   D   Transverse Mercator Projection
© Oxford University Press   E

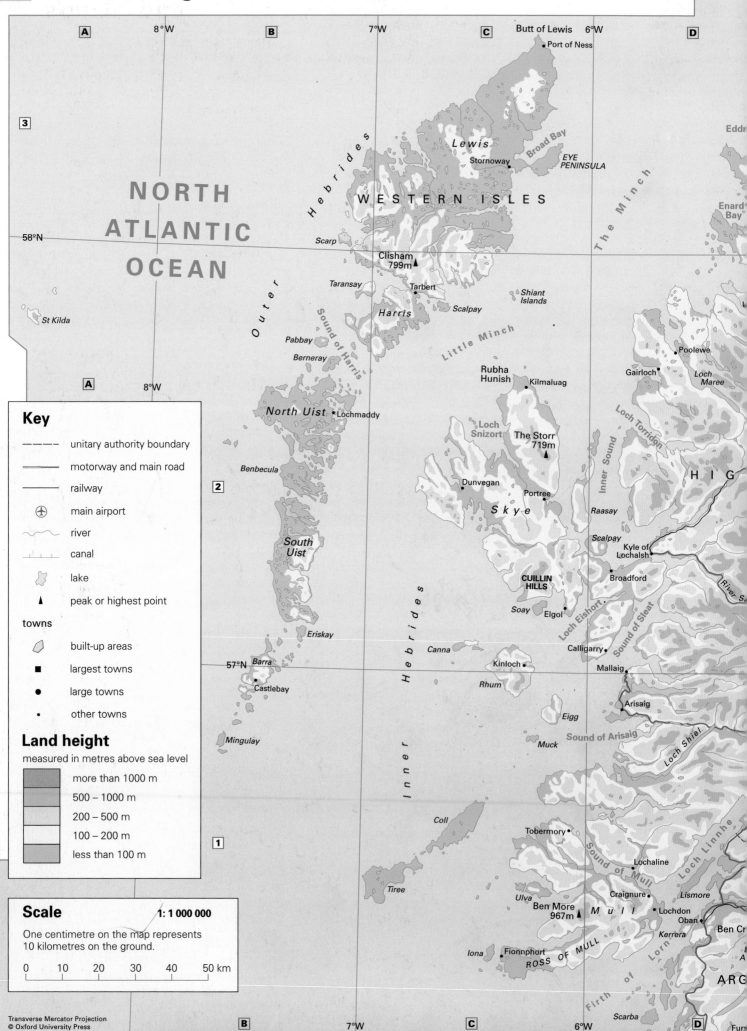

Key

unitary authority boundary

motorway and main road

railway

main airport

river

canal

lake

peak or highest point

towns

built-up areas

largest towns

large towns

other towns

Land height

measured in metres above sea level

more than 1000 m

500 – 1000 m

200 – 500 m

100 – 200 m

less than 100 m

Scale

1: 1 000 000

One centimetre on the map represents
10 kilometres on the ground.

0 10 20 30 40 50 km

Transverse Mercator Projection
© Oxford University Press

NORTH
ATLANTIC
OCEAN

58°N

57°N

St Kilda

Scarp

Taransay

Pabbay

Berneray

North Uist

Lochmaddy

Benbecula

South
Uist

Eriskay

Barra

Castlebay

Mingulay

Iona

Tiree

Coll

Hebrides

Outer

Inner

Hebrides

Sound of Harris

Lewis

Broad Bay

Stornoway

EYE
PENINSULA

WESTERN ISLES

Clisham
799m

Tarbert

Harris

Scalpay

Shiant
Islands

Little Minch

Rubha
Hunish

Kilmaluag

Loch
Snizort

The Storr
719m

Dunvegan

Portree

Skye

Raasay

Scalpay

Kyle of
Lochalsh

Broadford

CUILLIN
HILLS

Soay

Elgol

Loch Eishort

Calligarry

Sound of Sleat

Canna

Kinloch

Rhum

Eigg

Muck

Sound of Arisaig

Arisaig

Mallaig

Butt of Lewis

Port of Ness

The Minch

Eddr

Enard
Bay

Poolewe

Gairloch

Loch
Maree

Loch Torridon

Inner Sound

HIG

River S

Loch Shiel

Tobermory

Lochaline

Craignure

Ulva

Ben More
967m

Mull

Lochdon

Lismore

Oban

Kerrera

Ben Cr

Fionnphort

ROSS OF MULL

Sound of Mull

Firth of Lorn

Iona

Scarba

Fur

A R G

8°W

7°W

6°W

North Sea

© Oxford University Press

Key

–·–·–·	international boundary
–– ––	national boundary
–·–·–	county, district or unitary authority boundary
——	motorway and main road
——	railway
✈	main airport
∿	river
⊢⊢⊢	canal
	lake
▲	peak or highest point

towns

	built-up areas
■	largest towns
●	large towns
·	other towns

Land height

measured in metres above sea level

	more than 1000 m
	500 – 1000 m
	200 – 500 m
	100 – 200 m
	less than 100 m

Transverse Mercator Projection
© Oxford University Press

Map labels

Belfast, Edinburgh

Iona, Fionnphort, ROSS OF MULL, Kerrera, Oban, Dalma
Colonsay, Scalasaig, Oronsay, Scarba, ARGYLL AND, Inveraray, Furnace, Lochgilphead, Loch Fyne
Port Askaig, Craighouse, Kilmory, Tarbert, Tighnabruaic, Bute, Rothesay
I s l a y, Gigha, Ardminish, Clachan, Claonaig, Lochranza
Portnahaven, Ardbeg, Port Ellen, Mull of Oa, Goat Fell 874 m▲, Arran, Brodic
KINTYRE, NORTH AYRSH, Campbeltown

Malin Head, Tory Island, Tory Sound, INISHOWEN PENINSULA, ▲ Slieve Snaght 615m, Rathlin Island, Rathlin Sound, Mull of Kintyre, Southend, Fair Head, Ailsa Crai
Errigal Mountain 752m ▲, Creeslough, Lough Swilly, Buncrana, Lough Foyle, Portrush, Portstewart, Coleraine, River Bush, Ballycastle, MOYLE, North Channel, Ballantrae
Kilmacrenan, Limavady, COLERAINE, Ballymoney, ANTRIM MOUNTAINS, Corsewall Point
Letterkenny, R. Swilly, Londonderry, LONDONDERRY, LIMAVADY, Dungiven, River Bann, BALLYMONEY, River Bann, River Main, BALLYMENA, Stranraer
DONEGAL, Ballybofey, River Finn, Strabane, Sawel 683m ▲, Maghera, Lough Beg, Ballymena, LARNE, Larne, Portpatrick
STRABANE, MAGHERAFELT, Magherafelt, 529m ▲, Randalstown, ANTRIM, M22, NEWTOWNABBEY, Island Magee, CARRICKFERGUS, Carrickfergus
Newtownstewart, River Derg, NORTHERN IRELAND, COOKSTOWN, Antrim, Newtownabbey, BELFAST, Belfast Lough, Bangor, Donaghadee, Dru
Donegal, Lough Derg, Omagh, Cookstown, Lough Neagh, Lough Crumlin, Belfast, NORTH DOWN, Newtownards, Gal
Ballyshannon, OMAGH, Coalisland, CRAIGAVON, Lisburn, CASTLEREAGH, ARDS, ARDS PENINSULA, Strangford Lough
Lower Lough Erne, DUNGANNON, Dungannon, R. Blackwater, Lurgan, M1, LISBURN, Dromore
Lough Melvin, FERMANAGH, Enniskillen, Portadown, Craigavon, Banbridge, River Bann, DOWN, Downpatrick
Lough Macnean Upper, Upper Lough Erne, Armagh, BANBRIDGE, St John's Point
LEITRIM, Shannon, Lough Macnean Lower, Clones, MONAGHAN, Monaghan, Keady, ARMAGH, Newtownhamilton, Slieve Donard 852m ▲, Newcastle
Lough Allen, R. Erne, Castleblayney, NEWRY AND MOURNE, Newry, Warrenpoint, Kilkeel, Carlingford Lough
REPUBLIC OF IRELAND, Lough Oughter, Cavan, Crossmaglen, LOUTH, Dundalk

8°W, 7°W, 6°W, 56°N, 55°N, 54°N

Scale 1: 1 000 000

One centimetre on the map represents
10 kilometres on the ground.

0 10 20 30 40 50 km

Lockerbie · 3°W · C · 2°W · D

NORTHUMBERLAND

Cramlin

Newcastle upon Tyn

Gatesh

Wash

Chest

le-Stre

Durh

M6

55°N · Annan

River Irthing · Haltwhistle · Hexham

Carlisle · Brampton

Newton Stewart · Castle Douglas · 4°W · B · Kirkbean

Glenluce · Dalbeattie

Wigtown · Gatehouse of Fleet

Kirkcudbright

Whithorn

Luce Bay

Wigtown Bay

Mull of Galloway

Solway Firth

Wigton

River Eden

River Ellen

Cross Fell 893m

PENNINES

DURHAM · Spennym

Bishop Auckland

Newton Ay

River Wear

Maryport

R. Derwent · Cockermouth

931m Skiddaw

Penrith

Mickle Fell 790m

Appleby-in-Westmorland

River Tees

Consett

Durh

R. Derwent

Workington

Keswick · Derwent Water

CUMBRIA

Brough

Barnard Castle

DARL

Darlin

Whitehaven

St Bees Head

Helvellyn 950m

Ullswater

Kirkby Stephen

Richmond

54°N

Seascale

978m Scafell Pike · Windermere

LAKE DISTRICT

Ambleside · Windermere

Kendal

River Swale

R. Ure · Leyburn

NORTH YORKSHI

Coniston Water

Whernside 737m

River Wharfe

Dalton-in-Furness

Morecambe Bay

Carnforth

R. Greta · 723m Ingleborough

Pen-y-Ghent 693m

Great Whernside 704m

Barrow-in-Furness

Morecambe · Lancaster

Heysham · 560m Ward's Stone

River

FOREST OF BOWLAND

River Aire · Skipton · Harr

Fleetwood

River Wyre

Barnoldswick

Ilkley · Keighley

Clitheroe

Irish Sea

BLACKPOOL

LANCASHIRE · M55 · River Ribble

Colne · Nelson

Bradford

Blackpool

Preston

Blackburn

BLACKBURN WITH DARWEN

Burnley

Halifax

WES

Lytham St Anne's

Leyland · Chorley

Brighouse

Huddersfield

Dev

YORKS

Southport

M6

Bury

Rochdale

M62

Formby

Skelmersdale

Bolton

M61

Oldham

Manchester

Wigan

GREATER MANCHESTER

Kirkby

Salford

Bootle · MERSEYSIDE

St Helens

Sale

Stockport

Wallasey

Warrington

Cheadle

The Peak 636m

Liverpool

Widnes

WARRINGTON

Birkenhead

R. Mersey

Runcorn

HALTON

M53

Ellesmere Port

Northwich

Macclesfield

Buxton

Holyhead

ISLE OF ANGLESEY

Llandudno

Rhyl

Conwy

River Dee

Chester

CHESHIRE

Winsford

Bakewell

DER

River Dove

Holy Island

Bangor

Colwyn Bay

FLINTSHIRE

Flint

Crewe

Kidsgrove

Carmel Head

Amlwch

Caernarfon Bay

Anglesey

Bethesda

R. Conwy

Denbigh

Mold

CONWY

Wrexham

WREXHAM

Newcastle-under-Lyme

STOKE-ON-TRENT

Stoke-on-Trent

Snowdon 1085m

DENBIGHSHIRE

River Clwyd

Whitchurch

ENGLAN

Portmadog

LLEYN PENINSULA

Blaenau Ffestiniog

Llangollen

River Dee

Oswestry

Market Drayton

M6

Uttoxeter

Burton upon Tren

Pwllheli

Bala

Bala Lake

CAMBRIAN MOUNTAINS

Harlech

GWYNEDD

POWYS

Lake Vyrnwy

R. Vyrnwy

WREXHAM

Stafford

STAFFORDSHIRE

Rugeley

Barmouth

53°N

Cardigan Bay

Dolgellau · Cader Idris 892m

R. Dyfi · Machynlleth

WALES

Welshpool

Shrewsbury

SHROPSHIRE

R. Severn

Newport

TELFORD AND WREKIN

Telford

407m The Wrekin

M54

Cannock

Lichfiel

Tamworth

Wolverhampton

4°W · A · B · 3°W · C · 2°W

© Oxford University Press

Key

- – – national boundary
- –·– county or unitary authority boundary
- motorway and main road
- railway
- ⊕ main airport
- river
- canal
- lake
- ▲ peak or highest point

towns
- built-up areas
- ■ largest towns
- ● large towns
- · other towns

Land height

measured in metres above sea level

- more than 1000 m
- 500 – 1000 m
- 200 – 500 m
- 100 – 200 m
- less than 100 m
- below sea level

Scale   1: 1 000 000

One centimetre on the map represents 10 kilometres on the ground.

0 10 20 30 40 50 km

Transverse Mercator Projection
© Oxford University Press

Wales

Irish Sea

Irish Sea

Formby

MERSE

Boo
Wallase
Liver
Birkenhe

A
Malahide
Howth
Dublin
Dún Laoghaire
Bray
Greystones

REPUBLIC OF
IRELAND

53°N
Wicklow

Arklow

Irish
Sea

Carmel Head
Amlwch
Holyhead
Holy
Island
ISLE OF
ANGLESEY
Anglesey
Caernarfon
Bay
Caernarfon
Snowdon
1085m
Bangor
Bethesda
Llandudno
Conwy
Colwyn
Bay
Rhyl
CONWY
Denbigh
FLINTSHIRE
Flint
River Dee
River Clwyd
DENBIGHSHIRE
Wrexh
W

LLEYN PENINSULA
Porthmadog
Pwllheli
Harlech
Barmouth
Blaenau
Ffestiniog
GWYNEDD
Aran Fawddy
905m
Dolgellau
Cader Idris
892m
Machynlleth
R. Conwy
Bala
Bala
Lake
Lake
Vyrnwy
R. Vyrnwy
Llangollen
River Dee
Oswestr
Welshpool
R. Dyfi
WALES
R. Severn
Mor
SHRO

Cardigan
Bay

2
52°N

Aberystwyth
CEREDIGION
Aberaeron
New Quay
River Teifi
Cemaes Head
Cardigan
River Teifi
Newcastle Emlyn
Lampeter
Plynlimon
752m
Llanidloes
Rhayader
Llandrindod
Wells
POWYS
Builth Wells
MYNYDD
EPPYNT
CAMBRIAN MOUNTAINS
R. Wye
Kni
Newtown

St George's Channel

Strumble Head
St David's Head
St David's
PEMBROKESHIRE
Haverfordwest
St Brides
Bay
Milford
Haven
Pembroke
Tenby
Fishguard
MYNYDD
PRESELI
Carmarthen
R. Tywi
Llandovery
Llandeilo
CARMARTHENSHIRE
R. Tywi
Ammanford
Kidwelly
Burry
Port
Carmarthen
Bay
Pontardulais
Llanelli
Swansea
GOWER
Worms Head
Neath
Port Talbot
SWANSEA
NEATH
PORT TALBOT
Port
Talbot
Bridgend
BRIDGEND
R. Usk
River Usk
Llandovery
Brecon
811m
BRECON
BEACONS
886m
Abergav
Merthyr
Tydfil
Aberdare
RHONDDA
CYNON
MERTHYR
TYDFIL
Rhondda
TAFF
Pontypridd
Caerphilly
CAERPHILLY
CARDIFF
THE VALE OF
GLAMORGAN
Barry
Ebb
BLAENAU
GWENT
Abertille
Pontyp
Cwm
New
Ca

1

NORTH

ATLANTIC

OCEAN

Lundy

Ilfracombe
DEVON
Lynton
EXMOOR
Dunkery
Beacon
519m
Minehead
Weston-su
M
Bridgwater
Bay

Bristol Channel

6°W
5°W
4°W

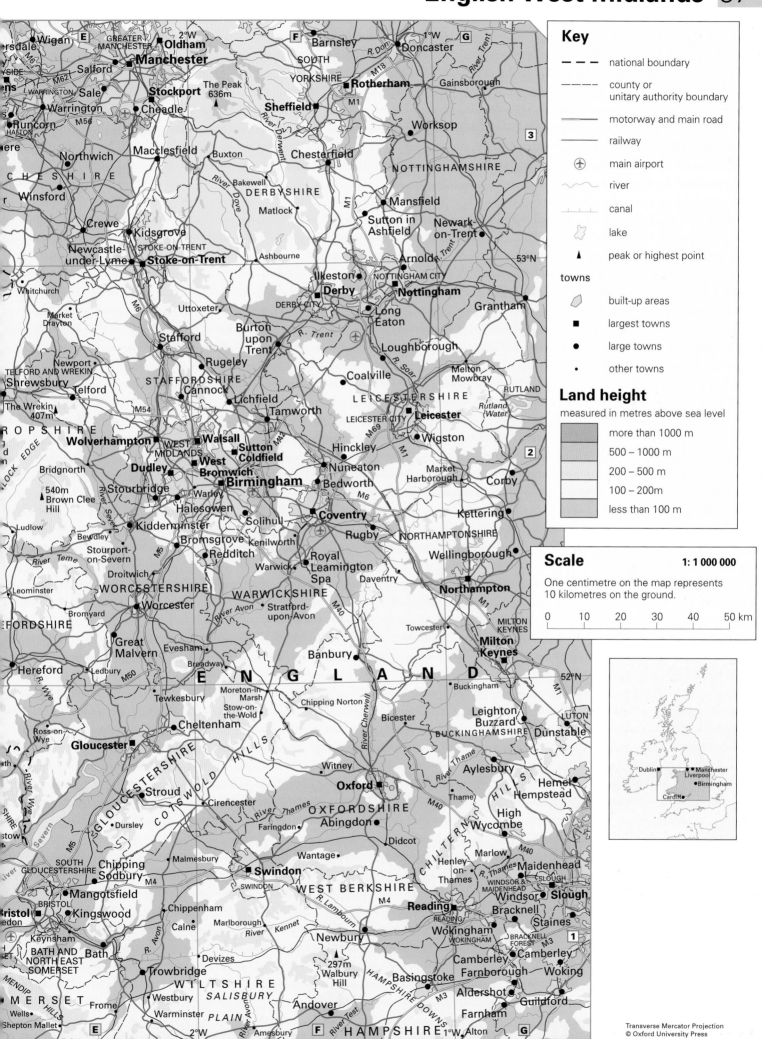

Key

- – – national boundary
- – – – county or unitary authority boundary
- ═══ motorway and main road
- ─── railway
- ⊕ main airport
- river
- canal
- lake
- ▲ peak or highest point

towns

- built-up areas
- ■ largest towns
- ● large towns
- • other towns

Land height

measured in metres above sea level

- more than 1000 m
- 500 – 1000 m
- 200 – 500 m
- 100 – 200m
- less than 100 m

Scale   1: 1 000 000

One centimetre on the map represents 10 kilometres on the ground.

0   10   20   30   40   50 km

Transverse Mercator Projection
© Oxford University Press

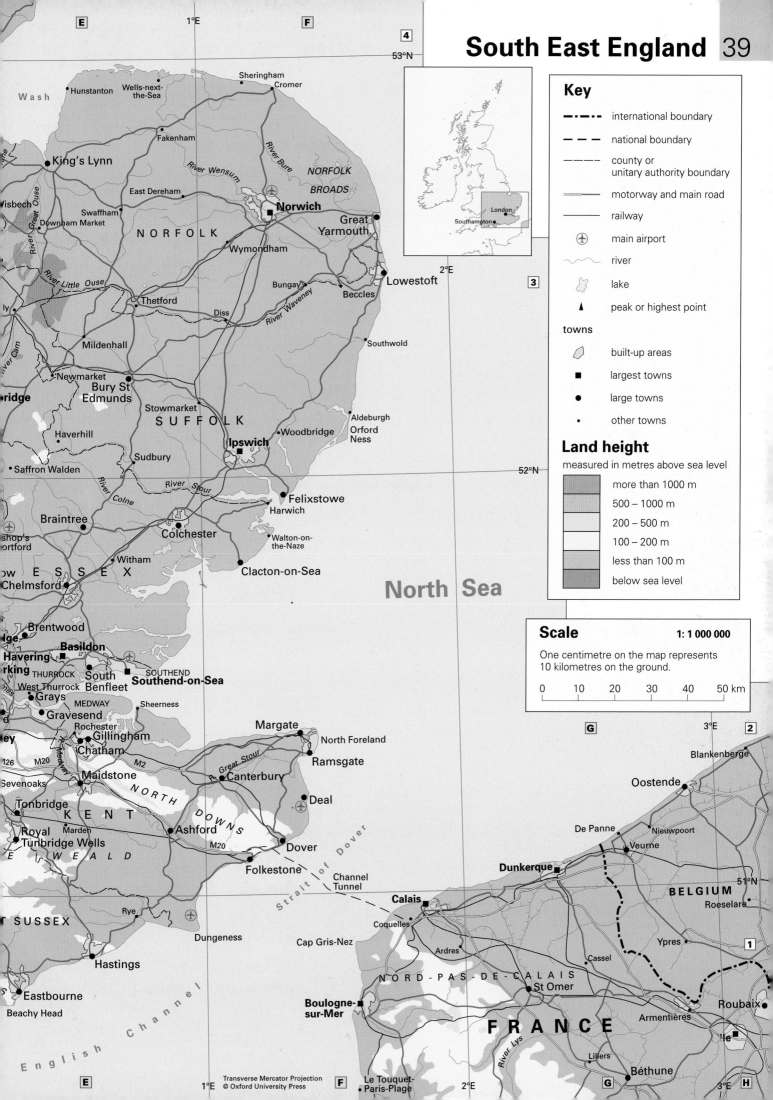

Key

- — · · — international boundary
- — — — national boundary
- — · — county or unitary authority boundary
- motorway and main road
- railway
- ✈ main airport
- river
- lake
- ▲ peak or highest point

towns

- built-up areas
- ■ largest towns
- ● large towns
- • other towns

Land height

measured in metres above sea level

- more than 1000 m
- 500 – 1000 m
- 200 – 500 m
- 100 – 200 m
- less than 100 m
- below sea level

Scale   1: 1 000 000

One centimetre on the map represents
10 kilometres on the ground.

0 10 20 30 40 50 km

London
Southampton

North Sea

English Channel

Wash

Hunstanton
Wells-next-the-Sea
Sheringham
Cromer
King's Lynn
Fakenham
River Wensum
River Bure
NORFOLK BROADS
Wisbech
Swaffham
East Dereham
Norwich
Downham Market
River Great Ouse
NORFOLK
Wymondham
Great Yarmouth
River Little Ouse
Lowestoft
Bungay
Beccles
Mildenhall
Thetford
Diss
River Waveney
Southwold
River Cam
Newmarket
Bury St Edmunds
Stowmarket
SUFFOLK
Aldeburgh
Orford Ness
bridge
Haverhill
Sudbury
Woodbridge
Ipswich
Saffron Walden
River Stour
Felixstowe
River Colne
Harwich
Braintree
Colchester
Walton-on-the-Naze
shop's
ortford
Witham
Clacton-on-Sea
ow ESSEX
Chelmsford
Brentwood
Basildon
Havering
rking
THURROCK
South Benfleet
SOUTHEND
Southend-on-Sea
West Thurrock
Grays
MEDWAY
Sheerness
Gravesend
Rochester
Gillingham
Margate
North Foreland
y
Chatham
Great Stour
Ramsgate
126
M20
Sevenoaks
Maidstone
M2
Canterbury
Tonbridge
NORTH DOWNS
Deal
Marden
R. Great Stour
Royal Tunbridge Wells
KENT
Ashford
Dover
WEALD
M20
Folkestone
Rye
Channel Tunnel
SUSSEX
Strait of Dover
Calais
Hastings
Dungeness
Coquelles
BELGIUM
Eastbourne
Cap Gris-Nez
Ardres
Blankenberge
Beachy Head
Oostende
De Panne
Nieuwpoort
Veurne
Dunkerque
NORD-PAS-DE-CALAIS
St Omer
Ypres
Roeselare
Cassel
Roubaix
Boulogne-sur-Mer
FRANCE
Armentières
le
Le Touquet-Paris-Plage
River Lys
Lillers
Béthune

Transverse Mercator Projection
© Oxford University Press

Key

- — ·— ·— international boundary
- — — — — county or unitary authority boundary
- motorway and main road
- railway
- ✈ main airport
- ～ river
- ┼┼┼ canal
- lake
- ▲ peak or highest point

towns

- built-up areas
- ■ largest towns
- ● large towns
- · other towns

Land height

measured in metres above sea level

- more than 1000 m
- 500 – 1000 m
- 200 – 500 m
- 100 – 200 m
- less than 100 m

NORTH ATLANTIC OCEAN

NORTH ATLANTIC OCEAN

Bristol Chann

51°N

50°N

49°N

4°W

5°W

6°W

Lundy

Ilfracombe

Lynton

Minehe
Dunkery B
▲ 519m

River Exe

Braunton

Barnstaple *E X M O O R*

Bideford Bay

South Molton

River Taw

Hartland Point

Bideford

Great Torrington

Tiverto

River Torridge

D E V O N

Cull

Bude Bay

Bude

Holsworthy

Hatherleigh

Crediton

Boscastle

Okehampton

Yes Tor
619

River

Exeter

Ex

Trevose Head

Padstow

Launceston

Brown Willy
▲ 420m

BODMIN MOOR

DARTMOOR

Teign

Bovey Tracey

Da

Wadebridge

River Camel

R. *Tamar*

River Tavy

Tavistock

Newton Abbot

Teignmouth

Newquay

Bodmin

River Fowey

Liskeard

Buckfastleigh

R. Dart

To

TORBA

St Agnes

CORNWALL

Lostwithiel

Saltash

PLYMOUTH

Totnes

Fal

St Austell

Fowey

Looe

Torpoint

Plymouth

Dartmouth

B

St Ives

Truro

River

Kingsbridge

Start Bay

Redruth
Camborne

Bigbury Bay

Start Po

St Just

Penryn

Salcombe

Penzance

Falmouth

Sennen
Land's End

Helston

Mount's Bay

Mullion

Bryher
St Martin's
Tresco
St Mary's
Hugh Town
Isles of Scilly

Lizard

Lizard Point

Cardiff
Southampton

Isles of Scilly

Channel Islands

Scale

1 : 1 000 000

One centimetre on the map represents 10 kilometres on the ground.

0 10 20 30 40 50 km

THE
GLAM

D

C

4°W

5°W

6°W

Transverse Mercator Projection
© Oxford University Press

Cardiff
Clevedon
3°W
BRISTOL
Bristol Kingswood
M4
Chippenham
Calne
2°W
E
M5
Keynsham
Bath
BATH AND NORTH EAST SOMERSET
ston-super-Mare
NORTH WEST SOMERSET
Devizes
Trowbridge
WILTSHIRE
SALISBURY PLAIN
Walbury Hill 297m
F
water Bay
MENDIP HILLS
Wells
Shepton Mallet
Westbury
Warminster
HAMPSHIRE DOWNS
Basingstoke
Camberley
Farnborough
Aldershot
1°W
G
Woking Epsom
SURREY
Bridgwater
Glastonbury
Frome
Andover
Farnham
Guildford
Dorking
ANTOCK HILLS
R. Parrett
S O M E R S E T
River Tone
Wincanton
Mere
Shaftesbury
River Test
Stockbridge
River Itchen
R. Itchen
Alton
NORTH DOWNS
Haslemere
4
unton
Ilchester
Shaftesbury
Winchester
HAMPSHIRE
51°N
Horsham
ngton
M5
River Yeo
Yeovil
Sherborne
Salisbury
Romsey
Eastleigh
Petersfield
WEST SUSSEX
Chard
Ilminster
Crewkerne
River Axe
Axminster
D O R S E T
Blandford Forum
Wimborne Minster
River Avon
Ringwood
Totton
SOUTHAMPTON
Southampton
Fawley
Waterlooville
Havant
SOUTH DOWNS
Arundel
Chichester
Worthing
ton
Bridport
Lyme Regis
Dorchester
River Frome
Wareham
POOLE
Poole
BOURNEMOUTH
Bournemouth
Christchurch
Lymington
Fareham
Gosport
PORTSMOUTH
Portsmouth
Cowes
Bognor Regis
Littlehampton
Seaton
idmouth
Lyme Bay
Weymouth
Swanage
The Needles
ISLE OF WIGHT
Newport
Ryde
Sandown
Shanklin
The Solent
Selsey Bill
St Alban's Head
Portland Bill
St Catherine's Point
3

E n g l i s h   C h a n n e l

50°N

Alderney
Auderville
Cap de la Hague
Barfleur
Cherbourg
Baie de la Seine
2
Guernsey
St Peter-Port
Sark
CHANNEL
Valognes
F R A N C E
ISLANDS
Jersey
St Helier
Carteret
Lessay
Carentan
Isigny-sur-Mer
Bayeux
Coutainville
Coutances
River Vire
St-Lô
Caen
River Orne
49°N
1

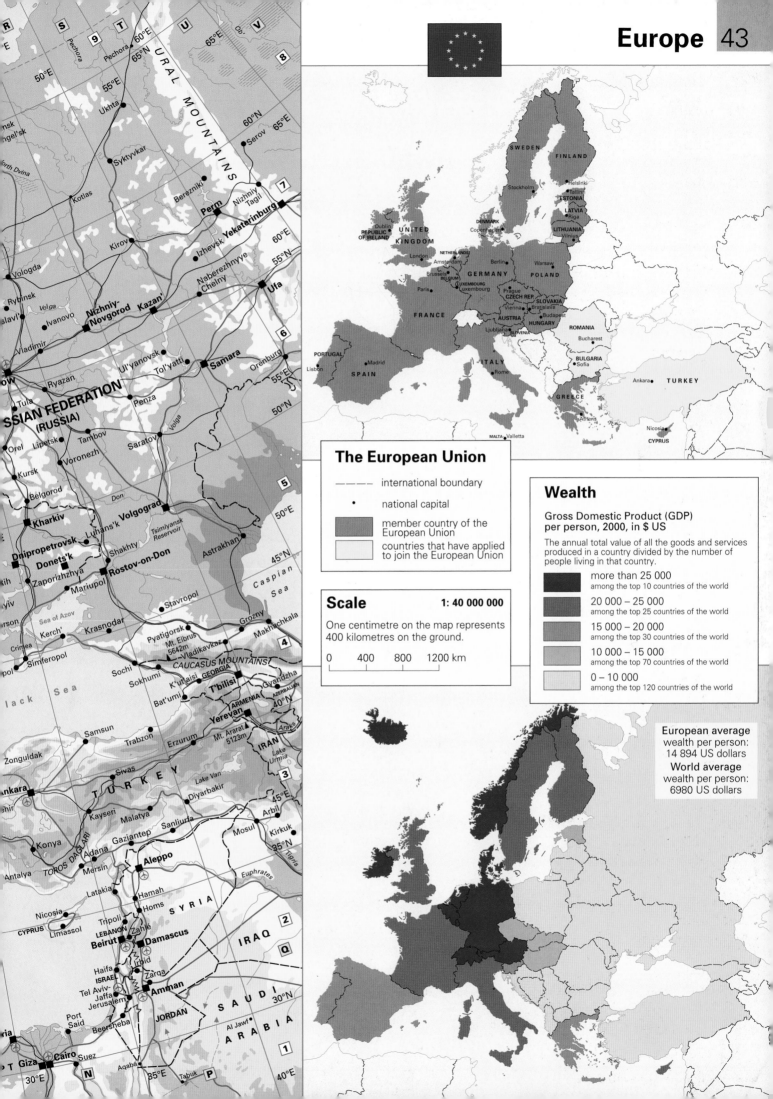

The European Union

- – – – international boundary
- • national capital
- member country of the European Union
- countries that have applied to join the European Union

Scale
1 : 40 000 000

One centimetre on the map represents 400 kilometres on the ground.

0 400 800 1200 km

Wealth

Gross Domestic Product (GDP) per person, 2000, in $ US

The annual total value of all the goods and services produced in a country divided by the number of people living in that country.

- **more than 25 000** — among the top 10 countries of the world
- **20 000 – 25 000** — among the top 25 countries of the world
- **15 000 – 20 000** — among the top 30 countries of the world
- **10 000 – 15 000** — among the top 70 countries of the world
- **0 – 10 000** — among the top 120 countries of the world

European average wealth per person: 14 894 US dollars

World average wealth per person: 6980 US dollars

Climatic regions

Very dry

with no reliable rain

with a little rain

Influenced by the sea: warm summers, mild winters

with dry summers (Mediterranean type)

with no dry season

Cool

rain all year

Cold polar

no warm season and fairly dry

Mountain

height of the land strongly affects the climate

Ocean currents

→ warm

→ cold

Climate recording stations

• climate recording stations for which graphs are shown

Almeria (6 m)

Barcelona (93 m)

Paris (75 m)

Warsaw (110 m)

Stockholm (44 m)

Ecosystems

Vegetation types are those which would occur naturally without interference by people.

coniferous forest

deciduous and mixed forest

evergreen trees and shrubs

temperate grasslands

semi-desert

tundra

ice

mountains

Scale

1: 40 000 000

One centimetre on the map represents 400 kilometres on the ground.

0   400   800   1200 km

Conical Orthomorphic Projection
© Oxford University Press

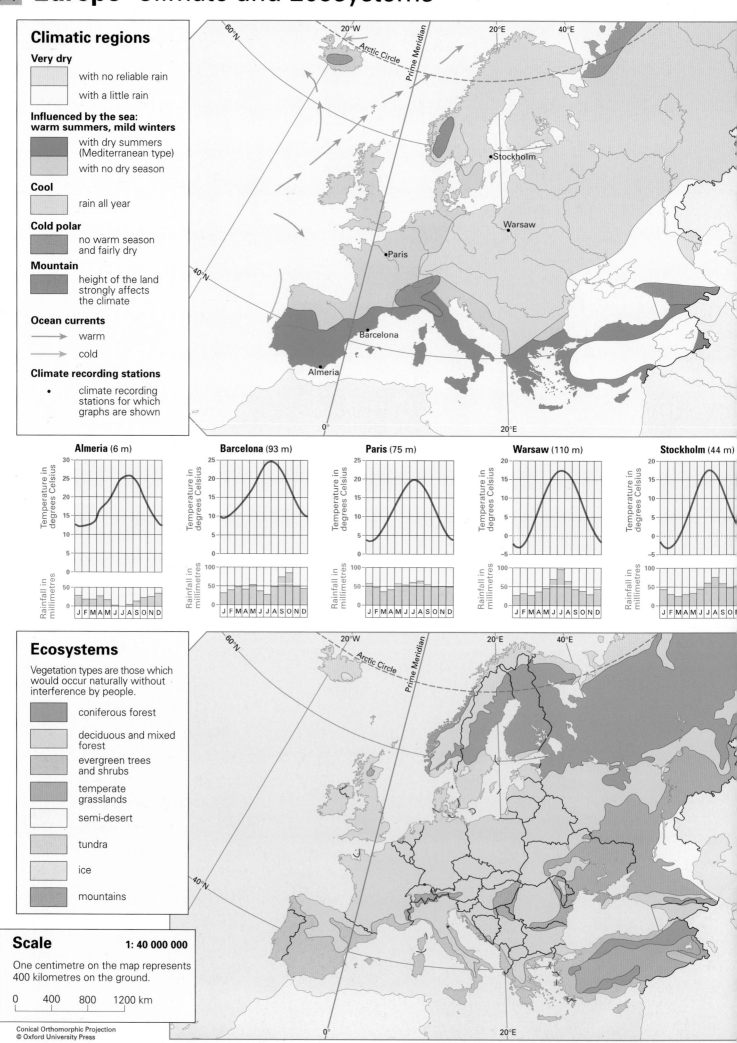

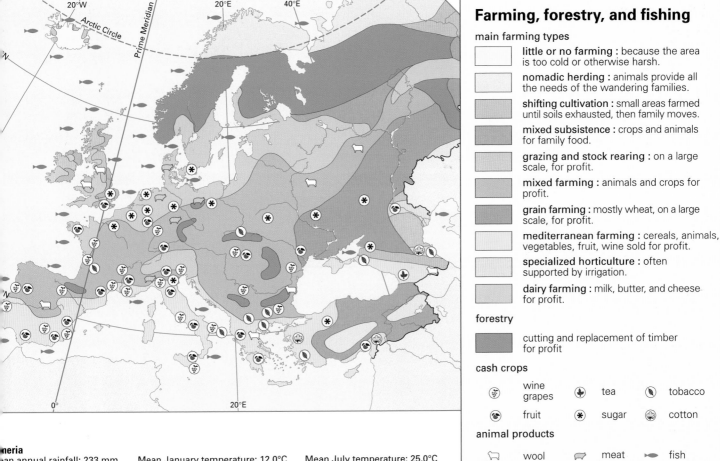

Farming, forestry, and fishing

main farming types

	little or no farming : because the area is too cold or otherwise harsh.
	nomadic herding : animals provide all the needs of the wandering families.
	shifting cultivation : small areas farmed until soils exhausted, then family moves.
	mixed subsistence : crops and animals for family food.
	grazing and stock rearing : on a large scale, for profit.
	mixed farming : animals and crops for profit.
	grain farming : mostly wheat, on a large scale, for profit.
	mediterranean farming : cereals, animals, vegetables, fruit, wine sold for profit.
	specialized horticulture : often supported by irrigation.
	dairy farming : milk, butter, and cheese for profit.

forestry

	cutting and replacement of timber for profit

cash crops

⊛	wine grapes	♣	tea	◉	tobacco
◉	fruit	✳	sugar	⊛	cotton

animal products

🐑	wool	🐂	meat	⊷	fish

meria
an annual rainfall: 233 mm   Mean January temperature: 12.0°C   Mean July temperature: 25.0°C

rcelona
an annual rainfall: 587 mm   Mean January temperature: 9.5°C   Mean July temperature: 24.5°C

ris
an annual rainfall: 589 mm   Mean January temperature: 3.5°C   Mean July temperature: 20.0°C

rsaw
an annual rainfall: 525 mm   Mean January temperature: -3.0°C   Mean July temperature: 19.5°C

ckholm
an annual rainfall: 524 mm   Mean January temperature: -3.0°C   Mean July temperature: 18.0°C

Scale   **1 : 40 000 000**

One centimetre on the map represents 400 kilometres on the ground.

0   400   800   1200 km

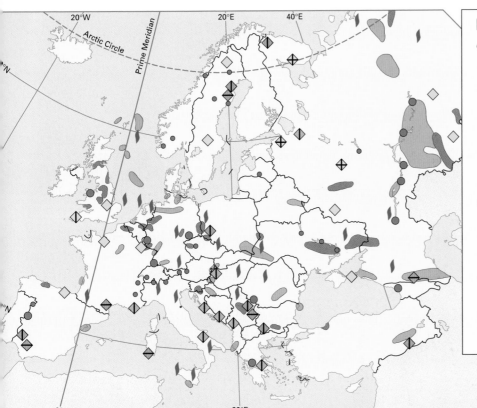

Energy and minerals

energy

	coalfield
	oil field (with associated gas, and sometimes off shore)
	gas field

hydro-electric power stations

●	largest (over 1000 megawatts)
•	smaller (500 – 1000 megawatts)

minerals (main mining areas)

◇	iron ore
◈	silver
◇	tin
◈	copper
◈	bauxite
⊕	phosphates

Conical Orthomorphic Projection
© Oxford University Press

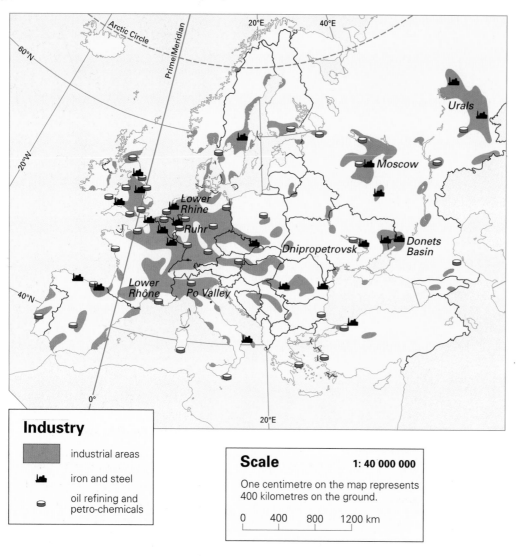

Industry

 industrial areas

iron and steel

oil refining and petro-chemicals

Scale   1: 40 000 000

One centimetre on the map represents 400 kilometres on the ground.

0   400   800   1200 km

Population structure of the United Kingdom

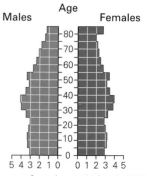

Age

Males   Females

percent of total population in 2000
Total population : 59.5 million

Population structure of France

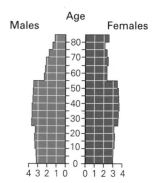

Age

Males   Females

percent of total population in 2000
Total population : 59.3 million

global warming
addition of greenhouse gases in tonnes of carbon per person
(look at the world map on page 17)

Environmental issues

sea pollution

areas severely polluted for all or part of the year

areas persistently affected by pollution

▼ deep sea dump sites

✳ major oil spills (over 100 000 tonnes)

✶ major oil spills (under 100 000 tonnes)

acid rain

A pH scale measures acidity. Unaffected rain water is slightly acidic with a pH of 5.6

pH less than 4.2 (most acidic)

pH 4.2 – 4.6

pH 4.6 – 5.0

air pollution

◆ cities where sulphur dioxide emissions are recorded and exceed recommended levels

industrial sites emitting the largest amounts of sulphur

◯ over 200 000 tonnes

○ 100 000 – 200 000 tonnes

○ 50 000 – 100 000 tonnes

∘ 30 000 – 50 000 tonnes

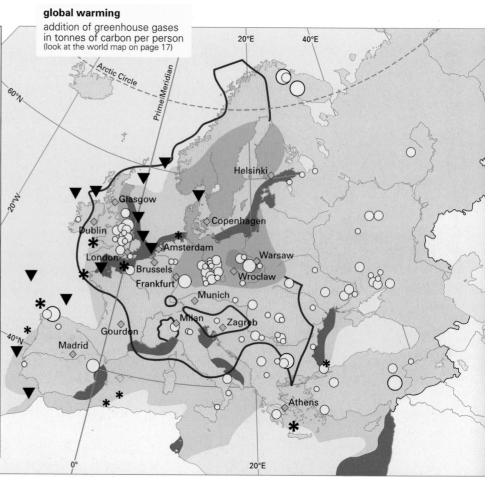

Conical Orthomorphic Projection
© Oxford University Press

Population structure of Germany

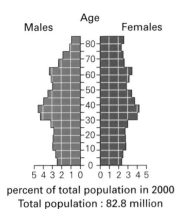

Males — Age — Females

percent of total population in 2000
Total population : 82.8 million

Population structure of Greece

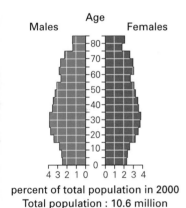

Males — Age — Females

percent of total population in 2000
Total population : 10.6 million

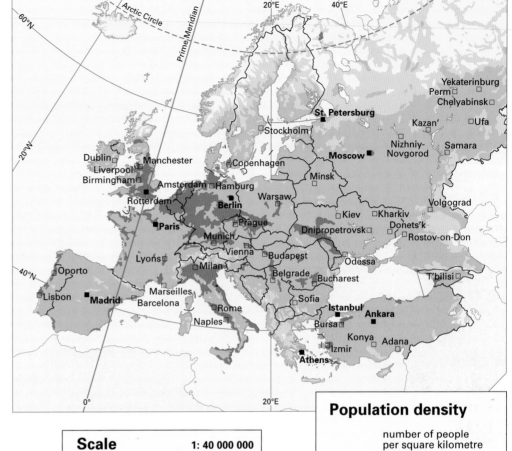

Scale 1: 40 000 000

One centimetre on the map represents
400 kilometres on the ground.

0   400   800   1200 km

Population density

number of people
per square kilometre

high		more than 100
moderate		10 – 100
sparse		1 – 10
very low		less than 1

■ major cities and built
up areas of at least
3 million people

□ cities with
1 – 3 million people

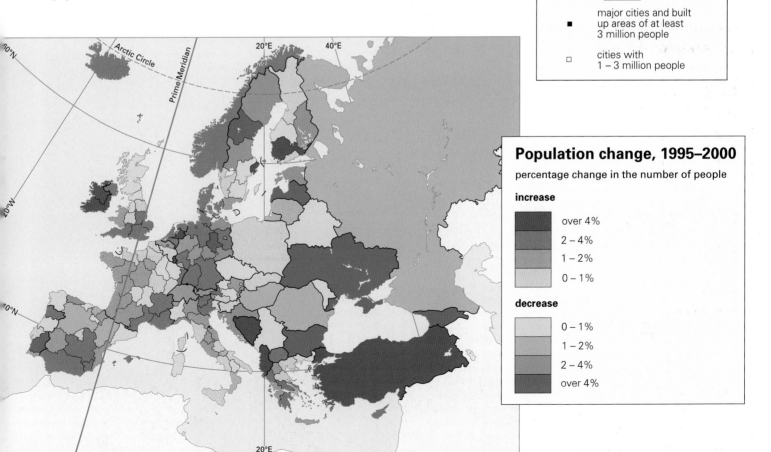

Population change, 1995–2000

percentage change in the number of people

increase

	over 4%
	2 – 4%
	1 – 2%
	0 – 1%

decrease

	0 – 1%
	1 – 2%
	2 – 4%
	over 4%

Conical Orthomorphic Projection
© Oxford University Pres

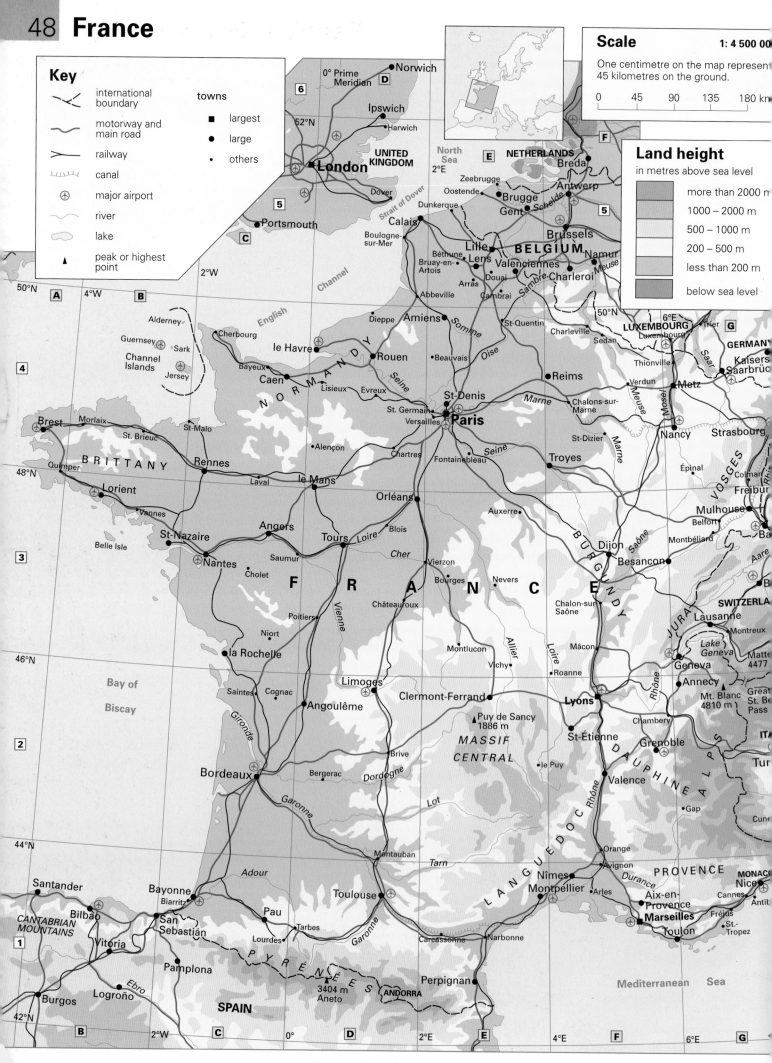

Key

- ⟩⟨ international boundary
- ∿ motorway and main road
- ⟩ railway
- ⊔⊔⊔ canal
- ⊕ major airport
- ∿ river
- ▱ lake
- ▲ peak or highest point

towns
- ■ largest
- ● large
- • others

Scale

1 : 4 500 000

One centimetre on the map represent 45 kilometres on the ground.

0   45   90   135   180 km

Land height

in metres above sea level

- more than 2000 m
- 1000 – 2000 m
- 500 – 1000 m
- 200 – 500 m
- less than 200 m
- below sea level

Norwich
Ipswich
Harwich
52°N
London
UNITED KINGDOM
North Sea 2°E
Portsmouth
Dover
Strait of Dover
Calais
Boulogne-sur-Mer
Dunkerque
Zeebrugge
Oostende
Brugge
Gent
Schelde
Antwerp
Breda
NETHERLANDS
Lille
Béthune
Lens
Bruay-en-Artois
Arras
Douai
Valenciennes
Cambrai
Sambre
Charleroi
BELGIUM
Brussels
Namur
Meuse
LUXEMBOURG
Luxembourg
Trier
GERMANY
50°N
6°E
Abbeville
Amiens
Somme
St-Quentin
Charleville
Sedan
Dieppe
Beauvais
Oise
Thionville
Kaisers
Saarbrüc
Cherbourg
le Havre
Rouen
Seine
Reims
Verdun
Metz
Saar
Mosel
Bayeux
Caen
NORMANDY
Lisieux
Evreux
St. Germain
St-Denis
Marne
Chalons-sur-Marne
Moselle
Nancy
Strasbourg
Versailles
Paris
Marne
St-Dizier
Brest
Morlaix
St. Brieuc
St-Malo
Alençon
Chartres
Fontainebleau
Seine
Troyes
Épinal
Colmar
VOSGES
Freibur
Quimper
BRITTANY
Rennes
Laval
le Mans
Orléans
Auxerre
Mulhouse
Belfort
48°N
Lorient
Vannes
Angers
Tours
Loire
Blois
Cher
Vierzon
Bourges
Nevers
Dijon
Saône
Montbéliard
Besançon
Ba
St-Nazaire
Saumur
BURGUNDY
Belle Isle
Nantes
Cholet
F R A N C E
Vienne
Châteauroux
Chalon-sur-Saône
SWITZERLA
JURA
Lausanne
Montreux
Poitiers
Niort
Allier
Mâcon
Lake Geneva
Matte
4477
la Rochelle
Loire
Roanne
Geneva
46°N
Bay of Biscay
Saintes
Cognac
Limoges
Clermont-Ferrand
Montlucon
Vichy
Lyons
Annecy
Great St. Be Pass
Angoulême
Gironde
Puy de Sancy
1886 m
St-Étienne
Chambery
Mt. Blanc
4810 m
ITA
MASSIF CENTRAL
le Puy
Grenoble
DAUPHINE ALPS
Tur
Bordeaux
Bergerac
Brive
Dordogne
Valence
Rhône
2
Garonne
Lot
44°N
Montauban
Tarn
Orange
Avignon
Durance
PROVENCE
MONACO
Nice
Adour
Toulouse
Nîmes
Arles
Cannes
Cune
Santander
Bayonne
Biarritz
Pau
LANGUEDOC
Rhône
Montpellier
Aix-en-Provence
Marseilles
Antib
Fréjus
St-Tropez
Toulon
Bilbao
Vitoria
San Sebastián
Tarbes
Garonne
Carcassonne
Narbonne
CANTABRIAN MOUNTAINS
Lourdes
Mediterranean Sea
Pamplona
PYRÉNÉES
Perpignan
Burgos
Logroño
Ebro
3404 m
Aneto
ANDORRA
SPAIN
42°N
English Channel
Alderney
Guernsey
Sark
Channel Islands
Jersey
50°N
2°W
0° Prime Meridian
4°W
2°W
0°
2°E
4°E
6°E

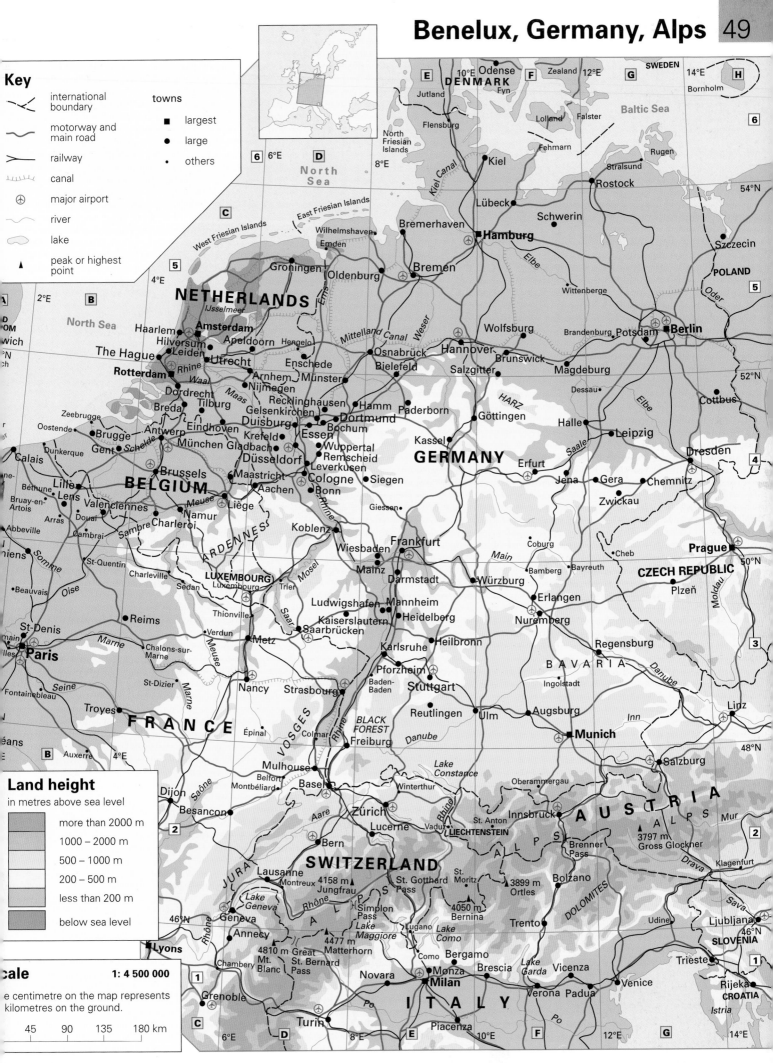

Key

	international boundary
	motorway and main road
	railway
	canal
	major airport
	river
	lake
▲	peak or highest point

towns

■ largest
● large
· others

Land height
in metres above sea level

	more than 2000 m
	1000 – 2000 m
	500 – 1000 m
	200 – 500 m
	less than 200 m
	below sea level

Scale
1: 4 500 000

e centimetre on the map represents
kilometres on the ground.

45   90   135   180 km

rthomorphic Projection   © Oxford University Press

SWEDEN

DENMARK
Jutland
Fyn
Odense
Zealand
Lolland
Falster
Bornholm
Flensburg
Fehmarn
Rugen
Baltic Sea
Kiel
Stralsund
Rostock
Lübeck
Schwerin
North Friesian Islands
Bremerhaven
Hamburg
Schwerin
Szczecin
POLAND
Wilhelmshaven
Emden
Bremen
Wittenberge
Groningen
Oldenburg
Wolfsburg
Brandenburg
Potsdam
Berlin

NETHERLANDS
IJsselmeer
West Friesian Islands
East Friesian Islands
North Sea
Mittelland Canal
Weser
Elbe
Oder

Haarlem
Amsterdam
Hilversum
Apeldoorn
Hengelo
Osnabrück
Hannover
Brunswick
Magdeburg
Dessau
Leipzig
Cottbus
The Hague
Leiden
Utrecht
Enschede
Bielefeld
Salzgitter
Halle
Dresden
Rotterdam
Rhine
Arnhem
Münster
Paderborn
Göttingen
HARZ
Saale
Dordrecht
Waal
Nijmegen
Recklinghausen
Hamm
Kassel
Erfurt
Jena
Gera
Chemnitz
Breda
Maas
Tilburg
Gelsenkirchen
Dortmund
Bochum
GERMANY
Zwickau
Zeebrugge
Antwerp
Eindhoven
Duisburg
Essen
Siegen
Oostende
Brugge
Schelde
München Gladbach
Krefeld
Wuppertal
Remscheid
Leverkusen
Gent
Düsseldorf
Aachen
Cologne
Bonn
Giessen
Calais
BELGIUM
Maastricht
Koblenz
Dunkerque
Brussels
Liège
Rhine
Lille
Béthune
Lens
Valenciennes
Namur
Meuse
Charleroi
Wiesbaden
Frankfurt
Main
Coburg
Cheb
Prague
Bruay-en-Artois
Douai
Sambre
ARDENNES
Mainz
Bamberg
Bayreuth
CZECH REPUBLIC
Arras
Cambrai
Darmstadt
Würzburg
Plzeň
Abbeville
St-Quentin
LUXEMBOURG
Mosel
Ludwigshafen
Mannheim
Erlangen
Moldau
iens
Somme
Luxembourg
Trier
Heidelberg
Nuremberg
Oise
Charleville
Sedan
Kaiserslautern
Saar
Karlsruhe
Heilbronn
Regensburg
Linz
Beauvais
St-Quentin
Thionville
Saarbrücken
BAVARIA
Danube
St-Denis
Reims
Verdun
Metz
Pforzheim
Stuttgart
Ingolstadt
Paris
Marne
Chalons-sur-Marne
Baden-Baden
Reutlingen
Ulm
Augsburg
Inn
main
Seine
St-Dizier
Nancy
Strasbourg
Danube
Munich
Salzburg
lles
Troyes
Épinal
Colmar
Rhine
BLACK FOREST
Freiburg
Lake Constance
Oberammergau
éans
Fontainebleau
VOSGES
Mulhouse
Winterthur
AUSTRIA
B
Auxerre
Belfort
Montbéliard
Basel
Aare
Zürich
Rhine
St. Anton
Innsbruck
ALPS
Mur
Dijon
Saône
Besancon
Lucerne
Vaduz
LIECHTENSTEIN
Brenner Pass
3797 m Gross Glockner
Drava
Klagenfurt
Bern
SWITZERLAND
St. Moritz
3899 m Ortles
Bolzano
DOLOMITES
Sava
JURA
Lausanne
Montreux
4158 m Jungfrau
St. Gotthard Pass
4050 m Bernina
Trento
Udine
Lake Geneva
ALPS
Simplon Pass
Lugano
Lake Como
Ljubljana
SLOVENIA
Geneva
Rhône
Lake Maggiore
Como
Bergamo
Lake Garda
Vicenza
Trieste
Annecy
4477 m Matterhorn
Monza
Brescia
Verona
Padua
Venice
Rijeka
CROATIA
Chambery
4810 m Mt. Blanc
Great St. Bernard Pass
Novara
Milan
Istria
Lyons
ITALY
Po
Grenoble
Turin
Piacenza
Po

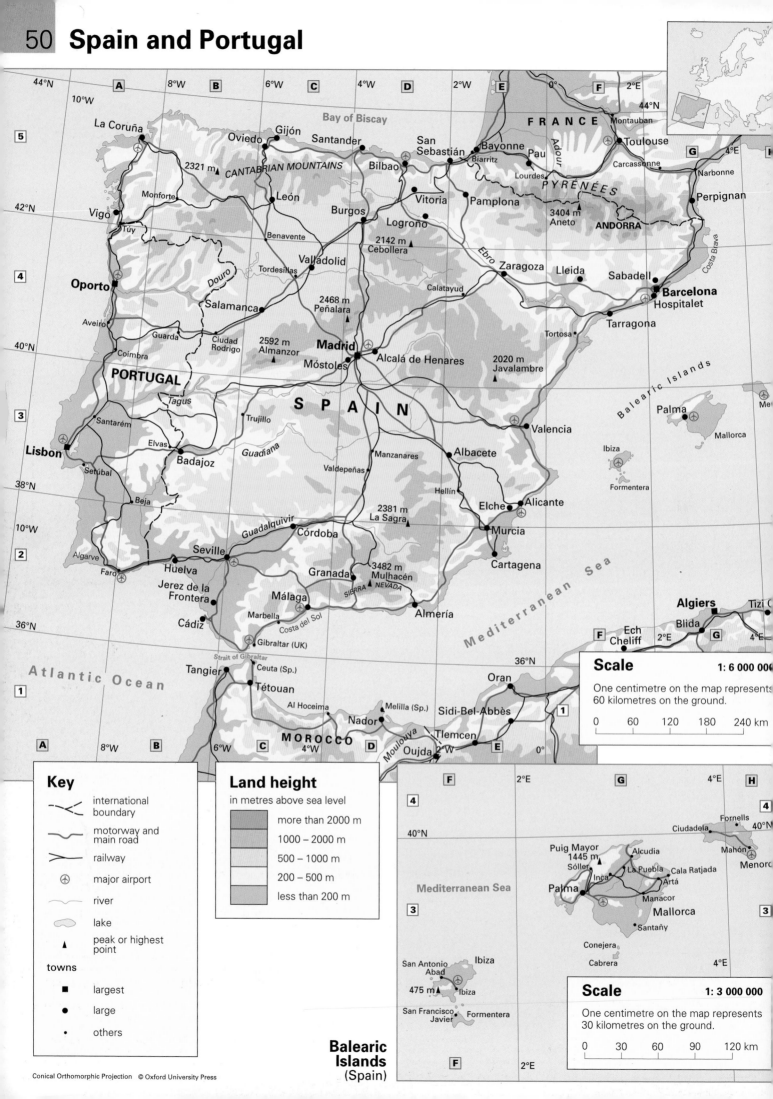

Key

- --·--·-- international boundary
- motorway and main road
- railway
- ✈ major airport
- ~~~~ river
- 🗺 lake
- ▲ peak or highest point

towns

- ■ largest
- ● large
- · others

Land height

in metres above sea level

- more than 2000 m
- 1000 – 2000 m
- 500 – 1000 m
- 200 – 500 m
- less than 200 m

Scale 1: 6 000 000

One centimetre on the map represents 60 kilometres on the ground.

| 0 | 60 | 120 | 180 | 240 km |

Scale 1: 3 000 000

One centimetre on the map represents 30 kilometres on the ground.

| 0 | 30 | 60 | 90 | 120 km |

Balearic Islands (Spain)

Conical Orthomorphic Projection © Oxford University Press

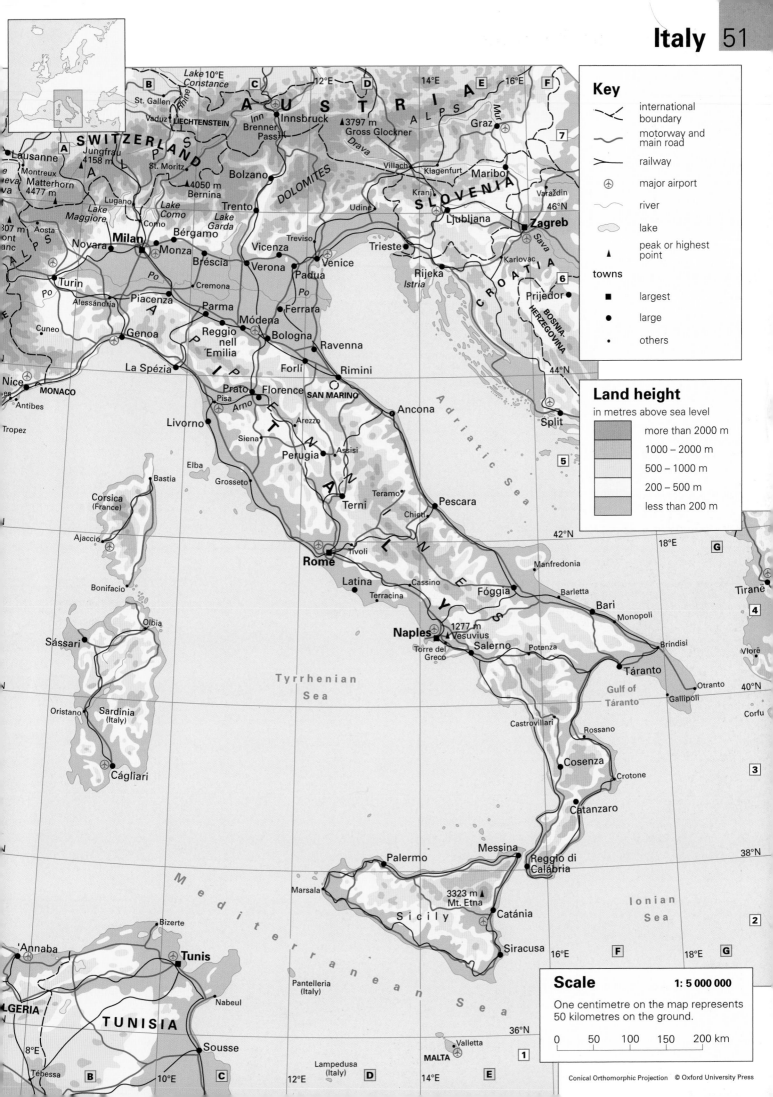

Key

⟋⟍	international boundary
⟋⟍	motorway and main road
⟋⟍	railway
⊕	major airport
⟋⟍	river
◯	lake
▲	peak or highest point

towns

■	largest
●	large
·	others

Land height

in metres above sea level

	more than 2000 m
	1000 – 2000 m
	500 – 1000 m
	200 – 500 m
	less than 200 m

Scale

1 : 5 000 000

One centimetre on the map represents 50 kilometres on the ground.

0   50   100   150   200 km

Conical Orthomorphic Projection   © Oxford University Press

SWITZERLAND
AUSTRIA
LIECHTENSTEIN
SLOVENIA
CROATIA
BOSNIA-HERZEGOVINA
TUNISIA
ALGERIA
MONACO
MALTA

St. Gallen
Vaduz
Innsbruck
Brenner Pass
Inn
▲3797 m Gross Glockner
Graz
Mur
Lake Constance
Rhine
Lausanne
Montreux
Geneva
Jungfrau ▲4158 m
Matterhorn ▲4477 m
Mont Blanc ▲4807 m
St. Moritz
▲4050 m Bernina
Bolzano
Trento
DOLOMITES
Villach
Klagenfurt
Maribor
Varaždin
Kranj
Udine
Ljubljana
Zagreb
Drava
Sava
Aosta
Lugano
Lake Maggiore
Lake Como
Como
Lake Garda
Treviso
Vicenza
Verona
Padua
Venice
Trieste
Rijeka
Istria
Karlovac
Prijedor
Novara
Milan
Monza
Bérgamo
Bréscia
Turin
Po
Cuneo
Alessándria
Piacenza
Cremona
Parma
Módena
Bologna
Ferrara
Po
Reggio nell'Emilia
Genoa
La Spézia
Ravenna
Forlí
Rimini
San Marino
Split
Nice
Antibes
Tropez
Prato
Pisa
Florence
Arno
Livorno
Elba
Arezzo
Siena
Perugia
Assisi
Ancona
Adriatic Sea
Bastia
Corsica (France)
Ajaccio
Bonifacio
Grosseto
Teramo
Terni
Chieti
Pescara
APENNINES
Rome
Tivoli
Latina
Terracina
Cassino
Fóggia
Manfredonia
Barletta
Bari
Monopoli
Bríndisi
Táranto
Gulf of Táranto
Otranto
Gallipoli
Tiranë
Vlorë
Corfu
Sássari
Olbia
Sardinia (Italy)
Oristano
Cágliari
Naples
▲1277 m Vesuvius
Torre del Greco
Salerno
Potenza
Tyrrhenian Sea
Castrovillari
Rossano
Cosenza
Crotone
Catanzaro
Messina
Reggio di Calábria
Palermo
Marsala
Sicily
▲3323 m Mt. Etna
Catánia
Siracusa
Ionian Sea
Mediterranean Sea
Bizerte
Annaba
Tunis
Tébessa
Sousse
Nabeul
Pantelleria (Italy)
Lampedusa (Italy)
Valletta
MALTA

Countries and capitals

— country boundary

---- disputed boundary

• capital city

The British Isles at the same scale

Scale   1: 80 000 000

One centimetre on the map represents 800 kilometres on the ground.

0   800   1600   2400 km

Countries map (top)

Prime Meridian · 0° · 20°E · 40°E · 80°N · 60°N

Kaliningrad (part of Russia)

• Moscow

RUSSIAN FEDERATION (RUSSIA)

• Ankara   **GEORGIA**   Astana •   **KAZAKHSTAN**

TURKEY   T'bilisi   Ulan Bator •

LEBANON   Yerevan • **AZERBAIJAN**   **MONGOLIA**

Beirut • **SYRIA**   Baku •   **UZBEKISTAN**   Bishkek

ISRAEL • Damascus • **ARMENIA**   Tashkent • **KYRGYZSTAN**   Beijing •

Jerusalem • Amman   **TURKMENISTAN**   Dushanbe •   **NORTH KOREA**

JORDAN   Baghdad •   Tehran • Ashgabat • **TAJIKISTAN**   **CHINA**   Pyongyang • • Tokyo

KUWAIT   **IRAN**   *Jammu and Kashmir*   Seoul • **JAPAN**

SAUDI • Kuwait   **AFGHANISTAN**   **SOUTH KOREA**

ARABIA **BAHRAIN** • Manama   Kabul • Islamabad

Riyadh • **QATAR** • Doha   **PAKISTAN**   New • **NEPAL**   **BHUTAN**

UNITED ARAB EMIRATES • Abu Dhabi   Delhi • Kathmandu • Thimphu • Taibei •

• Sana   **OMAN** • Muscat   Dhaka •   **TAIWAN**

YEMEN REPUBLIC   **INDIA**   **MYANMAR (BURMA)** **LAOS** • Hanoi   • Manila

Socotra (Yemen Rep.)   Yangon • Vientiane •   **PHILIPPINES**

Lakshadweep (India)   **BANGLADESH**   **THAILAND** **VIETNAM**

Andaman Islands (India)   Bangkok • **CAMBODIA**

  Phnom Penh •

MALDIVES   • Colombo   *Nicobar Islands (India)*   **BRUNEI**

• Malé   **SRI LANKA**   Kuala Lumpur • • Bandar Seri Begawan

MALAYSIA   **SINGAPORE** •   **INDONESIA**

Jakarta •   120°E   Dili • **EAST TIMOR**   140°E

Kuril Islands (Russia)

Ryukyu Islands (Japan)

Tropic of Cancer

Equator 0°   60°E   80°E   100°E

Arctic Circle

Land and water map (bottom)

Land height — in metres above sea level

- more than 5000 m
- 2000 – 5000 m
- 1000 – 2000 m
- 500 – 1000 m
- 200 – 500 m
- sea level – 200 m
- below sea level

▲ highest peaks with heights in metres

lakes

major rivers

marsh

ice cap

Prime Meridian · 0° · 20°E · 40°E · North Pole · 80°N · 60°N · 160°W · 180° · 40°N · 160°E

ARCTIC OCEAN   Barents Sea   Kara Sea   Bering Sea

Baltic Sea   Lake Onega   Lake Ladoga   North Dvina   **URAL MOUNTAINS**   **S i b e r i a**   Kolyma   Kamchatka Peninsula

Arctic Circle

Don   Volga   Ob   Yenisey   Irtysh   Lena   Amur   Sea of Okhotsk   Sakhalin

Black Sea   **CAUCASUS**   Caspian Sea   Aral Sea   Lake Baykal   Hokkaido

TAURUS MOUNTAINS   ▲5123 Mt. Ararat   Lake Balkhash   **ALTAI MOUNTAINS**   Sea of Japan

Dead Sea *(395m below sea level)*   **ZAGROS MOUNTAINS**   ▲5671 Mt. Demavand   ▼ Turpan Depression *(154m below sea level)*   Gobi Desert   Honshu

Euphrates   Tigris   **HINDU KUSH**   Tarim Basin   **KUNLUN SHAN**   Tsaidam Swamps   Hwang-Ho   East China Sea

Red Sea   The Gulf   ▲8611 K2   **TIBETAN PLATEAU**   Red Basin   Yangtze   Tropic of Cancer · 20°N · 160°E

Arabian Peninsula   Indus   **HIMALAYAS**   ▲ Mt. Everest 8848   Brahmaputra

Arabian Sea   **WESTERN GHATS**   **DECCAN**   Ganges   Irrawaddy   Salween   Bay of Bengal

PACIFIC OCEAN

Equator 0°   Sri Lanka   ▲4101 Mt. Kinabalu   Philippines   Taiwan   South China Sea   New Guinea

Mekong   Borneo   Sulawesi   ▲5030 Jaya Peak

INDIAN OCEAN   Sumatra   Java   Java Sea   Arafura Sea

60°E   80°E   100°E   120°E   140°E

Verkhoyansk
Mean annual rainfall : 136 m
Mean January temperature :
Mean July temperature : 13.

Mumbai
Mean annual rainfall : 1811
Mean January temperature :
Mean July temperature : 27.

Jakarta
Mean annual rainfall : 1799
Mean January temperature
Mean July temperature : 27.

Zenithal Equal Area Pr
© Oxford Universi

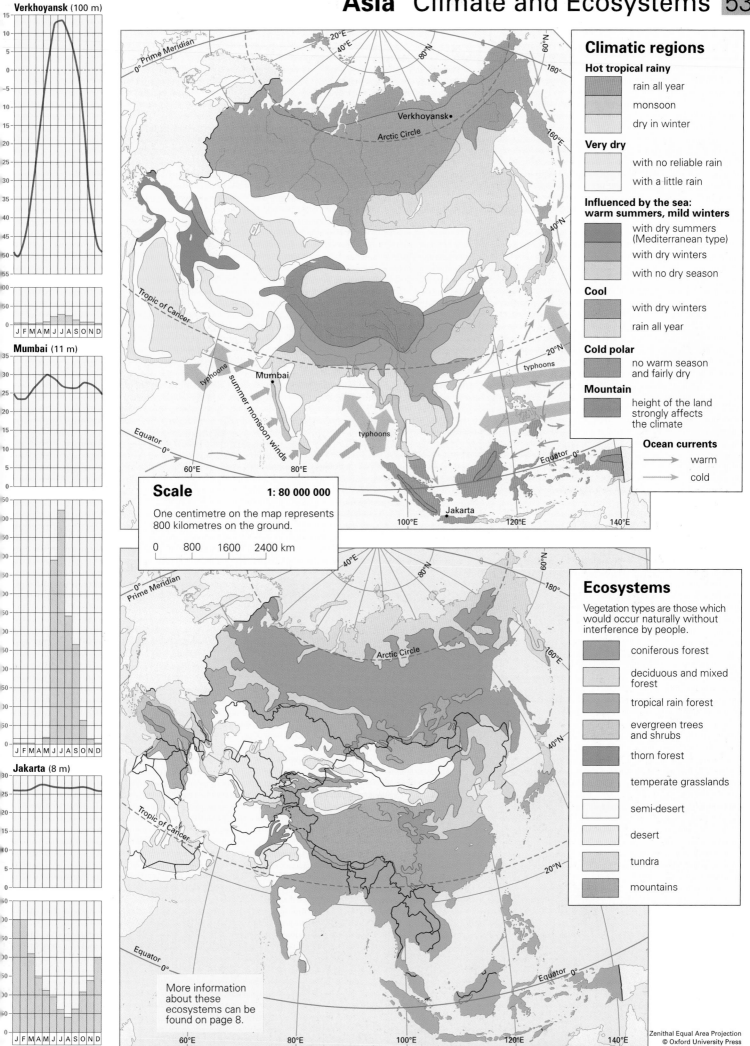

Verkhoyansk (100 m)

Mumbai (11 m)

Jakarta (8 m)

Scale 1: 80 000 000

One centimetre on the map represents
800 kilometres on the ground.

0   800   1600   2400 km

Climatic regions

Hot tropical rainy

rain all year

monsoon

dry in winter

Very dry

with no reliable rain

with a little rain

**Influenced by the sea:
warm summers, mild winters**

with dry summers
(Mediterranean type)

with dry winters

with no dry season

Cool

with dry winters

rain all year

Cold polar

no warm season
and fairly dry

Mountain

height of the land
strongly affects
the climate

Ocean currents

→ warm

→ cold

Ecosystems

Vegetation types are those which
would occur naturally without
interference by people.

coniferous forest

deciduous and mixed
forest

tropical rain forest

evergreen trees
and shrubs

thorn forest

temperate grasslands

semi-desert

desert

tundra

mountains

More information
about these
ecosystems can be
found on page 8.

Zenithal Equal Area Projection
© Oxford University Press

Farming, forestry, and fishing

main farming types

little or no farming : because the area is too dry or otherwise harsh.

nomadic herding : animals provide the needs of the wandering families.

shifting cultivation : small areas farmed until soils exhausted, then family moves.

mixed subsistence : crops and animals for family food.

rice subsistence : where heavy rainfall will allow a main crop of rice.

subsistance crops : mostly intensive with the aid of irrigation. Family food only.

grazing and stock rearing : on a large scale, for profit.

mixed farming : animals and crops for profit.

grain farming : mostly wheat, on a large scale, for profit.

plantation : well organized, specializing in one crop for profit, e.g. tea or rubber.

mediterranean farming : cereals, animals, vegetables, fruit, wine, surplus for profit.

specialized horticulture : mostly on oases supported by underground water.

dairy farming : milk, butter, and cheese for profit.

forestry

cutting and replacement of timber for profit

cash crops

ⓈÍ	coffee	♣	tea	◖	tobacco
◉	fruit	🌴	dates	✳	sugar
⊛	cotton	◎	rubber	◯	ground-nuts
⊤	palm products				

animal products

🐑 wool		🐖 meat		➤ fish	

Energy, Minerals, and Industry

energy

coalfield

oil field (with associated gas, and sometimes off shore)

gas field

hydro-electric power stations

● largest (over 3000 megawatts)

• smaller (500 – 3000 megawatts)

industry

🏭 main centres of industry

minerals (main mining areas)

◇	iron ore	◈	silver	⬦	gold
◈	tin	◇	nickel	◈	bauxite
◈	copper	◆	diamonds		
✦	phosphates				

Scale

1 : 80 000 000

One centimetre on the map represents 800 kilometres on the ground.

| 0 | 800 | 1600 | 2400 km |

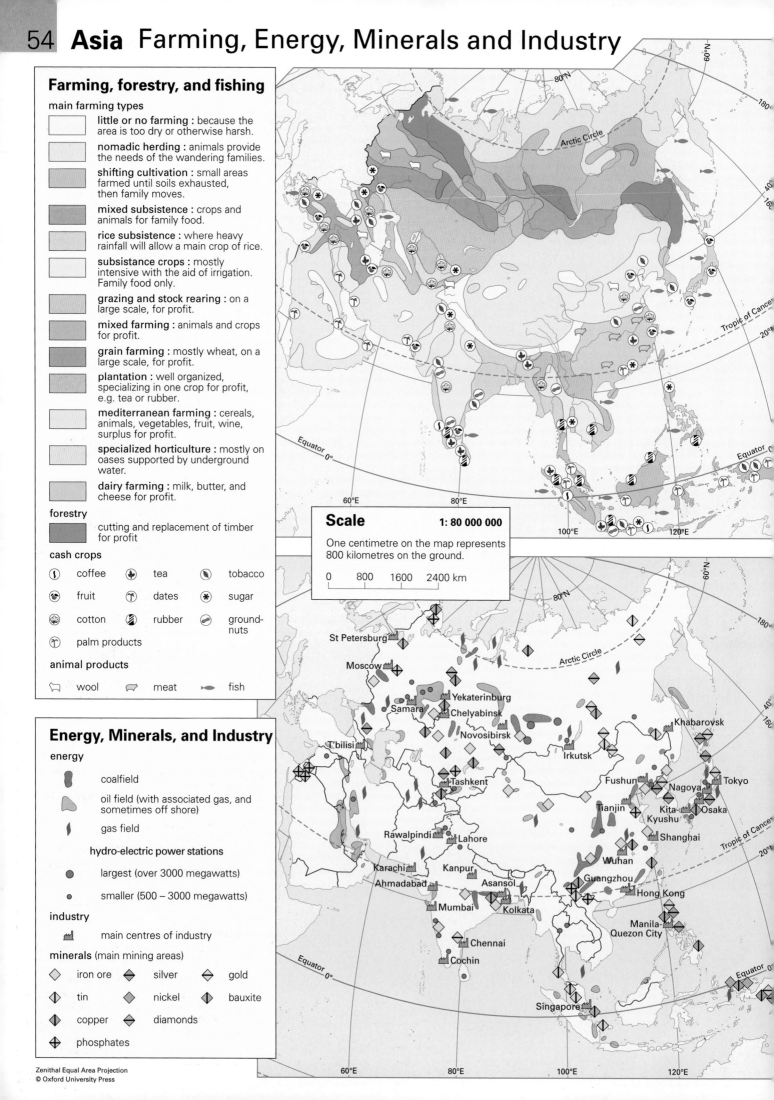

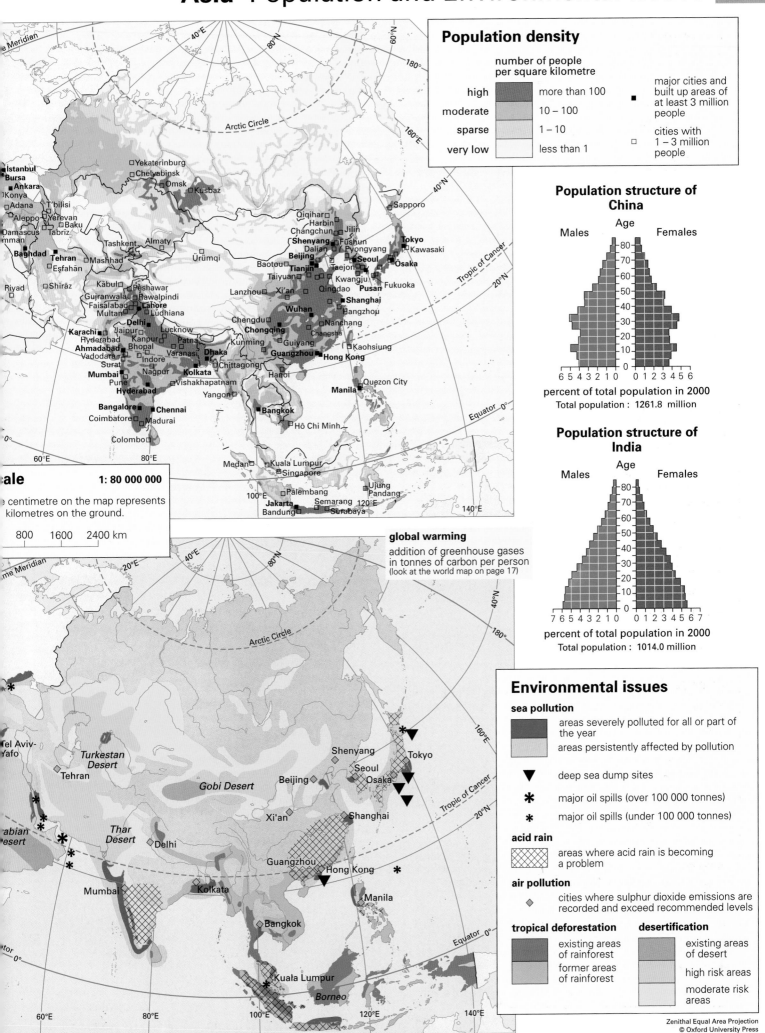

Population density

number of people per square kilometre

high	more than 100
moderate	10 – 100
sparse	1 – 10
very low	less than 1

■ major cities and built up areas of at least 3 million people

□ cities with 1 – 3 million people

Population structure of China
Males — Age — Females
6 5 4 3 2 1 0 0 1 2 3 4 5 6
percent of total population in 2000
Total population : 1261.8 million

Population structure of India
Males — Age — Females
7 6 5 4 3 2 1 0 0 1 2 3 4 5 6 7
percent of total population in 2000
Total population : 1014.0 million

Scale 1: 80 000 000
e centimetre on the map represents kilometres on the ground.
800   1600   2400 km

global warming
addition of greenhouse gases in tonnes of carbon per person (look at the world map on page 17)

Environmental issues

sea pollution
- areas severely polluted for all or part of the year
- areas persistently affected by pollution

▼ deep sea dump sites

✱ major oil spills (over 100 000 tonnes)

✻ major oil spills (under 100 000 tonnes)

acid rain
- areas where acid rain is becoming a problem

air pollution
◆ cities where sulphur dioxide emissions are recorded and exceed recommended levels

tropical deforestation
- existing areas of rainforest
- former areas of rainforest

desertification
- existing areas of desert
- high risk areas
- moderate risk areas

Zenithal Equal Area Projection
© Oxford University Press

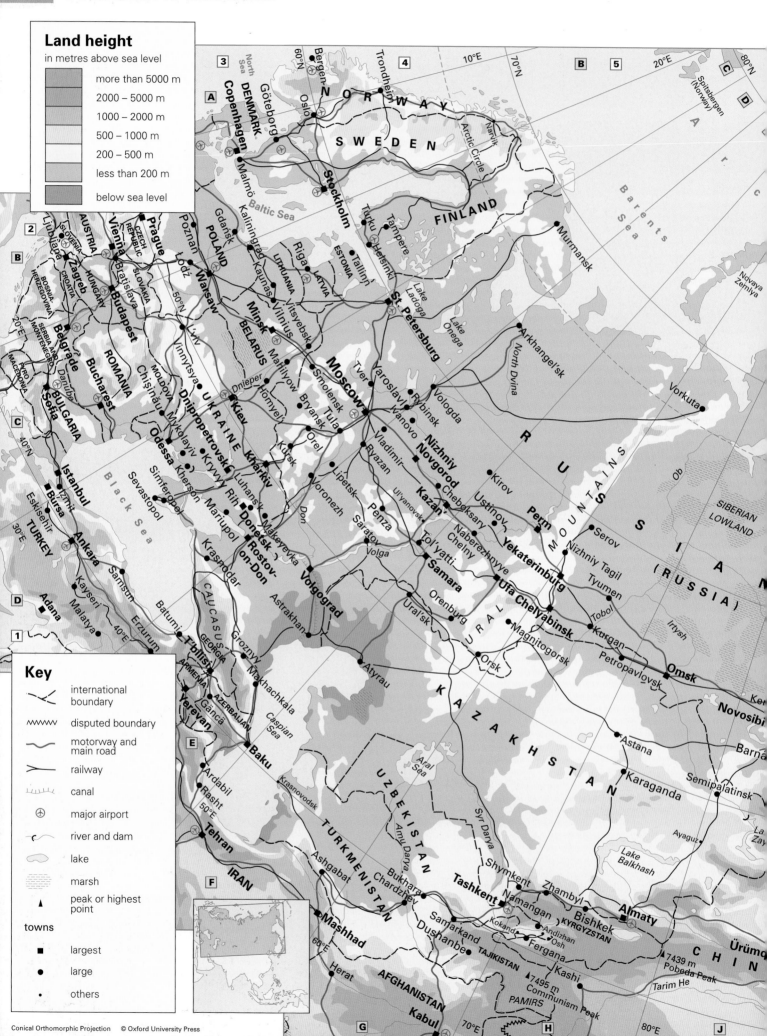

Land height

in metres above sea level

- more than 5000 m
- 2000 – 5000 m
- 1000 – 2000 m
- 500 – 1000 m
- 200 – 500 m
- less than 200 m
- below sea level

Key

- ⌇ international boundary
- ⌁⌁⌁ disputed boundary
- ⌒ motorway and main road
- ⟩ railway
- ⌓⌓ canal
- ⊕ major airport
- ⌒ river and dam
- ⬭ lake
- ⌆⌆ marsh
- ▲ peak or highest point

towns

- ■ largest
- ● large
- · others

Conical Orthomorphic Projection   © Oxford University Press

Scale 1: 20 000 000

One centimetre on the map represents
200 kilometres on the ground.

0 200 400 600 800 km

Key

international boundary	river and dam
disputed boundary	lake
motorway and main road	marsh
railway	peak or highest point
major airport	

towns

- ■ largest
- ● large
- · others

Land height

in metres above sea level

- more than 5000 m
- 2000 – 5000 m
- 1000 – 2000 m
- 500 – 1000 m
- 200 – 500 m
- less than 200 m
- below sea level

Scale 1: 20 000 000

One centimetre on the map represents 200 kilometres on the ground.

0   200   400   600   800 km

Conical Orthomorphic Projection © Oxford University Press

MONGOLIA
GOBI DESERT
ALTAI MOUNTAINS

TURKMENISTAN
UZBEKISTAN
Tashkent
Zhambyl
Bishkek
Shymkent
Namangan
KYRGYZSTAN
Almaty
Ürümqi
Hami
−154 m
Turpan Depression
Anxi
Zhangye
Jiayuguan
NAN SHAN
Lanzh
TIEN SHAN
Pobeda Peak
7439 m
TARIM PENDI
(Tarim Basin)
Qaidam Pendi
(Qaidam Basin)
Qinghai Hu
Xin
Bukhara
Chardzhev
Samarkand
TAJIKISTAN
Dushanbe
Kokand
Fergana
Andizhan
Osh
Kashi
Tarim He
CHINA
KUNLUN SHAN
Ashgabat
Atrek
Mashhad
Herat
7495 m
Communism Peak
PAMIRS
K2
8611 m
TIBETAN PLATEAU
Lhasa
Jinsha Jiang (Yangtze)
Lancang Jiang (Mekong)
Batang
Che
IRAN
AFGHANISTAN
Kabul
HINDU KUSH
Khyber Pass
JAMMU AND KASHMIR
Srinagar
Islamabad
Nu Jiang (Salween)
Zahedan
Kandahar
Quetta
Peshawar
Rawalpindi
Amritsar
Indus
Yarlung Zangbo Jiang (Tsangpo)
Annapurna
8073 m
HIMALAYAS
Mt. Everest
8848 m
Thimphu
BHUTAN
Brahmaputra
Dibrugarh
PAKISTAN
Faisalabad
Lahore
Ludhiana
Multan
Meerut
Delhi
Bareilly
NEPAL
Kathmandu
Guwahati
Kun
Irrawaddy
Sukkur
Bikaner
Jaipur
Agra
Gwalior
Lucknow
Kanpur
Patna
BANGLADESH
Imphal
THAR DESERT
Allahabad
Varanasi
Asansol
Ganges
Dhaka
Mandalay
Gwadar
Hyderabad
Tropic of Cancer
Ganges
Khulna
Chittagong
Salween
OMAN
Gulf of Oman
Karachi
Kandla
Bhopal
Narmada
Jabalpur
Jamshedpur
Kolkata
(Calcutta)
MYANMAR
(BURMA)
Ahmadabad
Indore
Nagpur
Raipur
Raipur
Cuttack
Chiang Mai
Vadodara
Porbandar
Surat
Pegu
THAIL
Arabian Sea
Mumbai
(Bombay)
Pune
Godavari
Bay of Bengal
Bassein
Moul
Solapur
Hyderabad
Vishakapatnam
Yangon
Kolhapur
Krishna
Vijayawada
Belgaum
Hubli
DECCAN
Andaman Sea
Mangalore
WESTERN GHATS
Bangalore
Chennai
(Madras)
Andaman Islands
(India)
Ban
(Krun
Lakshadweep
(Laccadive Islands)
Mysore
Salem
Calicut
Coimbatore
Cochin
Madurai
Jaffna
Isthmus of Kra
Trivandrum
Trincomalee
Nicobar Islands
(India)
MALDIVES
SRI LANKA
Colombo
Kandy
Banda Aceh
Me
INDON

INDIA

Indian Ocean

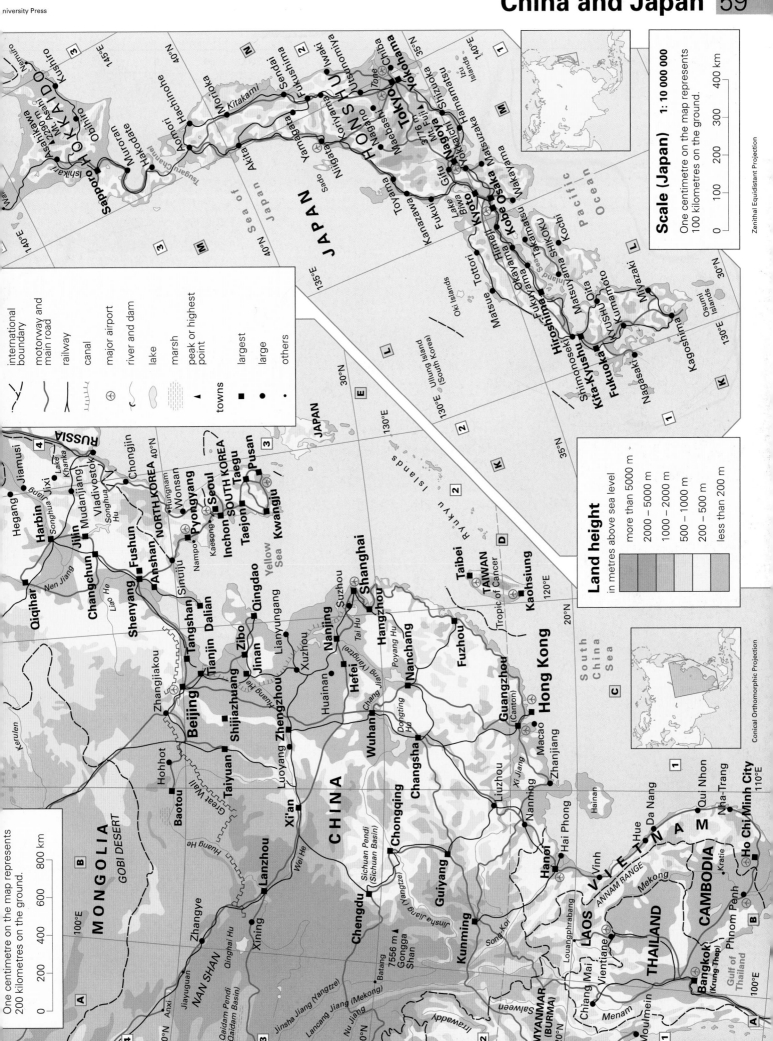

niversity Press

Scale (Japan) 1 : 10 000 000

One centimetre on the map represents 100 kilometres on the ground.

0 100 200 300 400 km

Zenithal Equidistant Projection

Legend

international boundary
motorway and main road
railway
canal
major airport
river and dam
lake
marsh
peak or highest point

towns
largest
large
others

Land height
in metres above sea level

more than 5000 m
2000 – 5000 m
1000 – 2000 m
500 – 1000 m
200 – 500 m
less than 200 m

Conical Orthomorphic Projection

One centimetre on the map represents 200 kilometres on the ground.

0 200 400 600 800 km

Map labels

HOKKAIDO
Nemuro
Asahikawa 2290 m
Kushiro
Obihiro
Tokachi
Muroran
Hakodate
Sapporo
Ishikari
Tsugaru Channel
HONSHU
Aomori
Hachinohe
Morioka
Kitakami
Akita
Yamagata
Sendai
Fukushima
Niigata
Iwaki
Koriyama
Utsunomiya
Maebashi
Nagano
TOKYO
Chiba
Yokohama
Mt. Fuji 3776 m
Shizuoka
Hamamatsu
Yokkaichi
Gifu
Nagoya
Kanazawa
Toyama
Fukui
Lake Biwa
Kyoto
Osaka
Kobe
Wakayama
Tottori
Matsue
Himeji
Okayama
Fukuyama
Matsuzaka
SHIKOKU
Takamatsu
Kochi
Matsuyama
Hiroshima
Oita
Shimonoseki
Kita-Kyushu
Fukuoka
KYUSHU
Kumamoto
Miyazaki
Nagasaki
Kagoshima
Osumi Islands
Oki Islands
Ullung Island (South Korea)
Ryukyu Islands
JAPAN
Sea of Japan
Pacific Ocean

RUSSIA
Hegang
Jiamusi
Jixi
Lake Khanka
Mudanjiang
Vladivostok
Chongjin
Harbin
Songhua Jiang
Jilin
Qiqihar
Nen Jiang
Changchun
Shenyang
Fushun
Anshan
NORTH KOREA
Hungnam
Wonsan
Pyongyang
Nampo
Kaesong
Sinuiju
Seoul
Inchon
SOUTH KOREA
Taejon
Taegu
Pusan
Kwangju
Yellow Sea

MONGOLIA
GOBI DESERT
Kerulen
Zhangjiakou
Hohhot
Baotou
Great Wall
NAN SHAN
Qaidam Pendi (Qaidam Basin)
Qinghai Hu
Xining
Lanzhou
Taiyuan
Beijing
Tianjin
Tangshan
Shijiazhuang
Zibo
Jinan
Dalian
Qingdao
Lianyungang
Liao He
Xuzhou
Luoyang
Zhengzhou
Huainan
Nanjing
Suzhou
Shanghai
Hangzhou
Tai Hu
Xi'an
Wei He
Huang He
CHINA
Hefei
Nanchang
Poyang Hu
Dongting Hu
Wuhan
Chang Jiang (Yangtze)
Changsha
Fuzhou
Taibei
TAIWAN
Tropic of Cancer
Kaohsiung
Nanchang
Guangzhou (Canton)
Hong Kong
Macao
Zhanjiang
Guiyang
Chongqing
Chengdu
7556 m Gongga Shan
Sichuan Pendi (Sichuan Basin)
Batang
Jinsha Jiang (Yangtze)
Lancang Jiang (Mekong)
Nu Jiang
Kunming
Guiyang
Liuzhou
Xi Jiang
Nanning
Hainan
South China Sea

MYANMAR (BURMA)
Irrawaddy
Salween
Chiang Mai
Menam
THAILAND
Bangkok (Krung Thep)
Moulmein
Gulf of Thailand
LAOS
Vientiane
Louangphrabang
Luang Prabang
CAMBODIA
Phnom Penh
Kratie
Mekong
VIETNAM
Hanoi
Hai Phong
Vinh
Hue
Da Nang
Qui Nhon
Nha-Trang
Ho Chi Minh City
ANNAM RANGE
Song Koi

Jiayuguan
Anxi
Zhangye

Key

towns
- ▲ peak or highest point
- ▪ largest
- ● large
- • others
- marsh

- international boundary
- motorway and main road
- railway
- ⊕ major airport
- river
- lake

Land height
in metres above sea level
- more than 2000 m
- 1000 – 2000 m
- 500 – 1000 m
- 200 – 500 m
- less than 200 m

Scale
1: 20 000 000

One centimetre on the map represents 200 kilometres on the ground.

Conical Orthomorphic Projection   © Oxford University Press

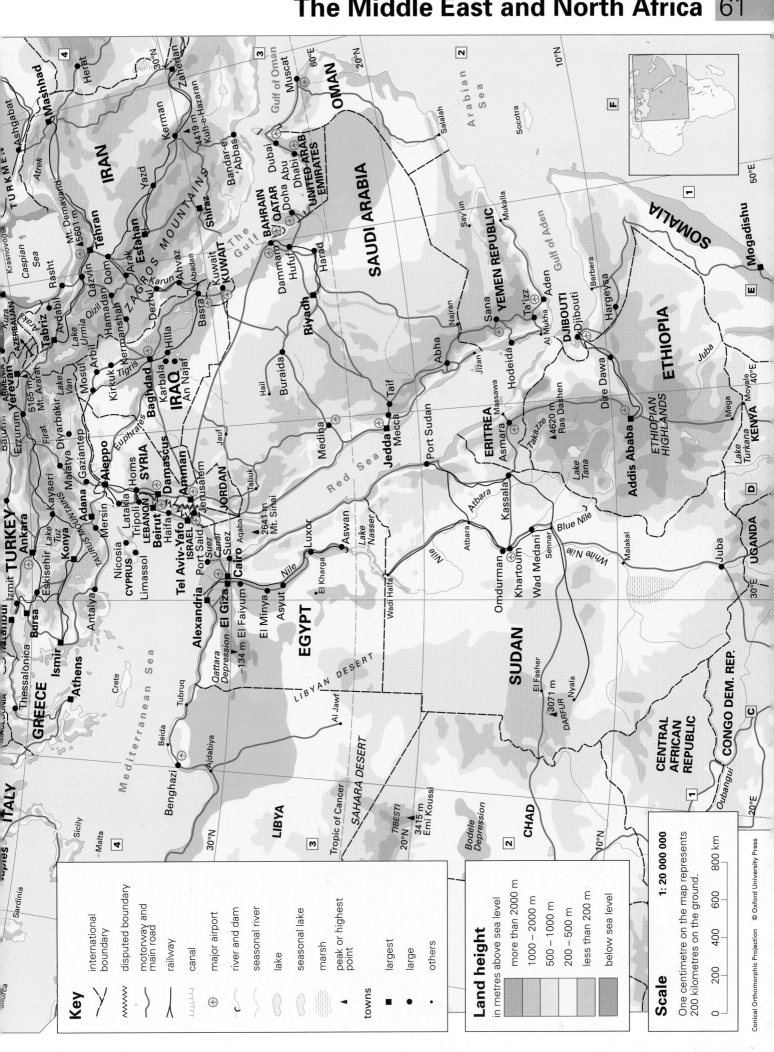

Key

⌇⌇	international boundary
wwww	disputed boundary
⌇	motorway and main road
	railway
	canal
⊕	major airport
	river and dam
	seasonal river
	lake
	seasonal lake
	marsh
▲	peak or highest point

towns

■	largest
●	large
·	others

Land height

in metres above sea level

	more than 2000 m
	1000 – 2000 m
	500 – 1000 m
	200 – 500 m
	less than 200 m
	below sea level

Scale

1: 20 000 000

One centimetre on the map represents 200 kilometres on the ground.

0 200 400 600 800 km

Conical Orthomorphic Projection   © Oxford University Press

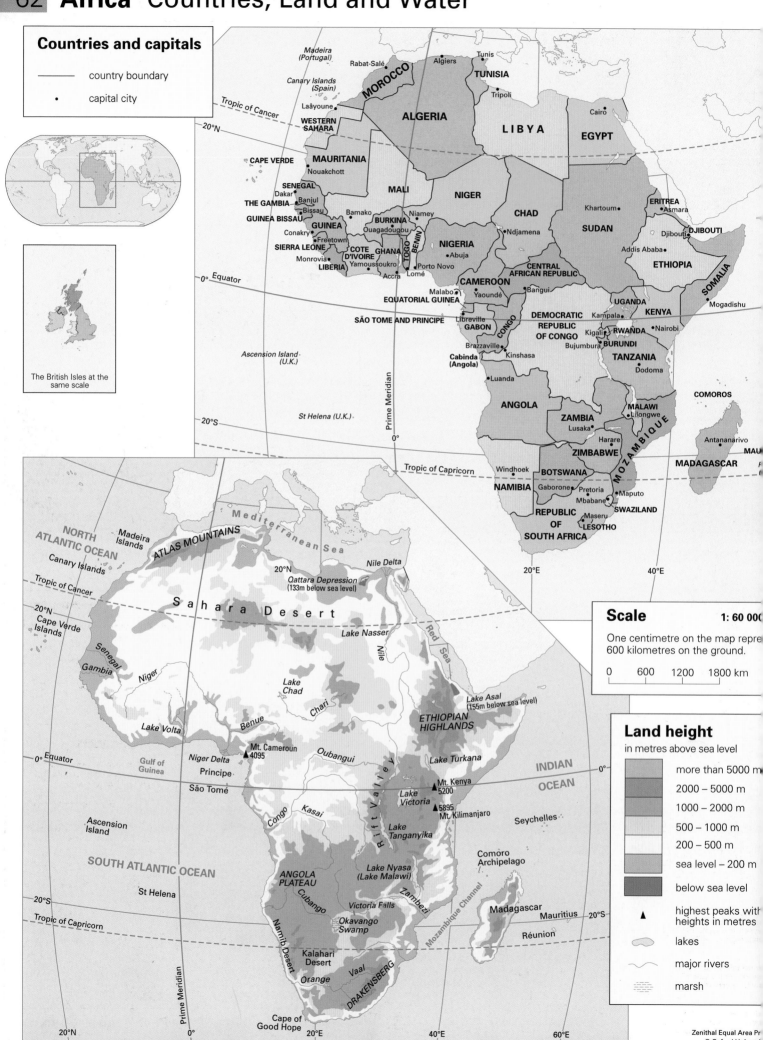

Countries and capitals

—— country boundary

• capital city

The British Isles at the same scale

Scale 1: 60 000

One centimetre on the map repre
600 kilometres on the ground.

0 600 1200 1800 km

Land height
in metres above sea level

more than 5000 m

2000 – 5000 m

1000 – 2000 m

500 – 1000 m

200 – 500 m

sea level – 200 m

below sea level

▲ highest peaks with
heights in metres

lakes

major rivers

marsh

Zenithal Equal Area Pr
© Oxford Universi

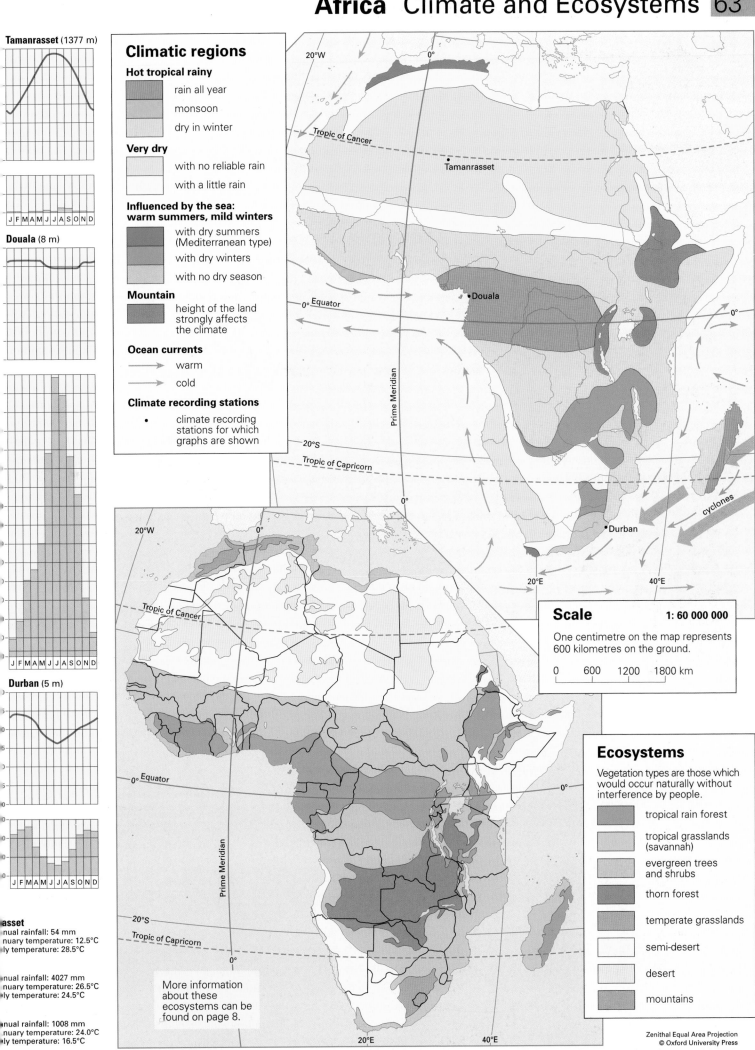

Tamanrasset (1377 m)

Douala (8 m)

Durban (5 m)

Climatic regions

Hot tropical rainy
- rain all year
- monsoon
- dry in winter

Very dry
- with no reliable rain
- with a little rain

Influenced by the sea: warm summers, mild winters
- with dry summers (Mediterranean type)
- with dry winters
- with no dry season

Mountain
- height of the land strongly affects the climate

Ocean currents
- → warm
- → cold

Climate recording stations
- • climate recording stations for which graphs are shown

Scale   1: 60 000 000

One centimetre on the map represents 600 kilometres on the ground.

0   600   1200   1800 km

Ecosystems

Vegetation types are those which would occur naturally without interference by people.

- tropical rain forest
- tropical grasslands (savannah)
- evergreen trees and shrubs
- thorn forest
- temperate grasslands
- semi-desert
- desert
- mountains

More information about these ecosystems can be found on page 8.

asset
- nual rainfall: 54 mm
- nuary temperature: 12.5°C
- ly temperature: 28.5°C

- nual rainfall: 4027 mm
- nuary temperature: 26.5°C
- ly temperature: 24.5°C

- nual rainfall: 1008 mm
- nuary temperature: 24.0°C
- ly temperature: 16.5°C

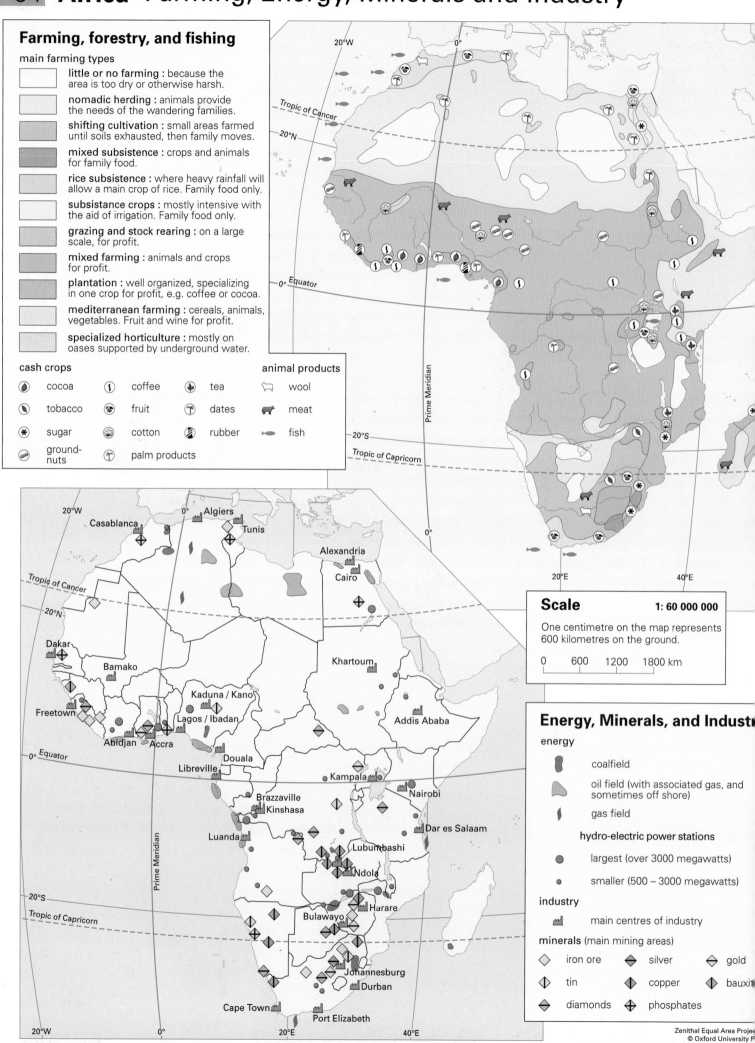

Farming, forestry, and fishing

main farming types

little or no farming : because the area is too dry or otherwise harsh.

nomadic herding : animals provide the needs of the wandering families.

shifting cultivation : small areas farmed until soils exhausted, then family moves.

mixed subsistence : crops and animals for family food.

rice subsistence : where heavy rainfall will allow a main crop of rice. Family food only.

subsistance crops : mostly intensive with the aid of irrigation. Family food only.

grazing and stock rearing : on a large scale, for profit.

mixed farming : animals and crops for profit.

plantation : well organized, specializing in one crop for profit, e.g. coffee or cocoa.

mediterranean farming : cereals, animals, vegetables. Fruit and wine for profit.

specialized horticulture : mostly on oases supported by underground water.

cash crops

- cocoa
- tobacco
- sugar
- ground-nuts
- coffee
- fruit
- cotton
- palm products
- tea
- dates
- rubber

animal products

- wool
- meat
- fish

Scale   1: 60 000 000

One centimetre on the map represents 600 kilometres on the ground.

0   600   1200   1800 km

Energy, Minerals, and Indust

energy

- coalfield
- oil field (with associated gas, and sometimes off shore)
- gas field

hydro-electric power stations

- largest (over 3000 megawatts)
- smaller (500 – 3000 megawatts)

industry

- main centres of industry

minerals (main mining areas)

- iron ore
- tin
- diamonds
- silver
- copper
- phosphates
- gold
- bauxi

Map labels (lower map): Casablanca, Algiers, Tunis, Alexandria, Cairo, Dakar, Bamako, Kaduna / Kano, Khartoum, Freetown, Lagos / Ibadan, Abidjan, Accra, Douala, Libreville, Kampala, Nairobi, Addis Ababa, Brazzaville, Kinshasa, Dar es Salaam, Luanda, Lubumbashi, Ndola, Harare, Bulawayo, Johannesburg, Durban, Cape Town, Port Elizabeth

Map labels (upper map): 20°W, Tropic of Cancer, 20°N, Equator, Prime Meridian, 20°S, Tropic of Capricorn, 20°E, 40°E

Zenithal Equal Area Proje
© Oxford University P

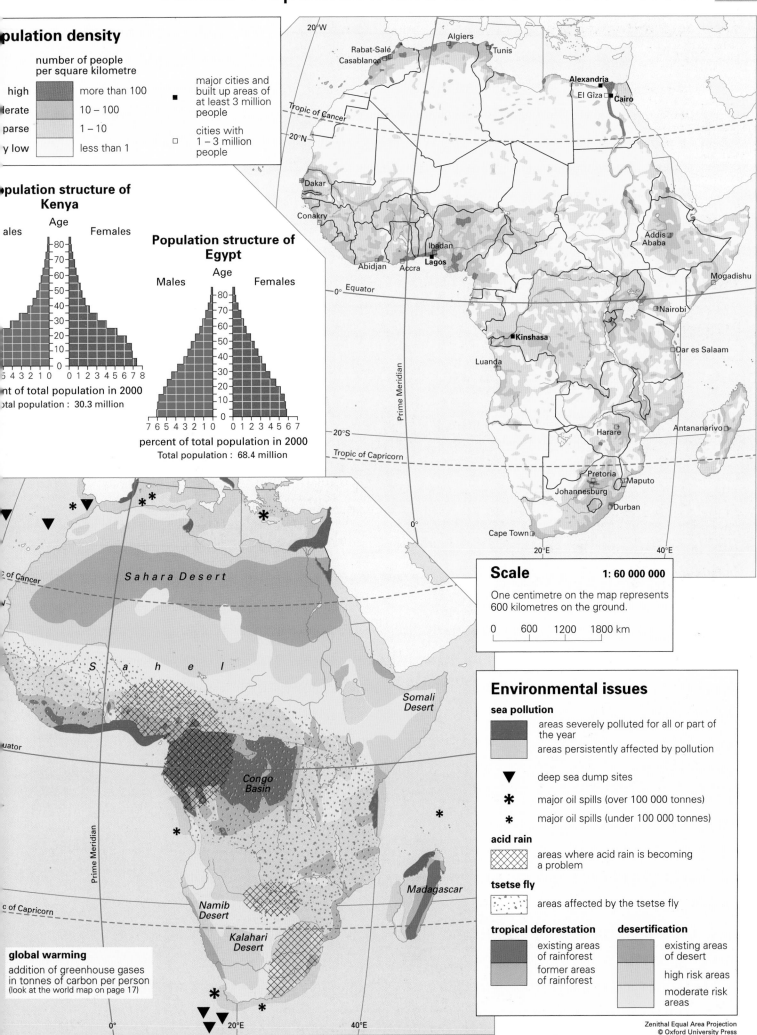

Population density

number of people
per square kilometre

high	more than 100
moderate	10 – 100
sparse	1 – 10
very low	less than 1

■ major cities and built up areas of at least 3 million people

□ cities with 1 – 3 million people

Population structure of Kenya

Males — Age — Females

80, 70, 60, 50, 40, 30, 20, 10, 0

...5 4 3 2 1 0 0 1 2 3 4 5 6 7 8

percent of total population in 2000
Total population : 30.3 million

Population structure of Egypt

Males — Age — Females

80, 70, 60, 50, 40, 30, 20, 10, 0

7 6 5 4 3 2 1 0 0 1 2 3 4 5 6 7

percent of total population in 2000
Total population : 68.4 million

Scale 1: 60 000 000

One centimetre on the map represents 600 kilometres on the ground.

0   600   1200   1800 km

Environmental issues

sea pollution

areas severely polluted for all or part of the year

areas persistently affected by pollution

▼ deep sea dump sites

✳ major oil spills (over 100 000 tonnes)

✳ major oil spills (under 100 000 tonnes)

acid rain

areas where acid rain is becoming a problem

tsetse fly

areas affected by the tsetse fly

tropical deforestation

existing areas of rainforest

former areas of rainforest

desertification

existing areas of desert

high risk areas

moderate risk areas

global warming

addition of greenhouse gases in tonnes of carbon per person
(look at the world map on page 17)

Zenithal Equal Area Projection
© Oxford University Press

Sahara Desert
Sahel
Congo Basin
Somali Desert
Namib Desert
Kalahari Desert
Madagascar

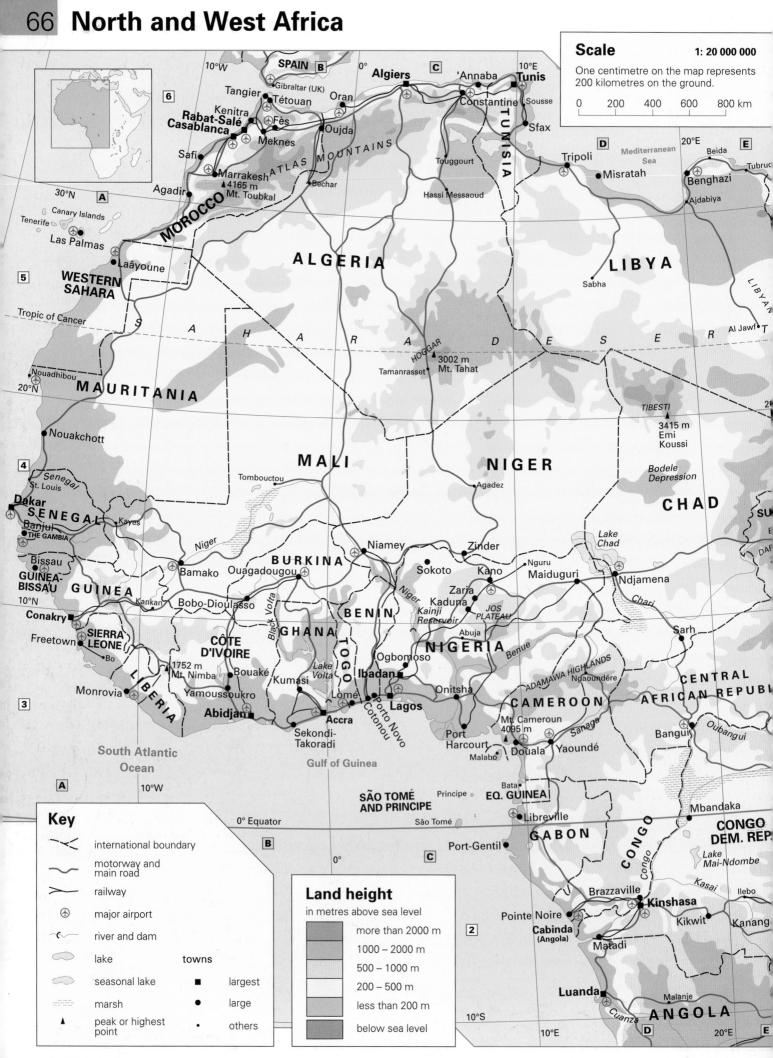

One centimetre on the map represents
200 kilometres on the ground.

0   200   400   600   800 km

Key

- international boundary
- motorway and main road
- railway
- major airport
- river and dam
- lake
- seasonal lake
- marsh
- peak or highest point

towns

- ■ largest
- ● large
- · others

Land height
in metres above sea level

- more than 2000 m
- 1000 – 2000 m
- 500 – 1000 m
- 200 – 500 m
- less than 200 m
- below sea level

Zenithal Equal Area Projection   © Oxford University Press

B 20°E C 30°E D 40°E ERITREA E 50°E

6

CHAD

El Fasher

▲3071 m
DARFUR
Nyala

SUDAN

White Nile

Sennar

Wad Medani

Blue Nile

Malakal

▲4620 m
Ras Dashen

Lake Tana

DJIBOUTI
Djibouti

Gulf of Aden

Berbera

10°N

ETHIOPIA

Addis Ababa

Dire Dawa

Hargeysa

ERIA

Sarh

Chari

Ngaoundéré
ADAMAWA HIGHLANDS

MEROON

a
Sanaga
Yaoundé

UINEA

Bangui

CENTRAL
AFRICAN REPUBLIC

Oubangui

Uele

Juba

ETHIOPIAN
HIGHLANDS

Lake
Turkana

Mega

Moyale

SOMALIA

Mogadishu

5

EASTERN RIFT VALLEY

Kisangani

Boyoma Falls

Mbandaka

Lake Albert

Mt. Ruwenzori
5118 m

Lake Edward

UGANDA
Kampala
Entebbe

Lake
Kyoga

KENYA

Kisumu

5200 m
▲Mt. Kenya

Nairobi

Equator 0°

GABON

CONGO

Brazzaville

Kinshasa

Congo

CONGO DEM. REP.

Lualaba

Lake
Mai-Ndombe

Kasai

Ilebo

Kikwit

Kananga

Mbuji-Mayi

Lake Kivu
Bukavu

RWANDA
Kigali

Bujumbura
BURUNDI

Kigoma

Lake
Victoria

Mwanza

Tabora

Dodoma

TANZANIA

5895 m
▲Mt. Kilimanjaro

Mombasa

Tanga

Zanzibar

Dar es Salaam

Indian

Ocean

4

nda
ola)

Matadi

WESTERN RIFT VALLEY

Kalemie

Lake
Tanganyika

Lake Rukwa

Lake
Mweru

Aldabra
Islands

10°S

uanda

Malanje

Cuanza

Kasai

Likasi

Lubumbashi

Lake
Bangweulu

Ruvuma

COMOROS

Moroni

Lobito
Benguela

Huambo

ANGOLA

Kitwe
Ndola

Kabwe

ZAMBIA

Lake Nyasa
(Lake Malawi)

MALAWI

Lilongwe

Moçambique

Nampula

Mahajanga

3

Lubango

Cubango

Cunene

Zambezi

Lusaka

Lake
Cabora Bassa

Blantyre

Zambezi

MOZAMBIQUE

Mozambique Channel

Toamasina

Etosha
Pan

Okavango
Swamp

Victoria
Falls

Lake
Kariba

Harare

ZIMBABWE

Beira

Antananarivo

20°S

NAMIB DESERT

NAMIBIA

Walvis Bay

Windhoek

KALAHARI
DESERT

BOTSWANA

Bulawayo

Limpopo

MADAGASCAR

Europa

Toliara

Tropic of Capricorn

2

Lüderitz

Gaborone

Pretoria
Johannesburg

HIGH VELD

Mbabane

Maputo

SWAZILAND

40°E

50°E

Atlantic Ocean

Orange

Vaal

Kimberley

Bloemfontein

Maseru

DRAKENSBERG

LESOTHO

3482 m

Pietermaritzburg

Durban

E

30°S

B 10°E

Cape
Town

Cape of
Good Hope

20°E

GREAT KARROO

Port Elizabeth

East London

REPUBLIC OF
SOUTH AFRICA

1

C 30°D

Scale 1: 20 000 000

One centimetre on the map represents
200 kilometres on the ground.

0 200 400 600 800 km

For explanations of the symbols and colours used on
this map look at the oppsite page.

Countries and capitals

——— country boundary

• capital city

The British Isles at the same scale

Scale   1: 44 000 000

One centimetre on the map represents 440 kilometres on the ground.

0   440   880   1320 km

Land height
in metres above sea level

more than 2000 m

1000 – 2000 m

500 – 1000 m

200 – 500 m

sea level – 200 m

below sea level

▲ highest peaks with heights in metres

lakes

major rivers

major seasonal rivers

coral reef

Modified Zenithal Equidistant Projection
© Oxford University Press

Map 1 labels:

Equator   0°   140°E   160°E   Equator

PAPUA NEW GUINEA   SOLOMON ISLANDS

Port Moresby   Honiara

VANUATU

Vila

New Caledonia (France)

Nouméa   Tropic of Capricorn

20°S   Tropic of Capricorn

AUSTRALIA

Norfolk Island (Australia)

Lord Howe Island (Australia)

Canberra

NEW ZEALAND   Wellington

100°E   120°E   140°E   160°E   180°

Map 2 labels:

Equator   0°   140°E   160°E   Equator

Jaya Peak 5030 ▲   New Guinea   Bismarck Sea   New Ireland

4508 ▲ Mt. Wilhelm   New Britain

Bougainville Island   Solomon Islands

Arafura Sea   Santa Cruz Islands

Timor Sea   Arnham Land   Gulf of Carpentaria   Cape York Peninsula   Great Barrier Reef   Coral Sea

Espiritu Santo

INDIAN OCEAN   Flinders   GREAT DIVIDING RANGE   New Caledonia   Loyalty Islands   Tropic of Capricorn

Great Sandy Desert   MACDONNELL RANGES   PACIFIC OCEAN

Mt Meharry 1251 ▲   Gibson Desert   Simpson Desert   Norfolk Island

20°S   HAMERSLEY RANGE   867 ▲ Ayers Rock   Sturt Desert   Lord Howe Island

Tropic of Capricorn   Lake Eyre   Darling

Great Victoria Desert   Lake Torrens   FLINDERS RANGE   Murrumbidgee   Tasman Sea

Nullarbor Plain   Murray   AUSTRALIAN ALPS ▲ 2230 Mt. Kosciusko   North Island

Great Australian Bight   Bass Strait   Cook Strait

SOUTHERN OCEAN   Tasmania   South Island   3764 ▲ Mt. Cook

Stewart Island

100°E   120°E   140°E   160°E   180°

40°S

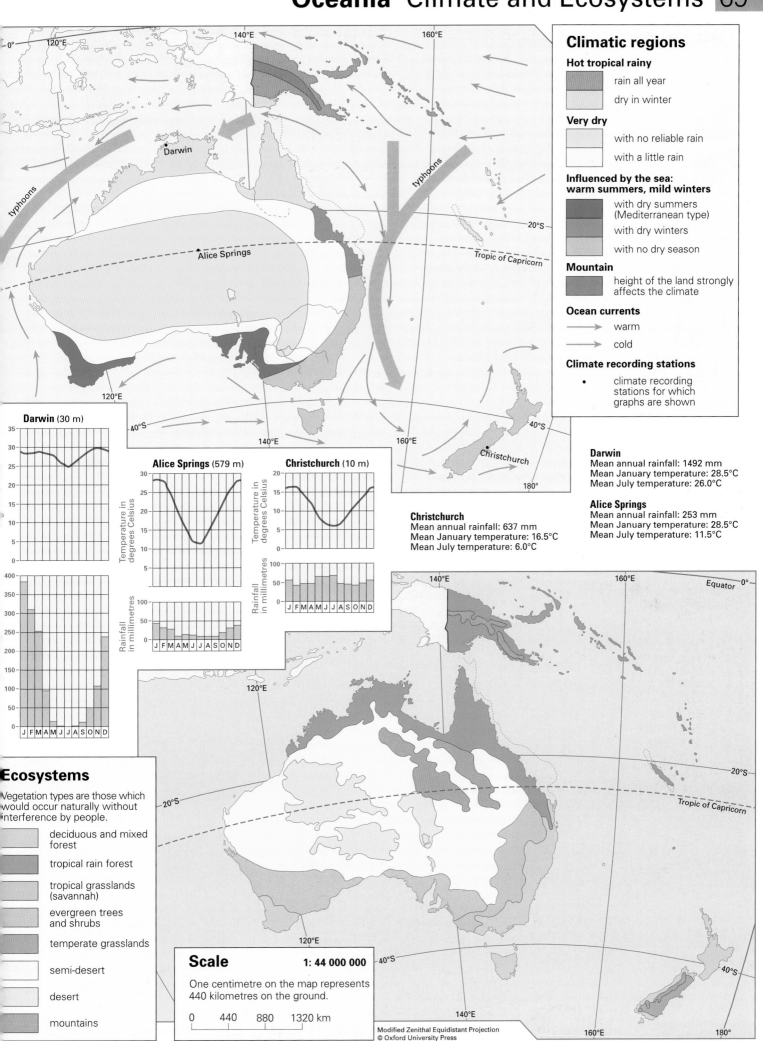

Climatic regions

Hot tropical rainy
- rain all year
- dry in winter

Very dry
- with no reliable rain
- with a little rain

Influenced by the sea: warm summers, mild winters
- with dry summers (Mediterranean type)
- with dry winters
- with no dry season

Mountain
- height of the land strongly affects the climate

Ocean currents
- → warm
- → cold

Climate recording stations
- • climate recording stations for which graphs are shown

Darwin (30 m)

Temperature in degrees Celsius
Rainfall in millimetres

J F M A M J J A S O N D

Alice Springs (579 m)

Temperature in degrees Celsius
Rainfall in millimetres

J F M A M J J A S O N D

Christchurch (10 m)

Temperature in degrees Celsius
Rainfall in millimetres

J F M A M J J A S O N D

Darwin
Mean annual rainfall: 1492 mm
Mean January temperature: 28.5°C
Mean July temperature: 26.0°C

Alice Springs
Mean annual rainfall: 253 mm
Mean January temperature: 28.5°C
Mean July temperature: 11.5°C

Christchurch
Mean annual rainfall: 637 mm
Mean January temperature: 16.5°C
Mean July temperature: 6.0°C

Ecosystems

Vegetation types are those which would occur naturally without interference by people.

- deciduous and mixed forest
- tropical rain forest
- tropical grasslands (savannah)
- evergreen trees and shrubs
- temperate grasslands
- semi-desert
- desert
- mountains

Scale   1: 44 000 000

One centimetre on the map represents 440 kilometres on the ground.

0   440   880   1320 km

Modified Zenithal Equidistant Projection
© Oxford University Press

Farming, forestry, and fishing

main farming types

	little or no farming : because the area is too dry or otherwise harsh.
	shifting cultivation : small areas farmed until soils exhausted, then family moves.
	mixed subsistence : crops and animals for family food.
	grazing and stock rearing : on a large scale, for profit.
	intensive grazing : fattening of lambs, mainly for meat, and of beef cattle. All for profit.
	mixed farming : animals and crops for profit.
	grain farming : mostly wheat but also other cereals, for profit.
	plantation : well organized, specializing in one crop for profit, e.g. sugar or cocoa.
	specialized horticulture : mostly supported by irrigation.
	dairy farming : milk, butter, and cheese for profit. Also lamb fattening in New Zealand.

forestry

	forestry for profit

cash crops

⊘	cocoa	ⓢ	coffee	✺	fruit
✳	sugar	⊛	cotton	ⓡ	rice
ⓣ	palm products				

animal products

🐑	wool	🐄 ⎱ meat		➤	fish

area irrigated by the River Murray Scheme

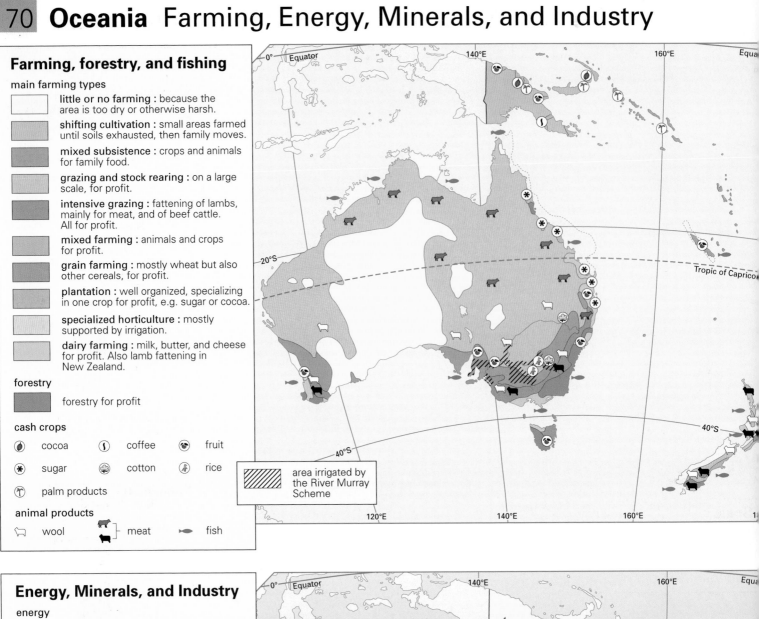

Energy, Minerals, and Industry

energy

▮	coalfield
◢	oil field (with associated gas, and sometimes off shore)
▸	gas field

hydro-electric power stations

●	largest (over 3000 megawatts)
•	smaller (500 – 3000 megawatts)

industry

🏭	main centres of industry

minerals (main mining areas)

◈	silver	◈	gold	◈	tin
◈	copper	◈	bauxite	◈	nickel
◈	zinc	◈	lead	◈	uranium
◈	diamonds	◇	iron ore (iron sands in New Zealand)		

Australian underground water supplies

	areas where artesian water is generally available
	areas where artesian water is available in places

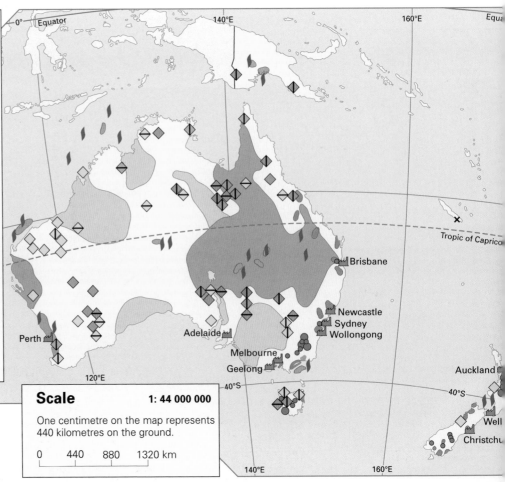

Scale   1: 44 000 000

One centimetre on the map represents 440 kilometres on the ground.

0	440	880	1320 km

Modified Zenithal Equidistant Projection
© Oxford University Press

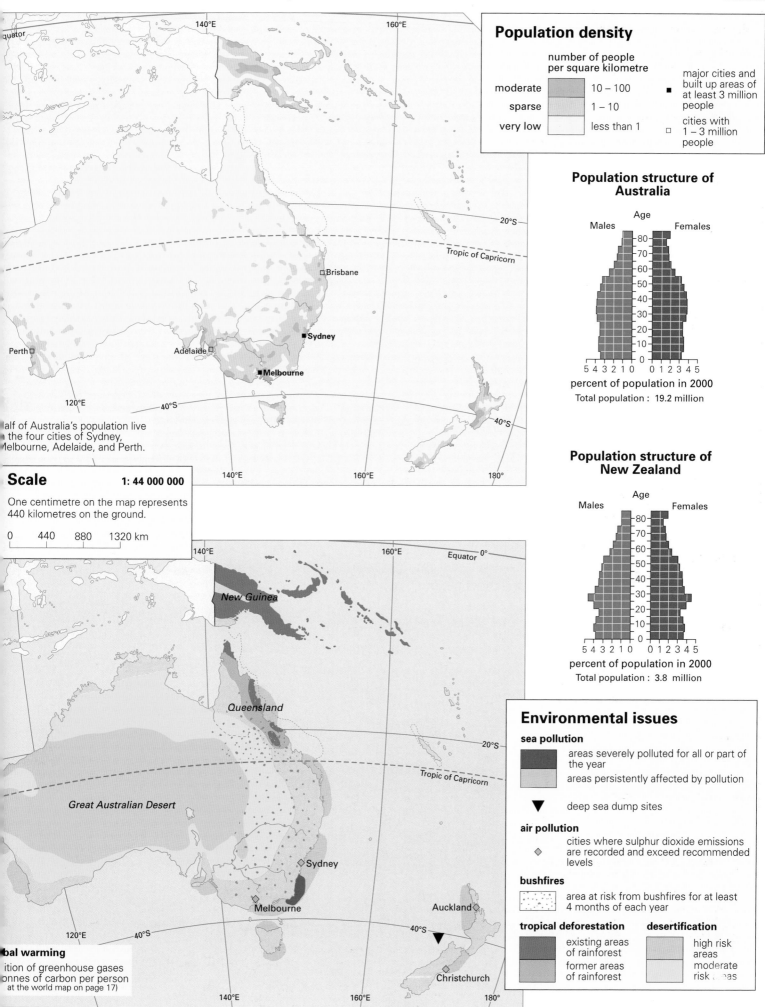

Population density

number of people per square kilometre

moderate	10 – 100	■ major cities and built up areas of at least 3 million people
sparse	1 – 10	
very low	less than 1	□ cities with 1 – 3 million people

Population structure of Australia

Age

Males — Females

80 70 60 50 40 30 20 10 0

5 4 3 2 1 0 — 0 1 2 3 4 5

percent of population in 2000

Total population : 19.2 million

Population structure of New Zealand

Age

Males — Females

80 70 60 50 40 30 20 10 0

5 4 3 2 1 0 — 0 1 2 3 4 5

percent of population in 2000

Total population : 3.8 million

Scale   1: 44 000 000

One centimetre on the map represents 440 kilometres on the ground.

0   440   880   1320 km

...alf of Australia's population live ...the four cities of Sydney, ...elbourne, Adelaide, and Perth.

Equator
140°E
160°E
20°S
Tropic of Capricorn
Brisbane
Sydney
Adelaide
Melbourne
Perth
120°E
40°S
40°S
140°E
160°E
180°

Environmental issues

sea pollution

■ areas severely polluted for all or part of the year

areas persistently affected by pollution

▼ deep sea dump sites

air pollution

◇ cities where sulphur dioxide emissions are recorded and exceed recommended levels

bushfires

⋰ area at risk from bushfires for at least 4 months of each year

tropical deforestation

existing areas of rainforest

former areas of rainforest

desertification

high risk areas

moderate risk areas

New Guinea
Queensland
140°E   160°E   Equator   0°
20°S
Tropic of Capricorn
Great Australian Desert
Sydney
Melbourne   Auckland
120°E   40°S   40°S
Christchurch
140°E   160°E   180°

...bal warming

...ition of greenhouse gases ...onnes of carbon per person ...at the world map on page 17)

Modified Zenithal Equidistant Projection
© Oxford University Press

Land height

in metres above sea level

more than 2000 m	
1000 – 2000 m	
500 – 1000 m	
200 – 500 m	
less than 200 m	
below sea level	

Key

international boundary	
state boundary	
motorway and main road	
railway	
major airport	
river	
seasonal river	
lake	
seasonal lake	
marsh	
coral reef	
peak or highest point	
towns	largest
	large
	others

Scale

1: 21 000 000

One centimetre on the map represents 210 kilometres on the ground.

Zenithal Equidistant Projection   © Oxford University

SOLOMON ISLANDS
Honiara

New Ireland
New Britain
Bougainville

PAPUA NEW GUINEA
Madang
Goroka
Lae
Wau
Mendi
Mount Hagen
Port Moresby
Kerema

5030 m Jaya Peak
IRIAN JAYA

INDONESIA
Ujung Pandang
Ambon
Buru
Seram
Aru Islands
Tanimbar Islands
EAST TIMOR
Dili
Timor
Kupang
Sumba
Sumbawa
Flores
Lombok
Bali
Java
Madura
Sulawesi
Borneo

Banda Sea
Arafura Sea
Timor Sea

Coral Sea
Great Barrier Reef

Torres Strait
Cape York
Gulf of Carpentaria

Cooktown
Cairns
Charters Towers
Townsville

Darwin
Katherine
Birdum
Daly
Victoria
Ord
Wyndham
Fitzroy
Derby
Broome

NORTHERN TERRITORY
Tennant Creek
Mt. Ziel 1510 m
MACDONNELL RANGES
Alice Springs
Finke
867 m Ayers Rock

QUEENSLAND
Flinders
Mount Isa
Cooper Creek
Longreach
Charleville
Cunnamulla

Brisbane
Gold Coast
Maryborough
Bundaberg
Rockhampton
Toowoomba
Grafton
Newcastle
Sydney
Wollongong

GREAT DIVIDING RANGE
GREAT DIVIDING RANGE

NEW SOUTH WALES
Bourke
Dubbo
Darling
Murrumbidgee
Murray
Broken Hill
Mildura
Canberra
2230 m Mt Kosciusko
SNOWY MTNS
Cape Howe

WESTERN AUSTRALIA
GREAT SANDY DESERT
GIBSON DESERT
GREAT VICTORIA DESERT
Lake Mackay
HAMERSLEY RANGE
1251 m Mt. Meharry
Marble Bar
Newman
Port Hedland
Roebourne
Carnarvon
Meekatharra
Mount Magnet
Murchison
Geraldton
Kalgoorlie
Esperance
Perth
Fremantle
Bunbury
Cape Leeuwin
Albany

SOUTH AUSTRALIA
SIMPSON DESERT
STURT DESERT
Lake Eyre
Lake Torrens
NULLARBOR PLAIN
FLINDERS RANGE
Port Augusta
Whyalla
Port Pirie
Port Lincoln
Adelaide
Spencer Gulf
Great Australian Bight

VICTORIA
Ballarat
Geelong
Melbourne
Bass Strait

TASMANIA
Burnie
Launceston

Tasman Sea
Southern Ocean
Indian Ocean

Tropic of Capricorn

Key

~~~ motorway and main road

~~~ railway

⊕ major airport

↜ river and dam

⬭ lake

▲ peak or highest point

towns

■ largest

● large

· others

Land height
in metres above sea level

more than 2000 m

1000 – 2000 m

500 – 1000 m

200 – 500 m

less than 200 m

Three Kings Islands

North Cape

Whangarei

Dargaville

Kaipara Harbour

Great Barrier Island

Hauraki Gulf

Auckland

Pukekohe

Waikato

Bay of Plenty

Hamilton

Tauranga

Whakatane

East Cape

Rotorua

Tokoroa

Rangitaiki

Taupo

Gisborne

New Plymouth

Lake Taupo

▲ 2797 m Ruapehu

Wanganui

Hawke Bay

Napier

Hawera

NORTH ISLAND

Hastings

Wanganui

Feilding

Palmerston North

Manawatu

Levin

Masterton

Tasman Sea

Cape Farewell

Tasman Bay

Nelson

Cook Strait

Wellington

Westport

Wairau

Blenheim

Greymouth

SOUTH ISLAND

SOUTHERN ALPS

Pegasus Bay

⊕ Christchurch

▲ 3764 m Mt. Cook

Rakaia

CANTERBURY PLAINS

Ashburton

Canterbury Bight

Lake Wanaka

Waitaki

Timaru

Lake Wakatipu

Milford Sound

Queenstown

Oamaru

Lake Te Anau

Clutha

Waiau

Gore

Cape Providence

Dunedin

Invercargill

Foveaux Strait

Southwest Cape

Stewart Island

South Pacific Ocean

165°E

170°E

175°E

35°S

40°S

45°S

180°

175°E

180°

Scale 1: 6 000 000

One centimetre on the map represents 60 kilometres on the ground.

0 60 120 180 240 km

Conical Orthomorphic Projection © Oxford University Press

Countries and capitals

— country boundary

• capital city

The British Isles at the same scale

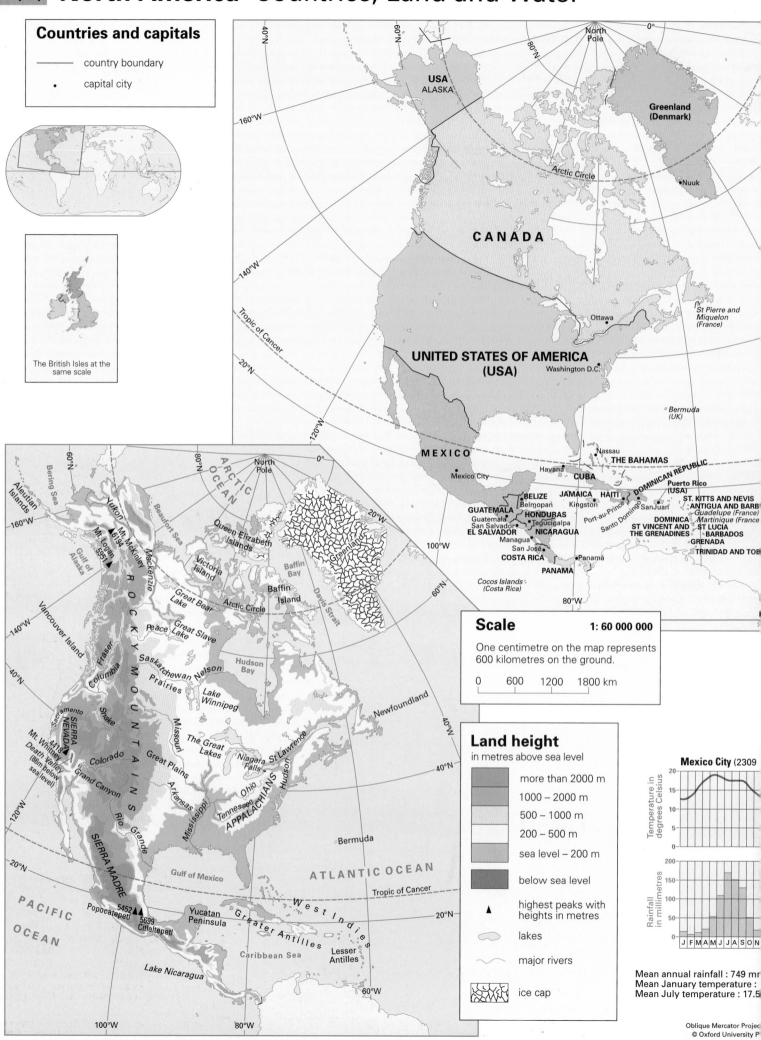

USA
ALASKA

Greenland
(Denmark)

•Nuuk

North Pole

Arctic Circle

C A N A D A

•Ottawa

St Pierre and Miquelon (France)

UNITED STATES OF AMERICA
(USA)

Washington D.C.•

•Bermuda (UK)

Nassau•

M E X I C O

THE BAHAMAS

•Mexico City

Havana•

CUBA

DOMINICAN REPUBLIC

Puerto Rico (USA)

•BELIZE

JAMAICA

HAITI

•SanJuan

ST. KITTS AND NEVIS

GUATEMALA

Belmopan•

Kingston•

Port-au-Prince•

Santo Domingo•

ANTIGUA AND BARB

Guatemala•

HONDURAS

DOMINICA

Guadelupe (France)

San Salvador•

•Tegucigalpa

Martinique (France

EL SALVADOR

NICARAGUA

ST VINCENT AND
THE GRENADINES

ST LUCIA

Managua•

BARBADOS

San José•

PANAMA

GRENADA

COSTA RICA

•Panamá

TRINIDAD AND TOB

PANAMA

Cocos Islands
(Costa Rica)

80°W

40°N, 60°N, 80°N, North Pole, 0°, Arctic Circle, Tropic of Cancer, 20°N, 160°W, 140°W, 120°W, 100°W

Scale   1: 60 000 000

One centimetre on the map represents
600 kilometres on the ground.

0   600   1200   1800 km

Land height
in metres above sea level

more than 2000 m

1000 – 2000 m

500 – 1000 m

200 – 500 m

sea level – 200 m

below sea level

▲ highest peaks with
heights in metres

lakes

major rivers

ice cap

Aleutian Islands

Bering Sea

ARCTIC OCEAN

North Pole

Beaufort Sea

Gulf of Alaska

Yukon

Mt McKinley 6194

Mt Logan 5951▲

▲

Mackenzie

Queen Elizabeth Islands

Victoria Island

Greenland

20°W

Vancouver Island

R O C K Y   M O U N T A I N S

Fraser

Columbia

Great Bear Lake

Arctic Circle

Baffin Island

Baffin Bay

Davis Strait

Peace

Great Slave Lake

Snake

Saskatchewan

Nelson

Prairies

Hudson Bay

SIERRA NEVADA ▲4418

Sacramento

Lake Winnipeg

Mt. Whitney 4418▲

Death Valley
(86m below sea level)

Grand Canyon

Colorado

Missouri

The Great Lakes

Niagara Falls

St Lawrence

Newfoundland

Great Plains

Hudson

Rio Grande

Arkansas

Ohio

Tennessee

Mississippi

APPALACHIANS

SIERRA MADRE

Bermuda

20°N

Gulf of Mexico

ATLANTIC OCEAN

Tropic of Cancer

PACIFIC OCEAN

Popocatepetl

5452▲▲
5699
Citlaltepetl

Yucatan Peninsula

W e s t   I n d i e s

20°N

G r e a t e r   A n t i l l e s

Lesser Antilles

Lake Nicaragua

Caribbean Sea

60°N, 80°N, 160°W, 140°W, 120°W, 40°N, 20°N, 100°W, 80°W, 60°N, 40°N

Mexico City (2309)

Temperature in degrees Celsius
20
15
10
5
0

J F M A M J J A S O N

Rainfall in millimetres
200
150
100
50

J F M A M J J A S O N

Mean annual rainfall : 749 mr
Mean January temperature :
Mean July temperature : 17.5

Oblique Mercator Projec
© Oxford University P

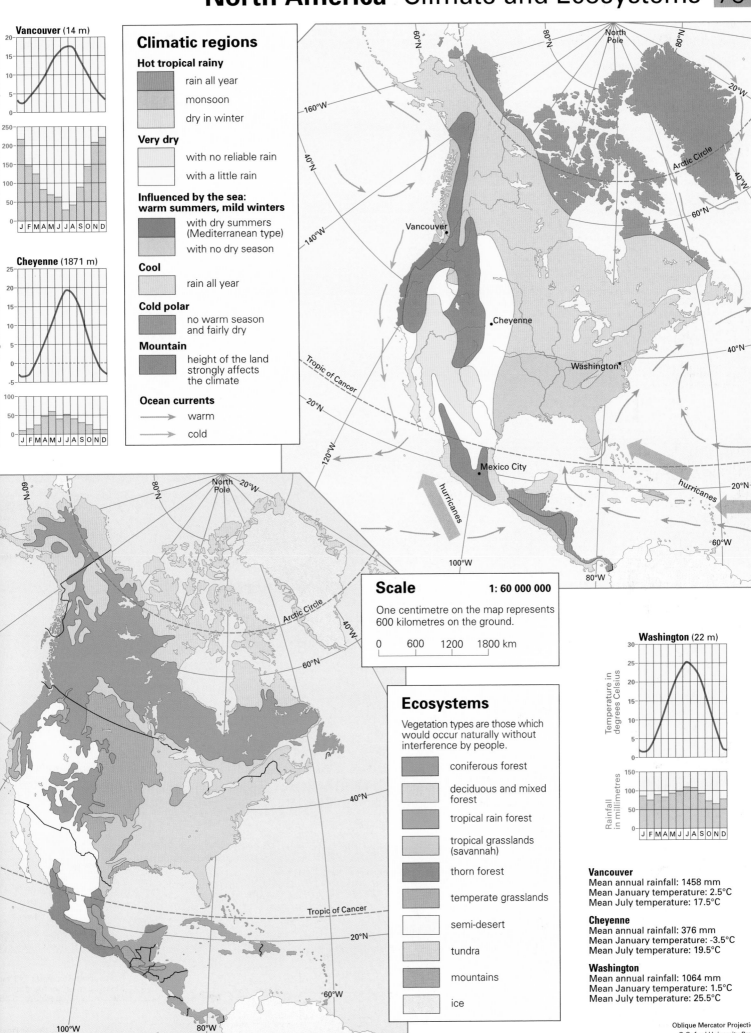

Vancouver (14 m)

Cheyenne (1871 m)

Climatic regions

Hot tropical rainy

rain all year

monsoon

dry in winter

Very dry

with no reliable rain

with a little rain

Influenced by the sea: warm summers, mild winters

with dry summers (Mediterranean type)

with no dry season

Cool

rain all year

Cold polar

no warm season and fairly dry

Mountain

height of the land strongly affects the climate

Ocean currents

→ warm

→ cold

Scale

1: 60 000 000

One centimetre on the map represents 600 kilometres on the ground.

0   600   1200   1800 km

Ecosystems

Vegetation types are those which would occur naturally without interference by people.

coniferous forest

deciduous and mixed forest

tropical rain forest

tropical grasslands (savannah)

thorn forest

temperate grasslands

semi-desert

tundra

mountains

ice

Washington (22 m)

Temperature in degrees Celsius

Rainfall in millimetres

Vancouver
Mean annual rainfall: 1458 mm
Mean January temperature: 2.5°C
Mean July temperature: 17.5°C

Cheyenne
Mean annual rainfall: 376 mm
Mean January temperature: -3.5°C
Mean July temperature: 19.5°C

Washington
Mean annual rainfall: 1064 mm
Mean January temperature: 1.5°C
Mean July temperature: 25.5°C

Oblique Mercator Projection
© Oxford University Press

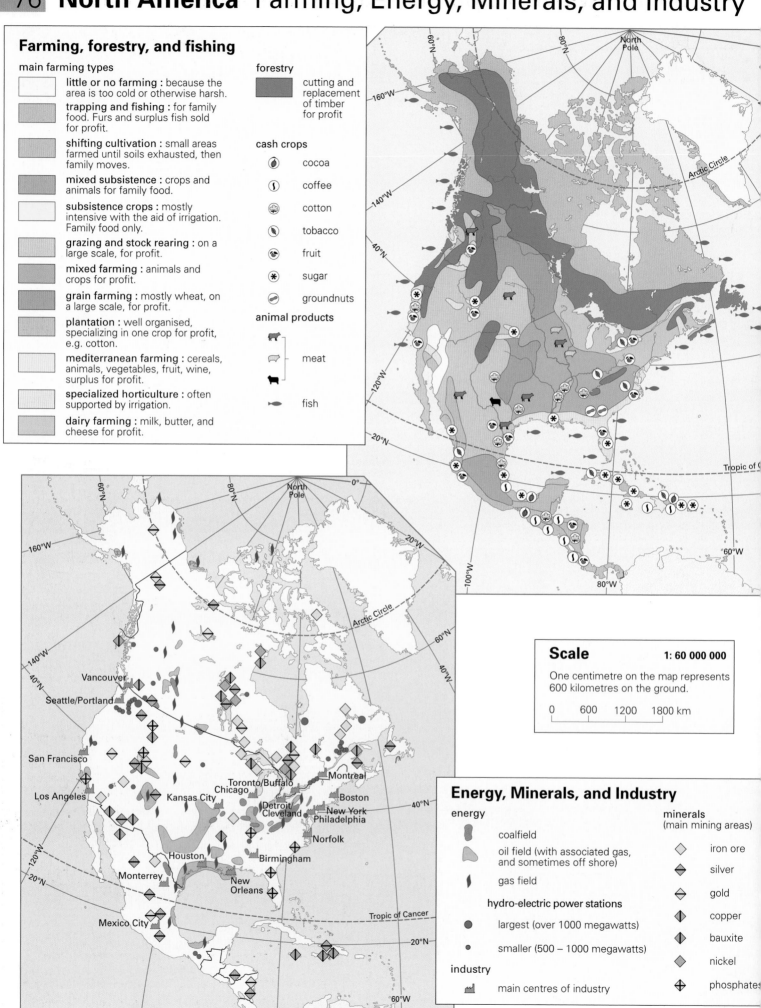

Farming, forestry, and fishing

main farming types

- **little or no farming** : because the area is too cold or otherwise harsh.
- **trapping and fishing** : for family food. Furs and surplus fish sold for profit.
- **shifting cultivation** : small areas farmed until soils exhausted, then family moves.
- **mixed subsistence** : crops and animals for family food.
- **subsistence crops** : mostly intensive with the aid of irrigation. Family food only.
- **grazing and stock rearing** : on a large scale, for profit.
- **mixed farming** : animals and crops for profit.
- **grain farming** : mostly wheat, on a large scale, for profit.
- **plantation** : well organised, specializing in one crop for profit, e.g. cotton.
- **mediterranean farming** : cereals, animals, vegetables, fruit, wine, surplus for profit.
- **specialized horticulture** : often supported by irrigation.
- **dairy farming** : milk, butter, and cheese for profit.

forestry

- cutting and replacement of timber for profit

cash crops

- cocoa
- coffee
- cotton
- tobacco
- fruit
- sugar
- groundnuts

animal products

- meat
- fish

Scale   1 : 60 000 000

One centimetre on the map represents 600 kilometres on the ground.

0   600   1200   1800 km

Energy, Minerals, and Industry

energy

- coalfield
- oil field (with associated gas, and sometimes off shore)
- gas field

hydro-electric power stations

- largest (over 1000 megawatts)
- smaller (500 – 1000 megawatts)

industry

- main centres of industry

minerals (main mining areas)

- iron ore
- silver
- gold
- copper
- bauxite
- nickel
- phosphates

Oblique Mercator Project
© Oxford University Pr

Population density

number of people per square kilometre

high		more than 100
moderate		10 – 100
sparse		1 – 10
very low		less than 1

■ major cities and built up areas of at least 3 million people

□ cities with 1 – 3 million people

Population structure of the United States

Age

Males | Females

80 70 60 50 40 30 20 10

5 4 3 2 1 0   0 1 2 3 4 5

percent of the population in 2000

Total population : 275.6 million

Population structure of Mexico

Age

Males | Females

80 70 60 50 40 30 20 10

7 6 5 4 3 2 1 0   0 1 2 3 4 5 6 7

percent of the population in 2000

Total population : 100.3 million

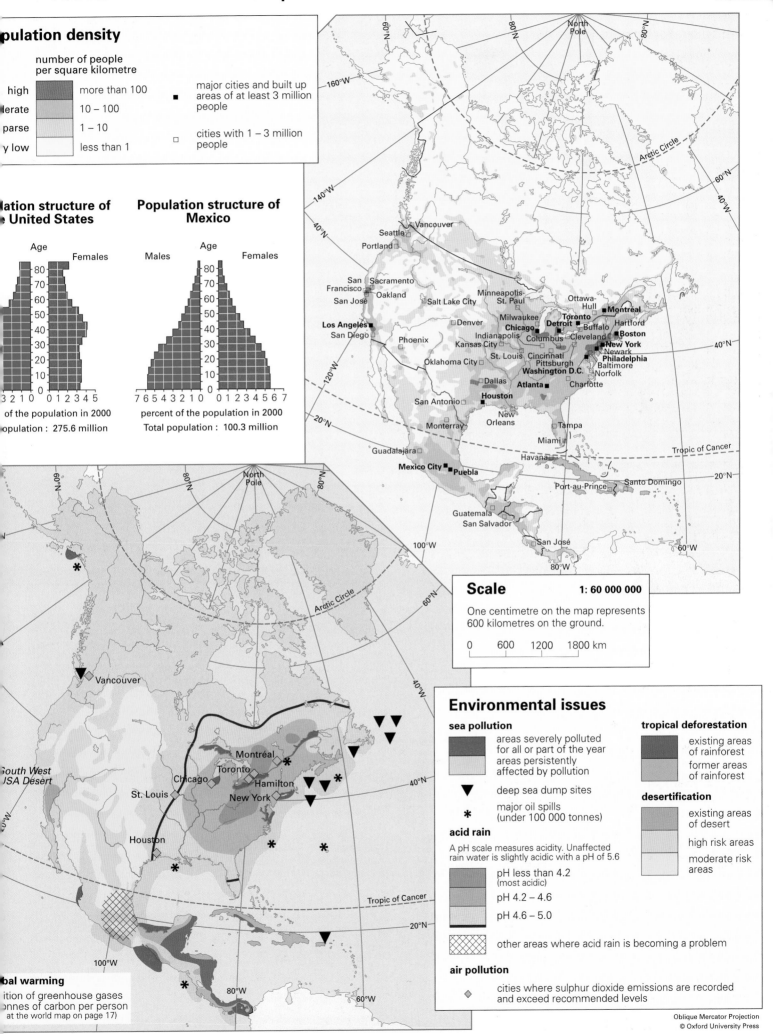

Scale   1: 60 000 000

One centimetre on the map represents 600 kilometres on the ground.

0   600   1200   1800 km

Environmental issues

sea pollution

areas severely polluted for all or part of the year

areas persistently affected by pollution

▼ deep sea dump sites

✳ major oil spills (under 100 000 tonnes)

acid rain

A pH scale measures acidity. Unaffected rain water is slightly acidic with a pH of 5.6

pH less than 4.2 (most acidic)

pH 4.2 – 4.6

pH 4.6 – 5.0

other areas where acid rain is becoming a problem

air pollution

◇ cities where sulphur dioxide emissions are recorded and exceed recommended levels

tropical deforestation

existing areas of rainforest

former areas of rainforest

desertification

existing areas of desert

high risk areas

moderate risk areas

global warming

emission of greenhouse gases (tonnes of carbon per person — at the world map on page 17)

South West USA Desert

Oblique Mercator Projection
© Oxford University Press

Key

international boundary
state or province boundary
motorway and main road
railway
canal

major airport
river and dam
lake
ice cap
marsh

peak or highest point

towns
largest
large
others

Land height

in metres above sea level

more than 2000 m
1000 – 2000 m
500 – 1000 m
200 – 500m
less than 200 m
below sea level

Scale

1 : 25 000 000

One centimetre on the map measures 250 kilometres on the ground.

0   250   500   750   1000 km

RUSSIAN FEDERATION (RUSSIA)

ICELAND
Reykjavík
Arctic Circle

GREENLAND

Mt. Forel 3360 m

Nuuk (Godthåb)

Atlantic Ocean

Cape Farewell

NEWFOUNDLAND AND LABRADOR

Schefferville
Smallwood Reservoir

Baffin Bay

Baffin Island

Southampton Island

Hudson Bay

Churchill

Ellesmere Island

Devon Island

Sverdrup Islands

Queen Elizabeth Islands

Parry Islands

Melville Island

Victoria Island

Banks Island

N U N A V U T

MANITOBA

Lynn Lake

Nelson

SASKATCHEWAN

Saskatchewan

Fort McMurray

Athabasca

Great Bear Lake

Great Slave Lake

Yellowknife

NORTHWEST TERRITORIES

Hay River

Peace

ALBERTA

Edmonton

Calgary

MACKENZIE MOUNTAINS

Mackenzie

Fort Simpson

Fort Liard

Mt. Robson 3954 m

R O C K Y   M O U N T A I N S

Arctic Ocean

Beaufort Sea

Prudhoe Bay

Inuvik

Dawson

YUKON TERRITORY

Whitehorse

Mt. Logan 5951 m

BRITISH COLUMBIA

COAST MOUNTAINS

Fraser

Prince Rupert

Mt. Waddington 4042 m

Vancouver Island

Victoria

Vancouver

Seattle

Tacoma

Mt. Rainier

BROOKS RANGE

A L A S K A

Yukon

Fairbanks

ALASKA RANGE

Mt. McKinley 6194 m

Anchorage

Seward

Kodiak Island

Gulf of Alaska

Pacific Ocean

Queen Charlotte Islands

Arctic Circle

Bering Strait

St. Lawrence

St. Matthew

Nunivak

Alaska Peninsula

Unimak Island

Bering Sea

North Pole

ICELAND

70°N

80°N

70°N

60°N

Arctic Circle

10°E
0°
10°W
20°W
30°W
40°W
60°W
80°W
100°W
120°W
140°W
160°W

170°E
180°
170°W
160°W
150°W
140°W

Zenithal Equidistant Projection

Abbreviations

CONN.	CONNECTICUT
DEL.	DELAWARE
MARY.	MARYLAND
MASS.	MASSACHUSETTS
MISS.	MISSISSIPPI
N.H.	NEW HAMPSHIRE
N.J.	NEW JERSEY
PENN.	PENNSYLVANIA
R.I.	RHODE ISLAND
VER.	VERMONT
W.VA.	WEST VIRGINIA

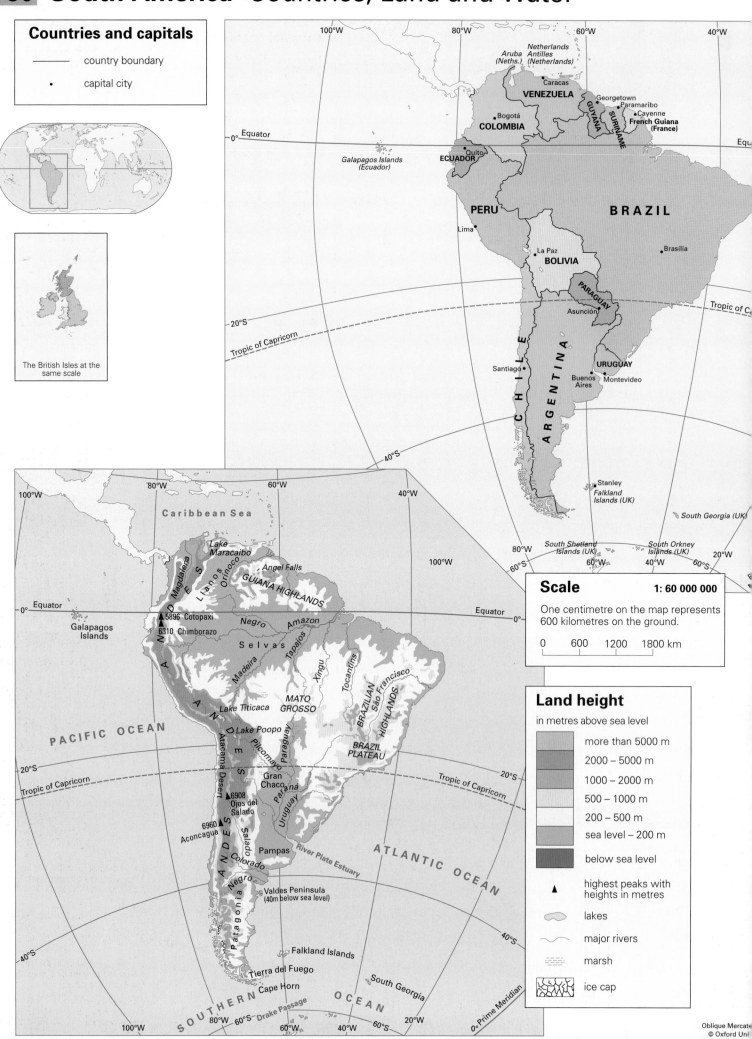

Countries and capitals

— country boundary

• capital city

The British Isles at the same scale

Netherlands Antilles (Netherlands)
Aruba (Neths.)
Caracas
•
VENEZUELA
Georgetown
•Paramaribo
•Cayenne
French Guiana (France)
GUYANA
SURINAME
•Bogotá
COLOMBIA
Equator
0°
Galapagos Islands (Ecuador)
Quito•
ECUADOR
PERU
B R A Z I L
Lima•
La Paz•
•Brasília
BOLIVIA
PARAGUAY
Asunción•
20°S
Tropic of Capricorn
Tropic of C.
URUGUAY
Santiago•
Buenos Aires
•Montevideo
C H I L E
A R G E N T I N A
40°S
•Stanley
Falkland Islands (UK)
South Georgia (UK)
South Shetland Islands (UK)
South Orkney Islands (UK)

Scale   1: 60 000 000

One centimetre on the map represents 600 kilometres on the ground.

0   600   1200   1800 km

Land height

in metres above sea level

	more than 5000 m
	2000 – 5000 m
	1000 – 2000 m
	500 – 1000 m
	200 – 500 m
	sea level – 200 m
	below sea level
▲	highest peaks with heights in metres
	lakes
	major rivers
	marsh
	ice cap

Caribbean Sea
Lake Maracaibo
Magdalena
Orinoco
Llanos
Angel Falls
GUIANA HIGHLANDS
Equator
▲5896 Cotopaxi
6310 Chimborazo
Galapagos Islands
Negro
Amazon
S e l v a s
Madeira
Tapajos
Xingu
Tocantins
BRAZILIAN
São Francisco
HIGHLANDS
MATO GROSSO
Lake Titicaca
Lake Poopo
Paraguay
Pilcomayo
BRAZIL PLATEAU
PACIFIC OCEAN
Atacama Desert
Gran Chaco
Paraná
Uruguay
20°S
Tropic of Capricorn
▲6908 Ojos del Salado
6960 ▲ Aconcagua
Salado
Colorado
Pampas
River Plate Estuary
ATLANTIC OCEAN
A N D E S
Negro
Valdes Peninsula (40m below sea level)
Patagonia
Falkland Islands
South Georgia
40°S
Tierra del Fuego
Cape Horn
S O U T H E R N   O C E A N
Drake Passage

Oblique Mercator
© Oxford Uni

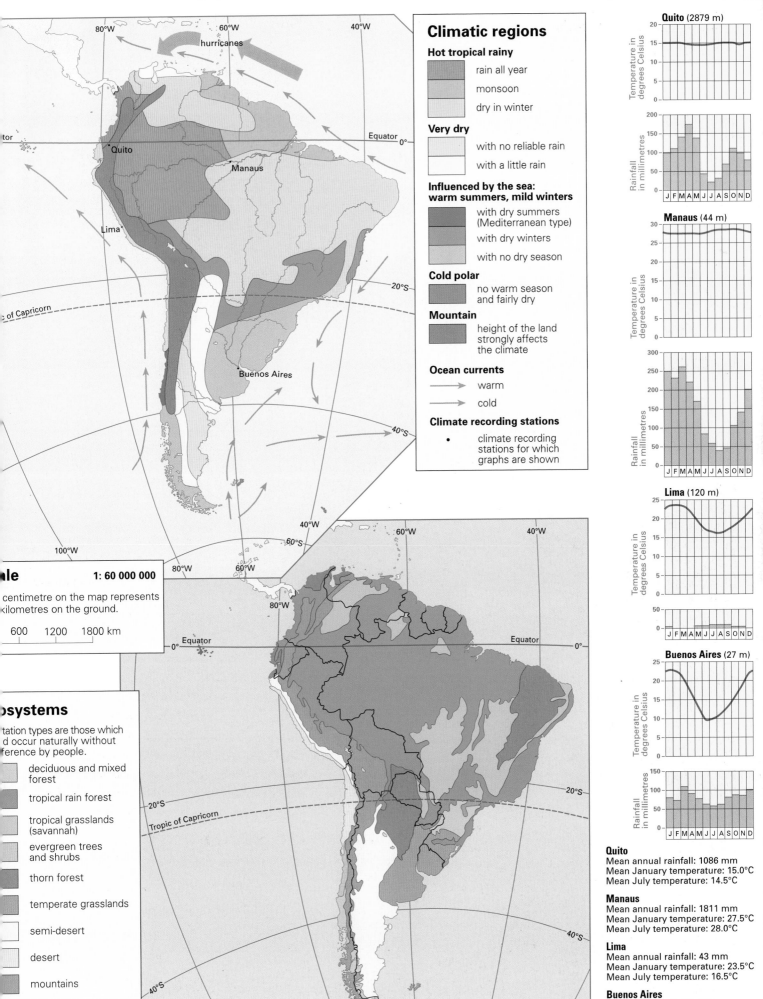

Climatic regions

Hot tropical rainy

- rain all year
- monsoon
- dry in winter

Very dry

- with no reliable rain
- with a little rain

Influenced by the sea: warm summers, mild winters

- with dry summers (Mediterranean type)
- with dry winters
- with no dry season

Cold polar

- no warm season and fairly dry

Mountain

- height of the land strongly affects the climate

Ocean currents

→ warm
→ cold

Climate recording stations

- • climate recording stations for which graphs are shown

Scale 1: 60 000 000

centimetre on the map represents kilometres on the ground.

600 1200 1800 km

Ecosystems

tation types are those which d occur naturally without ference by people.

- deciduous and mixed forest
- tropical rain forest
- tropical grasslands (savanna)
- evergreen trees and shrubs
- thorn forest
- temperate grasslands
- semi-desert
- desert
- mountains

Mercator Projection
University Press

Quito (2879 m)

Manaus (44 m)

Lima (120 m)

Buenos Aires (27 m)

Quito
Mean annual rainfall: 1086 mm
Mean January temperature: 15.0°C
Mean July temperature: 14.5°C

Manaus
Mean annual rainfall: 1811 mm
Mean January temperature: 27.5°C
Mean July temperature: 28.0°C

Lima
Mean annual rainfall: 43 mm
Mean January temperature: 23.5°C
Mean July temperature: 16.5°C

Buenos Aires
Mean annual rainfall: 950 mm
Mean January temperature: 23.0°C
Mean July temperature: 10.0°C

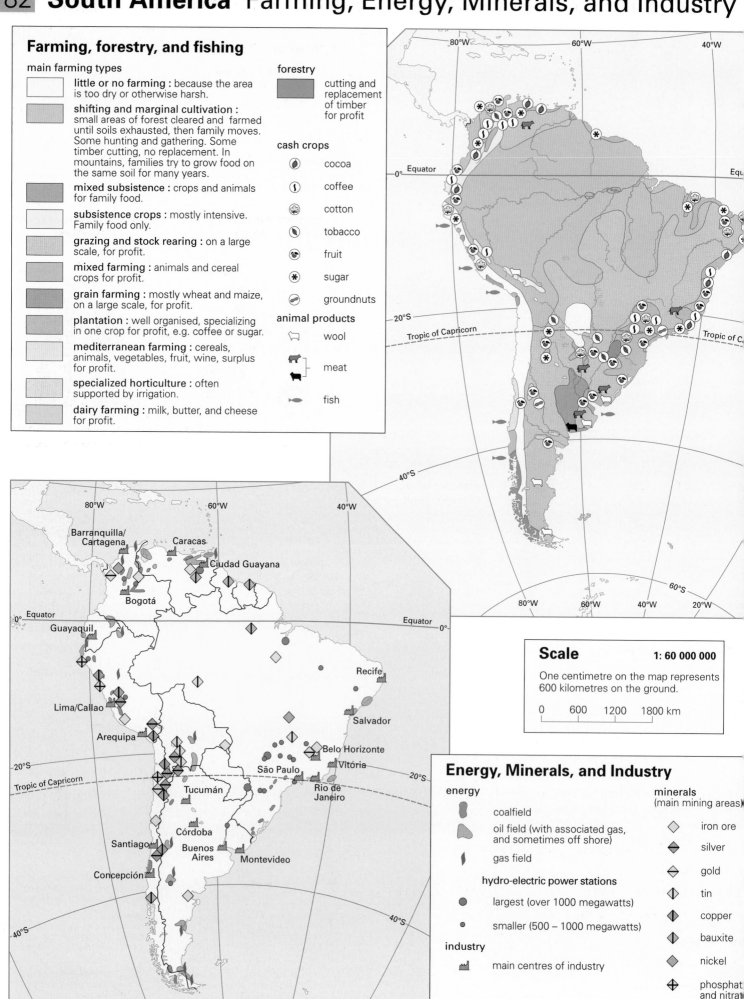

Farming, forestry, and fishing

main farming types

little or no farming : because the area is too dry or otherwise harsh.

shifting and marginal cultivation : small areas of forest cleared and farmed until soils exhausted, then family moves. Some hunting and gathering. Some timber cutting, no replacement. In mountains, families try to grow food on the same soil for many years.

mixed subsistence : crops and animals for family food.

subsistence crops : mostly intensive. Family food only.

grazing and stock rearing : on a large scale, for profit.

mixed farming : animals and cereal crops for profit.

grain farming : mostly wheat and maize, on a large scale, for profit.

plantation : well organised, specializing in one crop for profit, e.g. coffee or sugar.

mediterranean farming : cereals, animals, vegetables, fruit, wine, surplus for profit.

specialized horticulture : often supported by irrigation.

dairy farming : milk, butter, and cheese for profit.

forestry

cutting and replacement of timber for profit

cash crops

- cocoa
- coffee
- cotton
- tobacco
- fruit
- sugar
- groundnuts

animal products

- wool
- meat
- fish

Scale

1 : 60 000 000

One centimetre on the map represents 600 kilometres on the ground.

0   600   1200   1800 km

Energy, Minerals, and Industry

energy

- coalfield
- oil field (with associated gas, and sometimes off shore)
- gas field

hydro-electric power stations

- largest (over 1000 megawatts)
- smaller (500 – 1000 megawatts)

industry

- main centres of industry

minerals (main mining areas)

- iron ore
- silver
- gold
- tin
- copper
- bauxite
- nickel
- phosphat and nitrat (including guano)

Map labels: Barranquilla/Cartagena, Caracas, Ciudad Guayana, Bogotá, Guayaquil, Lima/Callao, Arequipa, Recife, Salvador, Belo Horizonte, Vitória, São Paulo, Rio de Janeiro, Tucumán, Córdoba, Santiago, Buenos Aires, Montevideo, Concepción

Population density

number of people
per square kilometre

high		more than 100
moderate		10 – 100
sparse		1 – 10
very low		less than 1

■ major cities and built up areas of at least 3 million people

□ cities with 1 – 3 million people

80°W 60°W 40°W

Barranquilla
Maracaibo
Caracas
Valencia
Medellín
Cali ■ Bogotá
ator
Quito
Guayaquil

Equator 0°

Belém
Manaus
Fortaleza
Recife
Lima
Salvador
La Paz
Brásília
Belo Horizonte
Nova Iguaçu
São Paulo
Rio de Janeiro
Curitiba
Córdoba
Porto Alegre
Rosario
Santiago ■
Buenos Aires

of Capricorn
Tropic of Capricorn 20°S

20°W

100°W 80°W 60°W 40°W

Scale 1: 60 000 000

One centimetre on the map represents 600 kilometres on the ground.

0   600   1200   1800 km

Population structure of Brazil

Age
Males   Females

80
70
60
50
40
30
20
10

6 5 4 3 2 1 0 0 1 2 3 4 5 6

percent of the population in 2000
Total population : 172.9 million

Population structure of Argentina

Age
Males   Females

80
70
60
50
40
30
20
10

6 5 4 3 2 1 0 0 1 2 3 4 5 6

percent of the population in 2000
Total population : 37.0 million

Environmental issues

sea pollution

	areas severely polluted for all or part of the year
	areas persistently affected by pollution

✳ major oil spills (over 100 000 tonnes)

✱ major oil spills (under 100 000 tonnes)

acid rain

▨ areas where acid rain is becoming a problem

air pollution

◆ cities where sulphur dioxide emissions are recorded and exceed recommended levels

tropical deforestation

	existing areas of rainforest
	former areas of rainforest

desertification

	existing areas of desert
	high risk areas
	moderate risk areas

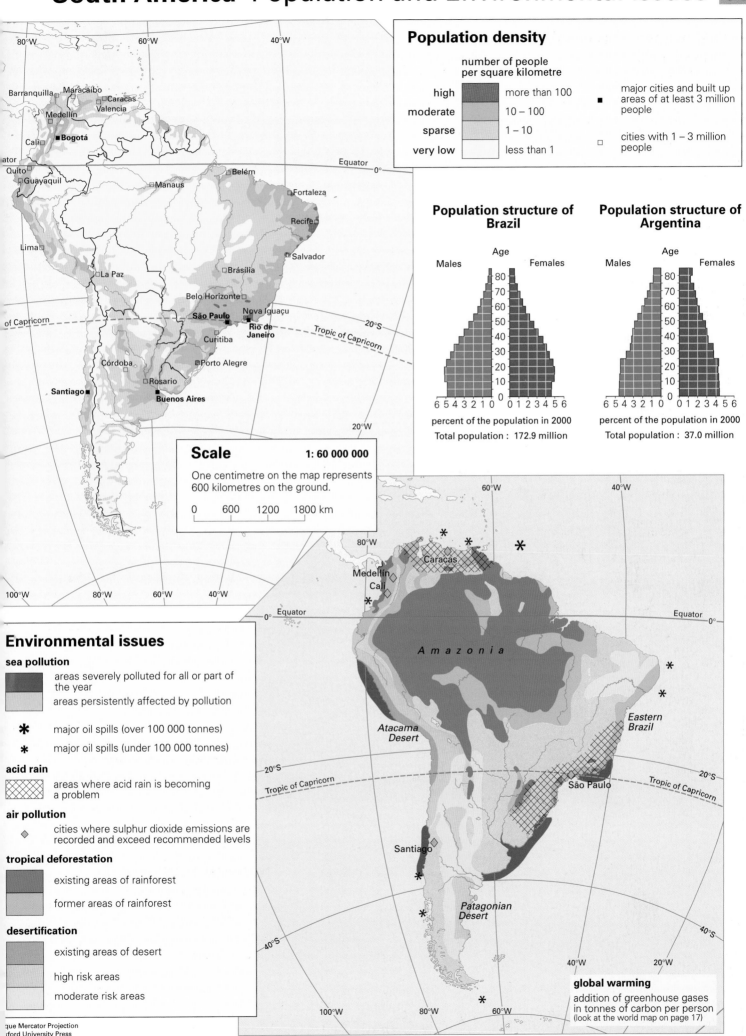

60°W 40°W

80°W
Caracas
Medellín
Cali
Equator 0°

Amazonia

Atacama Desert

Eastern Brazil

20°S
São Paulo
Tropic of Capricorn 20°S

Santiago

Patagonian Desert

40°S

100°W 80°W 60°W

40°W 20°W

40°S

global warming

addition of greenhouse gases in tonnes of carbon per person (look at the world map on page 17)

que Mercator Projection
xford University Press

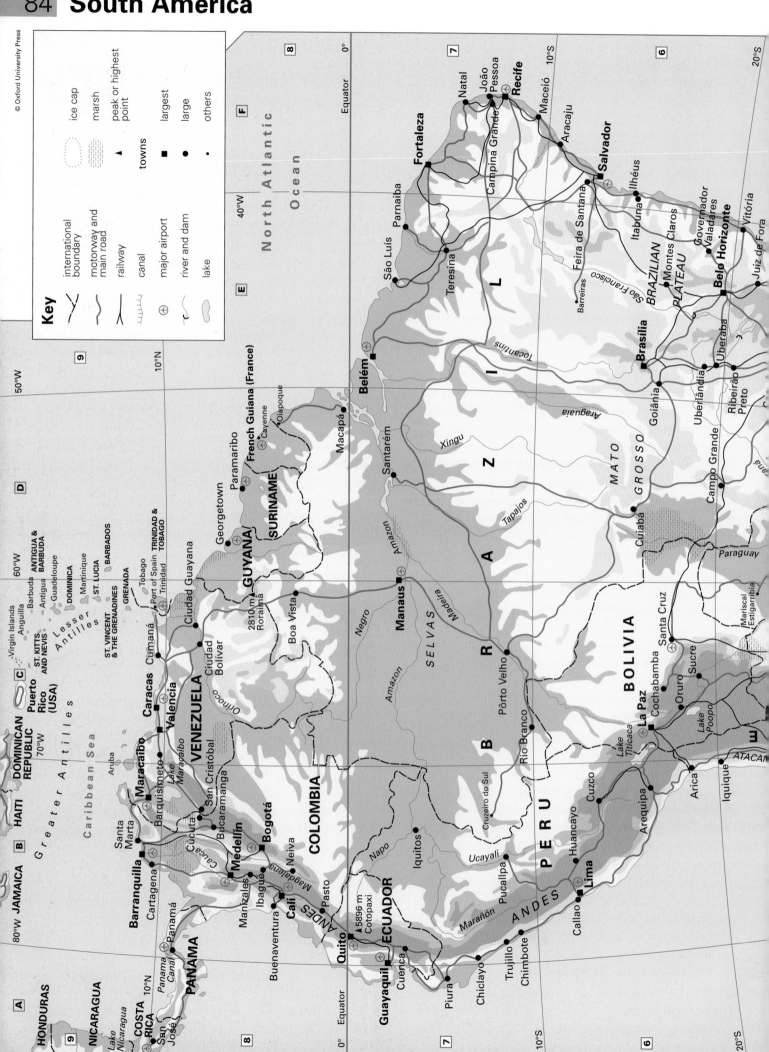

Key

ice cap	marsh
peak or highest point	
towns	largest
	large
	others

international boundary
motorway and main road
railway
canal
major airport
river and dam
lake

North Atlantic Ocean

Caribbean Sea

Greater Antilles

Lesser Antilles

HONDURAS
NICARAGUA
Lake Nicaragua
COSTA RICA
San José
PANAMA
Panama Canal
Panamá

JAMAICA
HAITI
DOMINICAN REPUBLIC
Virgin Islands
Anguilla
ST. KITTS AND NEVIS
Puerto Rico (USA)
Barbuda
ANTIGUA & BARBUDA
Antigua
Guadeloupe
DOMINICA
Martinique
ST. LUCIA
BARBADOS
ST. VINCENT & THE GRENADINES
GRENADA
Aruba
Tobago
TRINIDAD & TOBAGO
Port of Spain
Trinidad

COLOMBIA
Santa Marta
Barranquilla
Cartagena
Maracaibo
Lake Maracaibo
Barquisimeto
VENEZUELA
Valencia
Caracas
Cumaná
San Cristóbal
Cúcuta
Bucaramanga
Medellín
Manizales
Ibagué
Bogotá
Cali
Buenaventura
Neiva
Pasto
Cauca
Magdalena
ECUADOR
Quito
▲5896 m Cotopaxi
Guayaquil
Cuenca
ANDES
Piura
Chiclayo
Trujillo
Chimbote
Callao
Lima
PERU
Iquitos
Napo
Marañón
Ucayali
Pucallpa
Huancayo
Cuzco
Arequipa
Arica
Iquique
ATACAMA

Georgetown
GUYANA
Paramaribo
SURINAME
French Guiana (France)
Cayenne
Oiapoque
Macapá
Belém
Santarém
Boa Vista
2810 m Roraima
Ciudad Bolívar
Ciudad Guayana
Orinoco
Negro
Amazon
Manaus
SELVAS
Madeira
Xingu
Tapajos
Pôrto Velho
Rio Branco
Cruzeiro do Sul
B R A Z I L
Amazon
Tocantins
Araguaia
MATO GROSSO
Cuiabá
Campo Grande
Paraguay
BOLIVIA
La Paz
Cochabamba
Santa Cruz
Sucre
Oruro
Lake Poopó
Lake Titicaca
Mariscal Estigarribia

Fortaleza
Natal
João Pessoa
Campina Grande
Recife
Maceió
Aracaju
Salvador
Ilhéus
Itabuna
Parnaíba
São Luís
Teresina
Feira de Santana
Barreiras
São Francisco
Montes Claros
Governador Valadares
Belo Horizonte
Vitória
Juiz de Fora
BRAZILIAN PLATEAU
Brasília
Goiânia
Uberlândia
Uberaba
Ribeirão Preto

Equator

North Atlantic Ocean

Transverse Mercator Projection   © Oxford University Press

Land height
in metres above sea level

more than 5000 m
2000 – 5000 m
1000 – 2000 m
500 – 1000 m
200 – 500 m
less than 200 m

Scale

1: 21 000 000

One centimetre on the map represents
210 kilometres on the ground.

| 0 | 210 | 420 | 630 | 840 km |

Pacific
Ocean

South Atlantic
Ocean

Southern Ocean

Florianópolis
Caxias do Sul
Pôrto Alegre
Pelotas
Rio Grande
URUGUAY
Montevideo
River Plate
Estuary
Mar del Plata
La Plata
Rosario
Buenos Aires
Paraná
Santa Fé
Córdoba
Santiago del Estero
Salado
Uruguay
Paraná
San Juan
Mendoza
Aconcagua
6960 m
Viña del Mar
Valparaíso
Santiago
Talca
Talcahuano
Concepción
Temuco
Valdivia
Osorno
Puerto Montt
Chiloé Island
Chillán
Colorado
Negro
ARGENTINA
Bahía Blanca
PATAGONIA
Comodoro Rivadavia
Esquel
Juan Fernández Islands

Punta Arenas
Tierra del Fuego
Cape Horn

Stanley
Falkland Islands (UK)

South Georgia (UK)

South Orkney Islands (UK)

Antarctic Circle

South Shetland Islands (UK)

Antarctic Peninsula

ANTARCTICA

30°S
40°S
50°S
60°S

90°W
80°W
70°W
60°W
50°W
40°W
30°W

A B C D E F

1 2 3 4 5

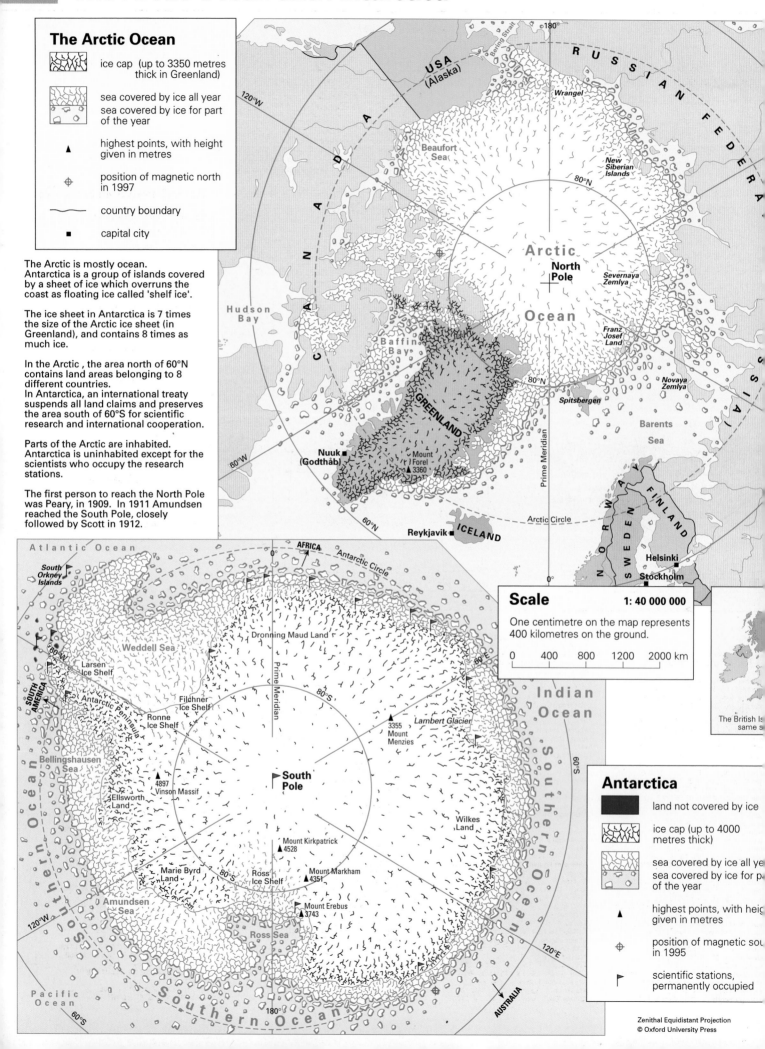

The Arctic Ocean

- ice cap (up to 3350 metres thick in Greenland)
- sea covered by ice all year
- sea covered by ice for part of the year
- ▲ highest points, with height given in metres
- ⊕ position of magnetic north in 1997
- country boundary
- ■ capital city

The Arctic is mostly ocean.
Antarctica is a group of islands covered by a sheet of ice which overruns the coast as floating ice called 'shelf ice'.

The ice sheet in Antarctica is 7 times the size of the Arctic ice sheet (in Greenland), and contains 8 times as much ice.

In the Arctic , the area north of 60°N contains land areas belonging to 8 different countries.
In Antarctica, an international treaty suspends all land claims and preserves the area south of 60°S for scientific research and international cooperation.

Parts of the Arctic are inhabited. Antarctica is uninhabited except for the scientists who occupy the research stations.

The first person to reach the North Pole was Peary, in 1909. In 1911 Amundsen reached the South Pole, closely followed by Scott in 1912.

Scale

1: 40 000 000

One centimetre on the map represents 400 kilometres on the ground.

0   400   800   1200   2000 km

Antarctica

- land not covered by ice
- ice cap (up to 4000 metres thick)
- sea covered by ice all year
- sea covered by ice for part of the year
- ▲ highest points, with height given in metres
- ⊕ position of magnetic south in 1995
- ⚑ scientific stations, permanently occupied

Zenithal Equidistant Projection
© Oxford University Press

ow to use the index

find a place on an atlas map use either
grid code or latitude and longitude.

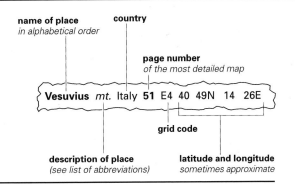

name of place
in alphabetical order

country

page number
of the most detailed map

Vesuvius *mt.* Italy **51** E4 40 49N 14 26E

grid code

description of place
(see list of abbreviations)

latitude and longitude
sometimes approximate

rid code

uvius is in grid square E4

Vesuvius *mt.* Italy **51** E4 40 49N 14 26E

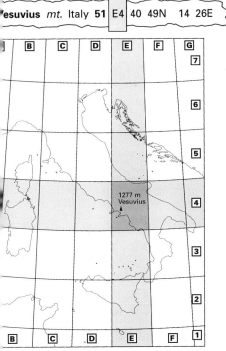

Latitude and longitude

Vesuvius is at latitude 40 49N longitude 14 26E

Vesuvius *mt.* Italy **51** E4 40 49N 14 26E

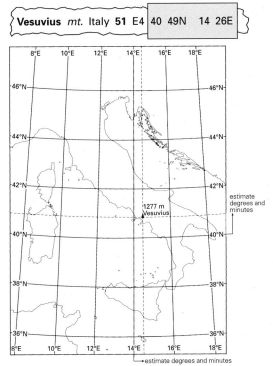

Abbreviations used in the index

admin.	administrative area
b.	bay or harbour
bor.	borough
c.	cape, point or headland
co.	county
est.	estuary
geog.reg.	geographical region
i.	island
is.	islands
l.	lake, lakes, lagoon
mt.	mountain
mts.	mountains
p.	peninsula
pk.	peak
plat.	plateau
pt.	point
r.	river
res.	reservoir
sd.	sound, strait or channel
sum.	summit
tn.	town
u.a.	unitary authority
vol.	volcano

hen Germany **49** D4 50 46N 6 06E
e *r.* Switzerland **49** D2 47 15N 7 30E
dan Iran **61** E4 30 20N 48 15E
eville France **48** D5 50 06N 1 51E
raeron Wales **36** C2 52 49N 44 43W
rchirder Scotland **31** G2 57 33N 2 38W
rdare Wales **36** D1 51 43N 3 27W
rdeen Scotland **31** G2 57 10N 2 04W
rdeen City *u.a.* Scotland **31** G2 57 10N 2 00W
rdeenshire *u.a.* Scotland **31** G2 57 10N 2 50W
rfeldy Scotland **31** F1 56 37N 3 54W
rgavenny Wales **36** D1 51 50N 3 00W
rtillery Wales **36** D1 51 45N 3 09W
rystwyth Wales **36** C2 52 25N 4 05W
a Saudi Arabia **61** E2 18 14N 42 31E
djan Côte d'Ivoire **66** B3 5 19N 4 01W
ngdon England **38** C2 51 41N 1 17W
yne Scotland **31** G2 57 05N 2 50W
Dhabi United Arab Emirates **61** F3 24 28N 25E
uja Nigeria **66** C3 9 10N 7 11E
pulco Mexico **79** K2 16 51N 99 56W
lins Island The Bahamas **79** M3 22 30N 74 30W
ncagua *mt.* Argentina **85** B4 32 40S 70 02W
amawa Highlands Africa **66** D3 7 00N 13 00E
na Turkey **43** P3 37 00N 35 19E
lis Ababa Ethiopia **61** D1 9 03N 38 42E
laide Australia **72** D2 34 55S 138 36E
en Yemen Republic **61** E2 12 50N 45 03E
en, Gulf of Indian Ocean **61** E2 12 50N 47 30E
ur *r.* France **48** C1 43 45N 0 30W
iatic Sea Mediterranean Sea **51** E5 43 00N 15 00E
ean Sea Mediterranean Sea **42** L3 39 00N 24 00E
GHANISTAN 58 B4
a India **58** C3 27 09N 78 00E
uascalientes Mexico **79** J3 21 51N 102 18W
madabad India **58** C3 23 03N 72 40E
vaz Iran **61** E4 31 17N 48 43E
sa Craig *i.* Scotland **32** D3 55 16N 5 07W

Aïn Sefra Algeria **42** F2 32 45N 0 35W
Airdrie Scotland **33** F3 55 52N 3 59W
Aire *r.* England **34** C2 54 00N 2 05W
Aix-en-Provence France **48** F1 43 31N 5 27E
Ajaccio Corsica **51** B4 41 55N 8 43E
Ajdabiya Libya **66** E6 30 46N 20 14E
Akita Japan **59** N2 39 44N 140 05E
Akureyri Iceland **42** C9 65 41N 18 04W
Alabama *state* USA **79** L4 32 00N 87 00W
Alaska *state* USA **78** D7 63 00N 150 00W
Alaska, Gulf of USA **78** E6 58 00N 147 00W
Alaska Peninsula USA **78** D6 56 30N 159 00W
Alaska Range *mts.* USA **78** D7/E7 62 30N 152 30W
Albacete Spain **50** E3 39 00N 1 52W
ALBANIA 42 L4
Albany Australia **72** B2 35 00S 117 53E
Alberta *province* Canada **78** H6 55 00N 115 00W
Albert, Lake Congo Dem. Rep./Uganda **67** D5 2 00N 31 00E
Ålborg Denmark **42** H7 57 05N 9 50E
Albuquerque USA **79** J4 35 05N 106 38W
Alcalá de Henares Spain **50** D4 40 28N 3 22W
Alcudia Balearic Islands **50** G3 39 51N 3 06E
Aldabra Islands Indian Ocean **67** E4 9 00S 46 00E
Aldeburgh England **39** F3 52 09N 1 35E
Alderney *i.* Channel Islands British Isles **41** E2 49 43N 2 12W
Aldershot England **38** D2 51 15N 0 47W
Aleppo Syria **61** D4 36 14N 37 10E
Alessándria Italy **51** B6 44 55N 8 37E
Alexandria Egypt **61** C4 31 13N 29 55E
Alexandria Scotland **33** E3 55 59N 4 36W
Algarve *geog. reg.* Portugal **50** A2 37 30N 8 00W
ALGERIA 66 C5
Algiers Algeria **66** C6 36 50N 3 00E
Al Hoceima Morocco **50** D1 35 14N 3 56W
Alicante Spain **50** E3 38 21N 0 29W
Alice Springs Australia **72** D3 23 41S 133 52E
Al Jawf Libya **66** E5 24 12N 23 18E
Allahabad India **58** D3 25 27N 81 50E
Allier *r.* France **48** E3 46 15N 3 15E
Alloa Scotland **33** F4 56 07N 3 49W
Almanzor *mt.* Spain **50** C4 40 15N 5 18W
Almaty Kazakhstan **56** H2 43 19N 76 55E

Almería Spain **50** D2 36 50N 2 26W
Al Mukha Yemen Republic **61** E2 13 20N 43 16E
Aln *r.* England **33** H3 55 30N 1 50W
Alnwick England **33** H3 55 25N 1 42W
Alps *mts.* Europe **49** D2/G2 46 00N 7 30E
Altai Mountains Mongolia **57** K2 47 00N 92 30E
Alton England **38** D2 51 09N 0 59W
Alyth Scotland **31** F1 56 37N 3 13W
Amazon *r.* Brazil **84** D7 2 30S 65 30W
Amble England **33** H3 55 20N 1 34W
Ambleside England **34** C3 54 26N 2 58W
Ambon Indonesia **60** D2 3 41S 128 10E
Amesbury England **38** C2 51 10N 1 47W
Amiens France **48** E4 49 54N 2 18E
Amlwch Wales **36** C3 53 25N 4 20W
Amman Jordan **61** D4 31 04N 46 17E
Ammanford Wales **36** D1 51 48N 3 58W
Amritsar India **58** C4 31 35N 74 56E
Amsterdam Netherlands **49** C5 52 22N 4 54E
Amu Darya *r.* Asia **56** G2 41 00N 61 00E
Amundsen Sea Southern Ocean **86** 72 00S 130 00W
Amur *r.* Asia **57** N3 54 00N 122 00E
Anchorage USA **78** E7 61 10N 150 00W
Ancona Italy **51** D5 43 37N 13 31E
Andaman Islands India **58** E2 12 00N 94 00E
Andaman Sea Indian Ocean **58** E2 13 00N 95 00E
Andes *mts.* South America **84/85** B8/C5 10 00S 77 00W
Andizhan Uzbekistan **56** H2 40 40N 72 12E
ANDORRA 50 F5
Andover England **38** C2 51 13N 1 28W
Andros *i.* The Bahamas **79** M3 24 00N 78 00W
Aneto Spain **50** F5 42 37N 0 40E
Angara *r.* Russia **57** K3 59 00N 97 00E
Angeles The Philippines **60** D4 15 09N 120 33E
Angers France **48** C3 47 29N 0 32W
Anglesey *i.* Wales **36** C3 53 13N 4 23W
ANGOLA 67 B3
Angoulême France **48** D2 45 40N 0 10E
Anguilla *i.* Leeward Islands **79** N2 18 14N 63 05W
Angus *u.a.* Scotland **31** F1/G1 56 45N 3 00W
Ankara Turkey **43** N3 39 55N 32 50E
'Annaba Algeria **66** C6 36 55N 7 47E
An Najaf Iraq **61** E4 31 59N 44 19E

Annam Range *mts.* Laos/Vietnam **60** B4 19 00N 104 00E
Annan Scotland **33** F2 54 59N 3 16W
Annan *r.* Scotland **33** F3 55 05N 3 20W
Annapurna *mt.* Nepal **58** D3 28 34N 83 50E
Annecy France **48** G2 45 54N 6 07E
Anshan China **59** D4 41 05N 122 58E
Anstruther Scotland **33** G4 56 14N 2 42W
Antalya Turkey **43** N3 36 53N 30 42E
Antananarivo Madagascar **67** E3 18 52S 47 30E
Antarctic Peninsula Antarctica **86** 68 00S 65 00W
Antibes France **48** G1 43 35N 7 07E
Antigua *i.* Antigua & Barbuda **84** C9 17 09N 61 49W
ANTIGUA AND BARBUDA 79 N2
Antofagasta Chile **84** B5 23 40S 70 23W
Antrim Northern Ireland **32** C2 54 43N 6 13W
Antrim *district* Northern Ireland **32** C2 54 45N 6 25W
Antrim Mountains Northern Ireland **32** C3/D2 55 00N 6 10W
Antwerp Belgium **49** C4 51 13N 4 25E
Anxi China **59** A5 40 32N 95 57E
Aomori Japan **59** N3 40 50N 140 43E
Aosta Italy **51** A6 45 43N 7 19E
Aparri The Philippines **60** D4 18 22N 121 40E
Apeldoorn Netherlands **49** C5 52 13N 5 57E
Appalachians *mts.* USA **79** L4 37 00N 82 00W
Appennines *mts.* Italy **51** C6/F4 44 30N 10 00E
Appleby-in-Westmorland England **34** C3 53 36N 2 29W
Aqaba Jordan **61** D3 29 32N 35 00E
Arabian Sea Indian Ocean **7** 17 00N 60 00E
Aracaju Brazil **84** F6 10 54S 37 07W
Arafura Sea Australia **72** D5 9 00S 133 00E
Araguaia *r.* Brazil **84** D6 12 30S 51 00W
Arak Iran **61** E4 34 05N 49 42E
Araks *r.* Asia **61** E4 39 30N 48 00E
Aral Sea Asia **56** G2 45 00N 60 00E
Aran Fawddy *mt.* Wales **36** D2 52 47N 3 41W
Ararat, Mount Turkey **43** Q3 39 44N 44 15E
Arbil Iraq **61** E4 36 12N 44 01E
Arbroath Scotland **31** G1 56 34N 2 35W
Arctic Ocean 86
Ardabil Iran **61** E4 38 15N 48 18E
Ardbeg Scotland **32** C3 55 39N 6 05W

Ardennes mts. Belgium **49** C4 50 10N 5 45E
Ardminish Scotland **32** D3 55 42N 5 44W
Ardres France **39** F1 50 51N 1 59E
Ards district Northern Ireland **32** D2 54 30N 5 30W
Ards Peninsula Northern Ireland **32** D2 54 25N 5 30W
Arequipa Peru **84** B6 16 25S 71 32W
Arezzo Italy **51** C5 43 28N 11 53E
ARGENTINA 85 C4
Argyll and Bute u.a. Scotland **32/33** D4/E4 56 10N 5 00W
Århus Denmark **42** J7 56 15N 10 10E
Arica Chile **84** B6 18 30S 70 20W
Arisaig Scotland **30** D1 56 51N 5 51W
Arisaig, Sound of Scotland **30** D1 56 50N 5 50W
Arizona state USA **79** H4 34 00N 112 00W
Arkansas r. USA **79** K4 35 00N 93 00W
Arkansas state USA **79** K4 34 00N 93 00W
Arkhangel'sk Russia **56** E4 64 32N 40 40E
Arklow Republic of Ireland **36** A2 52 48N 6 09W
Arles France **48** F1 43 41N 4 38E
Armagh Northern Ireland **32** C2 54 21N 6 39W
Armagh district Northern Ireland **32** C2 54 20N 6 40W
ARMENIA 43 Q4
Armentières France **39** G1 50 41N 2 53E
Arnhem Netherlands **49** E4 52 00N 5 53E
Arno r. Italy **51** C5 43 45N 11 00E
Arnold England **37** F2 53 00N 1 09W
Arran i. Scotland **32** D3 55 35N 5 15W
Arras France **48** E5 50 17N 2 46E
Artá Balearic Islands **50** G3 39 42N 3 20E
Arun r. England **38** D2 51 05N 0 30W
Arundel England **38** D1 50 51N 0 34W
Asahikawa Japan **59** N3 43 46N 142 23E
Asahi, Mount Japan **59** N3 43 42N 142 54E
Asansol India **58** D3 23 40N 86 59E
Ascension Island Atlantic Ocean **5** 7 57S 14 22W
Ashbourne England **37** F3 53 01N 1 43W
Ashburton New Zealand **73** C2 43 54S 171 45E
Ashford England **39** E2 51 09N 0 53E
Ashgabat Turkmenistan **56** F1 37 58N 58 24E
Ashington England **33** H3 55 11N 1 34W
Asmara Eritrea **61** D2 15 20N 38 58E
Assisi Italy **51** D5 43 04N 12 37E
Astana Kazakhstan **56** H3 51 10N 71 28E
Astrakhan Russia **56** E2 46 22N 48 04E
Asunción Paraguay **85** D5 25 15S 57 40W
Aswan Egypt **61** D3 24 05N 32 56E
Asyut Egypt **61** D3 27 14N 31 07E
Atacama Desert Chile **84/85** B5 22 30S 70 00W
Atbara Sudan **61** D2 17 42N 34 00E
Atbara r. Sudan **61** D2 17 00N 35 00E
Athabasca r. Canada **78** N6 57 30N 112 00W
Athens Greece **42** L3 38 00N 23 44E
Atlanta USA **79** L4 33 45N 84 23W
Atlantic Ocean 79 N4
Atlas Mountains Morocco **66** B6 32 00N 2 00W
Atrek r. Iran/Turkmenistan **61** F4 38 00N 57 00E
Atyrau Kazakhstan **56** F2 47 08N 51 59E
Auchterarder Scotland **31** F1 56 18N 3 43W
Auchtermuchty Scotland **33** F4 56 17N 3 15W
Auckland New Zealand **73** C3 36 51S 174 46E
Auderville France **41** F2 49 43N 1 56W
Augsburg Germany **49** F3 48 21N 10 54E
Austin USA **79** K4 30 18N 97 47W
AUSTRALIA 72
AUSTRIA 42 J5
Auxerre France **48** E3 47 48N 3 35E
Aveiro Portugal **50** A4 40 38N 8 40W
Aviemore Scotland **31** F2 57 12N 3 50W
Avignon France **48** F1 43 56N 4 48E
Avon r. Warwickshire/Worcestershire England **37** F2 52 15N 1 56W
Avon r. Wiltshire/Bath and North East Somerset/North Somerset England **38** B2 51 20N 2 05W
Avon r. Wiltshire/Hampshire/Dorset England **38** C1 50 55N 1 50W
Axe r. England **41** E3 50 50N 2 50W
Axminster England **41** E3 50 47N 3 00W
Ayaguz Kazakhstan **56** J2 47 59N 80 27E
Ayers Rock mt. Australia **72** D3 25 20S 131 01E
Aylesbury England **38** D2 51 50N 0 50W
Ayr Scotland **33** E3 55 28N 4 38W
Ayr r. Scotland **33** E3 55 30N 4 20W
Ayre, Point of c. Isle of Man British Isles **33** E2 54 25N 4 22W
AZERBAIJAN 56 E2
Azores is. Atlantic Ocean **4** 38 30N 28 00W
Azov, Sea of Asia **43** P5 46 00N 36 00E

B

Bacolod The Philippines **60** D4 10 38N 122 58E
Badajoz Spain **50** B3 38 53N 6 58W
Baden-Baden Germany **49** E3 48 45N 8 15E
Baffin Bay Canada **78** N8 72 00N 64 00W
Baffin Island Canada **78** M8 70 00N 75 00W
Baghdad Iraq **61** E4 33 20N 44 26E
BAHAMAS, THE 79 M3
Bahía Blanca Argentina **85** C4 38 45S 62 15W
BAHRAIN 61 F3
Baie de la Seine b. France **41** G2 49 40N 0 30W
Bakewell England **37** F3 53 13N 1 40W
Baku Azerbaijan **56** E2 40 22N 49 53E
Bala Wales **36** D2 52 54N 3 35W
Bala Lake Wales **36** D2 52 53N 3 38W
Balearic Islands Spain **50** F3/H4 40 00N 2 00E
Bali i. Indonesia **60** C2 8 30S 115 00E
Balikesir Turkey **42** M3 39 37N 27 51E
Balikpapan Indonesia **60** C2 1 15S 116 50E
Balkhash, Lake Kazakhstan **56** H2 46 00N 75 00E
Ballantrae Scotland **32** D3 55 06N 5 00W
Ballarat Australia **72** E2 37 33S 143 52E
Ballater Scotland **31** F2 57 03N 3 03W
Ballybofey Republic of Ireland **32** B2 54 48N 7 47W
Ballycastle Northern Ireland **32** C3 55 12N 6 15W
Ballymena Northern Ireland **32** C2 54 52N 6 17W
Ballymena district Northern Ireland **32** C2 54 55N 6 20W

Ballymoney Northern Ireland **32** C3 55 04N 6 31W
Ballymoney district Northern Ireland **32** C3 55 00N 6 30W
Ballyshannon Republic of Ireland **32** A2 54 30N 8 11W
Baltic Sea Europe **42** K7 55 15N 17 00E
Baltimore USA **79** M4 39 18N 76 38W
Bamako Mali **66** B4 12 40N 7 59W
Bamberg Germany **49** F3 49 54N 10 54E
Bamburgh England **33** H3 55 36N 1 42W
Banbridge Northern Ireland **32** C2 54 21N 6 16W
Banbridge district Northern Ireland **32** C2 54 20N 6 20W
Banbury England **38** C2 52 04N 1 20W
Banchory Scotland **31** G2 57 30N 2 30W
Banda Aceh Indonesia **60** A3 5 30N 95 20E
Bandar-e 'Abbas Iran **61** F3 27 12N 56 15E
Bandar Seri Begawan Brunei **60** C3 4 53N 114 57E
Banda Sea Indonesia **60** D2 5 50S 126 00E
Bandung Indonesia **60** B2 6 57S 107 34E
Bangalore India **58** C2 12 58N 77 35E
Bangka i. Indonesia **60** B2 2 30S 107 00E
Bangkok (Krung Thep) Thailand **60** B4 13 44N 100 30E
BANGLADESH 58 D3/E3
Bangor Northern Ireland **32** D2 54 40N 5 40W
Bangor Wales **36** C3 53 13N 4 08W
Bangui Central African Republic **67** B5 4 23N 18 37E
Bangweulu, Lake Zambia **67** C3 11 15S 29 45E
Banjarmasin Indonesia **60** C2 3 22S 114 33E
Banjul The Gambia **66** A4 13 28N 16 39W
Banks Island Canada **78** G8 73 15N 121 30W
Bann r. Northern Ireland **32** C2 54 55N 6 30W
Baotou China **59** K4 40 38N 109 59E
BARBADOS 79 P2
Barbuda i. Antigua & Barbuda **84** C9 17 41N 61 48W
Barcelona Spain **50** G4 41 25N 2 10E
Bareilly India **58** C3 28 20N 79 24E
Barents Sea Arctic Ocean **86** 75 00N 40 00E
Barfleur France **41** F2 49 40N 1 16W
Bari Italy **51** F4 41 07N 16 52E
Barito r. Indonesia **60** C2 2 00S 115 00E
Barking England **39** E2 51 33N 0 06E
Barletta Italy **51** F4 41 20N 16 17E
Barmouth Wales **36** C2 52 43N 4 03W
Barnard Castle England **34** D3 54 33N 1 55W
Barnaul Russia **56** J3 53 21N 83 45E
Barnet England **38** D2 51 39N 0 12W
Barnoldswick England **34** C2 53 56N 2 16W
Barnsley England **35** D2 53 34N 1 28W
Barnstaple England **40** C4 51 05N 4 04W
Barquisimeto Venezuela **84** C9 10 03N 69 18W
Barra i. Scotland **30** B1/2 57 00N 7 25W
Barranquilla Colombia **84** B9 11 10N 74 50W
Barreiras Brazil **84** E6 12 09S 44 58W
Barrow-in-Furness England **34** B3 54 07N 3 14W
Barry Wales **36** D1 51 24N 3 18W
Barton-upon-Humber England **35** E2 53 41N 0 27W
Basel Switzerland **49** D2 47 33N 7 36E
Basildon England **39** E2 51 34N 0 25W
Basingstoke England **38** C2 51 16N 1 05W
Basra Iraq **61** E4 30 30N 47 50E
Bassein Myanmar **58** E2 16 46N 94 45E
Bass Strait Australia **72** E2 39 51S 145 53E
Bastia France **51** B5 42 14N 9 26E
Bata Equatorial Guinea **66** C3 1 51N 9 49E
Batang China **59** J3 30 02N 99 01E
Batangas The Philippines **60** D4 13 46N 121 01E
Bath England **38** B2 51 23N 2 22W
Bath and North East Somerset u.a. England **38** B2 51 25N 2 30W
Bathgate Scotland **33** F3 55 55N 3 39W
Baton Rouge USA **79** K4 30 30N 91 10W
Batumi Georgia **56** E2 41 37N 41 36E
Bavaria admin. Germany **49** F3/G3 49 00N 12 00E
Bayeux France **48** C4 49 16N 0 42W
Baykal, Lake Russia **57** L3 54 00N 109 00E
Bayonne France **48** C1 43 30N 1 28W
Bayreuth Germany **49** F3 49 27N 11 35E
Beachy Head c. England **39** E1 50 44N 0 16E
Bearsden Scotland **33** E3 55 56N 4 20W
Beaufort Sea Arctic Ocean **78** E7 72 00N 140 00W
Beauly r. Scotland **31** E2 57 30N 4 30W
Beauvais France **48** E4 49 26N 2 05E
Beccles England **39** F3 52 28N 1 34E
Bechar Algeria **66** B6 31 35N 2 17W
Bedford England **38** D3 52 08N 0 29W
Bedfordshire co. England **38** D3 52 08N 0 29W
Bedworth England **37** F2 52 29N 1 28W
Beida Libya **66** E6 32 00N 21 30E
Beijing China **59** L4 39 55N 116 26E
Beinn Dearg mt. Scotland **31** E2 57 47N 4 56W
Beira Mozambique **67** D3 19 49S 34 52E
Beirut Lebanon **61** D4 33 52N 35 30E
Beja Portugal **50** B3 38 01N 7 52W
Bejaïa Algeria **42** H3 36 49N 5 03E
BELARUS 56 C3
Belém Brazil **84** E7 1 27S 48 29W
Belfast Northern Ireland **32** D2 54 35N 5 55W
Belfast district Northern Ireland **32** C2/D2 54 30N 5 58W
Belfast Lough est. Northern Ireland **32** D2 54 40N 5 45W
Belfort France **48** G3 47 38N 6 52E
Belgaum India **58** C2 15 54N 74 36E
BELGIUM 49
Belgrade Serbia and Montenegro **42** L4 44 50N 20 30E
Belitung i. Indonesia **60** B2 2 30S 107 30E
BELIZE 79 L2
Belize Belize **79** L2 17 29N 88 10W
Belle Isle i. France **48** B3 47 20N 3 10W
Bellingshausen Sea Southern Ocean **86** 71 00S 85 00W
Belmopan Belize **79** L2 17 13N 88 48W
Belo Horizonte Brazil **84** E6 19 54S 43 54W
Ben Alder mt. Scotland **31** E1 56 49N 4 28W
Benavente Spain **50** C5 42 00N 5 40W
Benbecula i. Scotland **30** B2 57 25N 7 20W

Ben Cruachan mt. Scotland **30** D1 56 26N 5 09W
Bengal, Bay of Indian Ocean **58** D2 17 00N 88 00E
Benghazi Libya **66** E6 32 07N 20 04E
Benguela Angola **67** B3 12 34S 13 24E
Ben Hope mt. Scotland **31** E3 58 24N 4 37W
BENIN 66 C4
Ben Klibreck mt. Scotland **31** E3 58 14N 4 22W
Ben Lawers mt. Scotland **31** E1 56 33N 4 15W
Ben Lomond mt. Scotland **33** E4 56 12N 4 38W
Ben More mt. Argyll and Bute Scotland **30** C1 56 25N 6 02W
Ben More mt. Stirling Scotland **31** E1 56 25N 4 32W
Ben More Assynt mt. Scotland **31** E3 58 07N 4 52W
Ben Nevis mt. Scotland **31** D1 56 48N 5 00W
Benue r. Nigeria/Cameroon **66** C3/D3 9 00N 10 00E
Ben Wyvis mt. Scotland **31** E2 57 40N 4 35W
Berbera Somalia **61** E2 10 28N 45 02E
Berezniki Russia **43** T7 59 26N 56 49E
Bérgamo Italy **51** B6 45 42N 9 40E
Bergen Norway **42** H8 60 23N 5 20E
Bergerac France **48** D2 44 50N 0 29E
Bering Sea Pacific Ocean **S3** 58 00N 170 00W
Bering Strait Russia/USA **78** C7 69 00N 169 00W
Berlin Germany **49** G5 52 32N 13 25E
Bermuda i. Atlantic Ocean **4** 32 50N 64 20W
Bern Switzerland **49** D2 46 57N 7 26E
Berneray i. Scotland **30** B2 57 42N 7 15W
Bernina mt. Europe **42** E6 46 23N 9 54E
Berwick-upon-Tweed England **33** G3 55 46N 2 00W
Besançon France **48** F3 47 14N 6 02E
Bethesda Wales **36** C3 53 11N 4 03W
Béthune France **48** E5 50 32N 2 38E
Beverley England **35** E2 53 51N 0 26W
Bewdley England **37** E2 52 22N 2 19W
Bexhill England **39** E1 50 51N 0 29E
Bexley England **39** E2 51 27N 0 09E
BHUTAN 58 D3/E3
Białystok Poland **42** L6 53 09N 23 10E
Biarritz France **48** C1 43 29N 1 33W
Bicester England **38** C2 51 54N 1 09W
Bideford England **40** C4 51 01N 4 13W
Bideford Bay England **40** C4 51 05N 4 25W
Bielefeld Germany **49** E5 52 02N 8 32E
Bigbury Bay England **40** D3 50 17N 4 00W
Biggar Scotland **33** F3 55 38N 3 32W
Biggleswade England **38** D3 52 05N 0 17W
Bikaner India **58** C3 28 01N 73 22E
Bilbao Spain **50** D5 43 15N 2 56W
Bintan i. Indonesia **60** B3 0 50N 104 30E
Birdum Australia **72** D4 15 39S 133 13E
Birkenhead England **34** B2 53 24N 3 02W
Birmingham England **37** F2 52 30N 1 50W
Birmingham USA **79** L4 33 30N 86 55W
Biscay, Bay of Atlantic Ocean **48** B2 45 30N 2 50W
Bishkek Kyrgyzstan **56** H2 42 53N 74 46E
Bishop Auckland England **34** D3 54 40N 1 40W
Bishop's Stortford England **39** E2 51 53N 0 09E
Biskra Algeria **42** H2 34 50N 5 41E
Bissau Guinea-Bissau **66** A4 11 52N 15 39W
Biwa, Lake Japan **59** M2 35 20N 135 20E
Bizerte Tunisia **51** B2 37 18N 9 52E
Blackburn England **34** C2 53 45N 2 29W
Blackburn with Darwen u.a. England **34** C2 53 43N 2 25W
Black Forest mts. Germany **49** E3 47 00N 8 00E
Black Mountains Wales **36** D1 51 55N 3 10W
Blackpool England **34** B2 53 50N 3 03W
Blackpool u.a. England **34** B2 53 51N 3 10W
Black Sea Europe **43** P4 43 00N 35 00E
Black Volta r. Africa **66** B3/4 10 00N 3 00W
Blackwater r. Northern Ireland **32** C2 54 30N 6 45W
Blackwater Reservoir Scotland **30** E1 56 41N 4 46W
Blaenau Ffestiniog Wales **36** D2 52 59N 3 56W
Blaenau Gwent u.a. Wales **36** D1 51 45N 3 10W
Blagoveshchensk Russia **57** N3 50 19N 127 30E
Blairgowrie Scotland **31** F1 56 36N 3 21W
Blandford Forum England **41** E3 50 52N 2 11W
Blantyre Malawi **67** D3 15 46S 35 00E
Blenheim New Zealand **73** C2 41 31S 173 57E
Blida Algeria **42** H3 36 30N 2 50E
Blois France **48** D3 47 36N 1 20E
Bloemfontein Republic of South Africa **67** C2 29 07S 26 14E
Blue Nile r. Ethiopia/Sudan **61** D2 12 00N 33 00E
Blyth England **33** H3 55 07N 1 30W
Blyth r. England **33** H3 55 10N 1 45W
Boa Vista Brazil **84** C8 3 23S 55 30W
Bobo Dioulasso Burkina **66** B4 11 11N 4 18W
Bochum Germany **49** D4 51 28N 7 11E
Bodele Depression Chad **66** D4 17 00N 17 50E
Bodmin England **40** C3 50 29N 4 43W
Bodmin Moor England **40** C3 50 35N 4 40W
Bodø Norway **42** J9 67 18N 14 26E
Bognor Regis England **38** D1 50 47N 0 41W
Bogor Indonesia **60** B2 6 34S 106 45E
Bogotá Colombia **84** B8 4 38N 74 05W
Boise USA **79** H5 43 38N 116 12W
BOLIVIA 84 C6
Bologna Italy **51** C6 44 30N 11 20E
Bolton England **34** C2 53 35N 2 26W
Bolzano Italy **51** C7 46 30N 11 22E
Bombay see Mumbai
Bonaire i. Lesser Antilles **79** N2 12 15N 68 27W
Bonar Bridge tn. Scotland **31** E2 57 53N 4 21W
Bo'ness Scotland **33** F4 56 01N 3 37W
Bonifacio Corsica **51** B4 41 23N 9 10E
Bonn Germany **49** D4 50 44N 7 06E
Bootle England **34** B2 53 28N 3 00W
Bordeaux France **48** C2 44 50N 0 34W
Borneo i. Indonesia/Malaysia **60** C3 1 00N 113 00E
Bornholm i. Denmark **49** H6 55 02N 15 00E
Boscastle England **40** C3 50 41N 4 42W
BOSNIA-HERZEGOVINA 42 K4
Boston England **35** E1 52 29N 0 01W
Boston USA **79** M5 42 20N 71 05W
Bothnia, Gulf of Finland/Sweden **42** L8 61 00N 19 10E
BOTSWANA 67 C2
Bouaké Côte d'Ivoire **66** B3 7 42N 5 00W
Bougainville i. Papua New Guinea **72** F5 6 15S 155 00E

Boulogne-sur-Mer France **48** D5 50 43N 1 37E
Bourges France **48** E3 47 05N 2 23E
Bourke Australia **72** E3 30 05S 145 58E
Bournemouth England **41** F3 50 43N 1 54W
Bournemouth u.a. England **41** F3 50 46N 1 52W
Bou Saâda Algeria **42** G3 35 10N 4 09E
Bovey Tracey England **40** D3 50 36N 3 40W
Boyoma Falls Congo Dem.Rep. **67** C5 0 18N 25 E
Bracknell England **38** D2 51 26N 0 46W
Bracknell Forest u.a. England **38** D2 51 22N 0 44W
Bradford England **34** D2 53 48N 1 45W
Braemar Scotland **31** F2 57 01N 3 23W
Brahmaputra r. India/Bangladesh **58** E3 27 00N 94 00E
Brăila Romania **42** M5 45 17N 27 58E
Braintree England **39** E2 51 53N 0 32E
Brampton England **34** C3 54 57N 2 44W
Brandenburg Germany **49** G5 52 25N 12 34E
Branderburgh Scotland **31** F2 57 43N 3 18W
Brasília Brazil **84** E6 15 45S 47 57W
Braşov Romania **42** M5 45 39N 25 35E
Bratislava Slovakia **42** K5 48 10N 17 10E
Bratsk Russia **57** L3 56 20N 101 50E
Braunton England **40** C4 51 07N 4 10W
Bray Republic of Ireland **36** A3 53 12N 6 06W
BRAZIL 84 C7/E7
Brazilian Plateau Brazil **84** E6 17 00S 44 00W
Brazzaville Congo **66** D2 4 14S 15 14E
Brechin Scotland **31** G1 56 44N 2 40W
Brecon Wales **36** D1 51 57N 3 24W
Brecon Beacons mts. Wales **36** D1 51 53N 3 31W
Breda Netherlands **49** C4 51 35N 4 46E
Bremen Germany **49** E5 53 05N 8 48E
Bremerhaven Germany **49** E5 53 33N 8 35E
Brenner Pass Austria/Italy **49** F2 47 02N 11 32E
Brent England **38** D2 51 34N 0 17W
Brentwood England **39** E2 51 38N 0 18E
Bréscia Italy **51** C6 45 33N 10 13E
Bressay i. Scotland **29** D3 60 08N 1 05W
Brest Belarus **42** L6 52 08N 23 40E
Brest France **48** A4 48 23N 4 30W
Bridgend Wales **36** D1 51 31N 3 35W
Bridgend u.a. Wales **36** D1 51 32N 3 35W
Bridgnorth England **37** E2 52 33N 2 25W
Bridgwater England **41** E4 51 08N 3 00W
Bridgwater Bay England **41** D4 51 15N 3 20W
Bridlington England **35** E3 54 05N 0 12W
Bridport England **41** E3 50 44N 2 46W
Brigg England **35** E2 53 34N 0 30W
Brighouse England **34** D2 53 42N 1 47W
Brighton England **38** D1 50 50N 0 10W
Brighton & Hove u.a. England **38** D1 50 52N 0 10W
Brindisi Italy **51** F4 40 37N 17 57E
Brisbane Australia **72** F3 27 28S 153 03E
Bristol England **38** B2 51 27N 2 35W
Bristol u.a. England **38** B2 51 30N 2 30W
Bristol Channel United Kingdom **36** C1/D1 51 20N 3 50W
British Columbia province Canada **78** G6 55 00N 128 00W
Brittany geog. reg. France **48** B4 48 00N 3 00W
Brive France **48** D2 45 09N 1 32E
Brixham England **40** D3 50 23N 3 30W
Broad Bay Scotland **30** C3 58 15N 6 10W
Broadford Scotland **30** D1 57 14N 5 54W
Broad Law mt. Scotland **33** F3 55 30N 3 22W
Broadway England **37** F2 52 02N 1 50W
Brodick Scotland **32** D3 55 35N 5 09W
Broken Hill tn. Australia **72** E2 31 57S 141 28E
Bromley England **39** E2 51 31N 0 01W
Bromsgrove England **37** E2 52 20N 2 03W
Bromyard England **37** E2 52 11N 2 30W
Brooks Range mts. U.S.A. **78** D7/E7 67 55N 155 E
Broome Australia **72** C4 17 57S 122 13E
Brora Scotland **31** F3 58 01N 3 51W
Brough England **34** C3 54 32N 2 19W
Brough Head Scotland **29** B2 59 09N 3 19W
Brown Clee Hill England **37** E2 52 27N 2 35W
Brown Willy sum. England **40** C3 50 35N 4 36W
Brugge Belgium **49** B4 51 13N 3 14E
BRUNEI 60 C3
Brunswick Germany **49** F5 52 15N 10 30E
Brussels Belgium **49** C4 50 50N 4 21E
Bryansk Russia **56** D3 53 15N 34 09E
Bryher i. England **40** A2 49 57N 6 21W
Bucaramanga Colombia **84** B8 7 08N 73 10W
Buchan Ness c. Scotland **31** H2 57 28N 1 47W
Bucharest Romania **42** M4 44 25N 26 07E
Buckfastleigh England **40** D3 50 29N 3 46W
Buckhaven Scotland **33** F4 56 11N 3 03W
Buckie Scotland **31** G2 57 40N 2 58W
Buckingham England **38** D2 52 00N 1 00W
Buckinghamshire co. England **38** D2 51 50N 0 48W
Budapest Hungary **42** K5 47 30N 19 03E
Bude England **40** C3 50 50N 4 33W
Bude Bay England **40** C3 50 50N 4 40W
Buenaventura Colombia **84** B8 3 54N 77 02W
Buenos Aires Argentina **85** D4 34 40S 58 30W
Buffalo USA **79** M5 42 52N 78 55W
Builth Wells Wales **36** D2 52 09N 3 24W
Bujumbura Burundi **67** C4 3 22S 29 19E
Bukavu Congo Dem. Rep. **67** C4 2 30S 28 50E
Bukhara Uzbekistan **56** G1 39 47N 64 26E
Bulawayo Zimbabwe **67** C2 20 10S 28 43E
BULGARIA 42 M4
Bunbury Australia **72** B2 33 20S 115 39E
Buncrana Republic of Ireland **32** B3 55 08N 7 27W
Bundaberg Australia **72** F3 24 53S 152 21E
Bungay England **39** F3 52 27N 1 26E
Buraida Saudi Arabia **61** E3 26 20N 43 59E
Bure r. England **39** F3 52 47N 1 20E
Burgas Bulgaria **42** M4 42 30N 27 29E
Burghead tn. Scotland **31** F2 57 42N 3 30W
Burgos Spain **50** D5 42 21N 3 41W
Burgundy geog. reg. France **48** F3 47 00N 5 00E
BURKINA 66 B4
BURMA see MYANMAR
Burnie Australia **72** E1 41 03S 145 55E
Burnley England **34** C2 53 48N 2 14W

y Port Wales 36 C1 51 42N 4 15W
a Turkey 42 M4 40 12N 29 04E
on upon Trent England 37 F2 52 48N 1 36W
i. Indonesia 60 D2 3 30S 126 30E
UNDI 67 C4
England 34 C2 53 36N 2 17W
St. Edmunds England 39 E3 52 15N 0 43E
n r. Northern Ireland 32 C3 55 10N 6 30W
i. Scotland 32 D3 55 50N 5 05W
, Sound of Scotland 32 D3 55 45N 5 10W
on i. Indonesia 60 D2 5 00S 122 45E
of Lewis c. Scotland 30 C3 58 30N 6 20W
ton The Philippines 60 D3 8 56N 125 31E
ton England 37 F3 53 15N 1 55W
goszcz Poland 42 K6 53 16N 18 00E

anatuan The Philippines 60 D4 15 30N 120 58E
inda province Angola 66 D2 5 00S 12 30E
ora Bassa, Lake Mozambique 67 D3 15 40S
   40E
rera i. Balearic Islands 50 G3 39 00N 2 59E
er Idris mt. Wales 36 D2 52 42N 3 54W
z Spain 50 B2 39 26N 6 18W
n France 48 C4 49 11N 0 22W
rnarfon Wales 36 C3 53 08N 4 16W
rnarfon Bay Wales 36 C3 53 05N 4 30W
rphilly Wales 36 D1 51 35N 3 14W
rphilly u.a. Wales 36 D1 51 37N 3 5W
ayan de Oro The Philippines 60 D3 8 29N 124 40E
liari Italy 51 B3 39 13N 9 08E
n Gorm mt. Scotland 31 F2 57 07N 3 40W
ngorms mts. Scotland 31 F2 57 10N 3 30W
ains Australia 72 E4 16 54S 145 45E
o Egypt 61 D4 30 03N 31 15E
ais France 48 D5 50 57N 1 52E
n Ratjada Balearic Islands 50 G3 39 43N 3 27E
atayud Spain 50 E4 41 21N 1 39W
bayog The Philippines 60 D4 12 04N 124 38E
cutta see Kolkata
gary Canada 78 H6 51 05N 114 05W
Colombia 84 B3 3 24N 76 30W
cut India 58 C2 11 15N 75 45E
fornia state USA 79 H4 36 00N 119 00W
fornia, Gulf of Mexico 79 H3 27 00N 111 00W
ander Scotland 33 E4 56 15N 4 13W
ao Peru 84 B6 12 05S 77 08W
igarry Scotland 30 D2 57 02N 5 58E
ne England 38 B2 51 57N 0 15W
naguey Cuba 79 M3 21 25N 77 55W
mberley England 38 D2 51 21N 0 45W
MBODIA 60 B4
nborne England 40 B3 50 12N 5 19W
nbrai France 48 E5 50 10N 3 14E
nbrian Mountains Wales 36 D2 52 15N 3 45W
nbridge England 39 E3 52 12N 0 07E
nbridgeshire co. England 38/39 D3/E3 52 30N
   0W
nel r. England 40 C3 50 30N 4 45W
MEROON 66 D3
neroun, Mount Cameroon 66 C3 4 13N 9 10E
npbeltown Scotland 32 D3 55 26N 5 36W
npina Grande Brazil 84 F7 7 15S 35 50W
npinas Brazil 84 E5 22 54S 47 06W
npo Grande Brazil 84 D5 20 24S 54 35W
npos Brazil 84 E5 21 46S 41 21W
npsie Fells hills Scotland 33 E4 56 00N 4 15W
nary Islands Spain 66 A5 28 30N 15 10W
naveral, Cape USA 79 L5 28 28N 80 28W
nberra Australia 72 E2 35 17S 149 09E
aisp mt. Scotland 31 D3 58 07N 5 03W
ana i. Scotland 30 C3 57 05N 6 35W
nnock England 37 E2 52 42N 2 01W
tabrian Mountains Spain 50 B5/C5 43 00N 5 30W
nterbury England 39 F2 51 17N 1 05E
nterbury Bight b. New Zealand 73 C2 44 00S
72 00E
nterbury Plains New Zealand 73 C2 43 45S 171 56E
n Tho Vietnam 60 B4 10 03N 105 46E
e de la Hague c. France 41 F2 49 44N 1 56W
e Town Republic of South Africa 67 B1 33 56S
   28E
PE VERDE 4
e Gris-Nez c. France 39 F1 50 52N 1 35E
acas Venezuela 84 C9 10 35N 66 56W
cassonne France 48 E1 43 13N 2 21E
diff Wales 36 D1 51 30N 3 13W
diff u.a. Wales 36 D1 51 32N 3 14W
rdigan Wales 36 C2 52 06N 4 40W
rdigan Bay Wales 36 C2 52 30N 4 30W
rentan France 41 F2 49 18N 1 15W
ibbean Sea Central America 79 M2 15 00N 75 00W
rlingford Lough est. Northern Ireland/
   Republic of Ireland 32 C2 54 05N 6 10W
rlisle England 34 C3 54 54N 2 55W
rmarthen Wales 36 C1 51 51N 4 20W
rmarthen Bay Wales 36 C1 51 40N 4 30W
rmarthenshire u.a. Wales 36 C1/D1 51 55N 4 00W
mel Head Wales 36 C3 53 24N 4 34W
narvon Australia 72 B3 24 53S 113 40E
rn Eige mt. Scotland 31 D2 57 18N 5 07W
nforth England 34 C3 54 08N 2 46W
noustie Scotland 31 G1 56 30N 2 44W
pathians mts. Europe 42 L5/M5 49 00N 22 00E
pentaria, Gulf of Australia 72 D4 14 39S 139 11E
rickfergus Northern Ireland 32 D2 54 43N 5 49W
rickfergus district Northern Ireland 32 D2 54 40N
   50W
tagena Colombia 84 B9 10 24N 75 33W
tagena Spain 50 E2 37 36N 0 59W
teret France 41 F2 49 22N 1 48W
spian Sea Asia 56 F2 41 00N 50 00E
ssel France 39 G1 51 40N 2 28E
ssino Italy 51 D4 41 29N 13 50E
stlebay Scotland 30 B1 56 57N 7 28W

Castleblaney Republic of Ireland 32 C2 54 07N 6 44W
Castle Douglas Scotland 33 F2 54 57N 3 56W
Castleford England 35 D2 43 44N 1 21W
Castlereagh district Northern Ireland 32 D2 54 35N
   5 50W
Castletown Isle of Man British Isles 33 E2 54 04N
   4 38W
Castrovillari Italy 51 F3 39 48N 16 12E
Catánia Italy 51 E2 37 31N 15 06E
Catanzaro Italy 51 F3 38 54N 16 36E
Cat Island The Bahamas 79 M3 24 30N 75 30W
Cauca r. Colombia 84 B8 7 40N 75 00W
Caucasus mts. Asia 56 E2 43 00N 43 00E
Cavan Republic of Ireland 32 B1 53 58N 7 21W
Caxias do Sul Brazil 85 D5 29 14S 51 10W
Cayenne French Guiana 84 D8 4 55N 52 18W
Cayman Islands Caribbean Sea 79 L2 19 20N 81 15W
Cebollera mt. Spain 50 D4 42 00N 2 40W
Cebu The Philippines 60 D4 10 17N 123 56E
Celebes Sea Indonesia 60 D3 3 00N 122 00E
Cemaes Head Wales 36 C2 53 10N 4 50W
CENTRAL AFRICAN REPUBLIC 67 B5/C5
Central Siberian Plateau Russia 57 L4 65 00N 110 00E
Ceredigion u.a. Wales 36 C2/D2 52 20N 4 00W
Ceuta territory Spain 50 C1 35 53N 5 19W
CHAD 66 D4
Chad, Lake West Africa 66 D4 13 50N 14 00E
Chagos Archipelago is. Indian Ocean 5 6 00S 72 00E
Châlons-sur-Marne France 48 F4 48 58N 4 22E
Chalon-sur-Saône France 48 F3 46 47N 4 51E
Chambéry France 48 F2 45 34N 5 55E
Changchun China 59 D4 43 50N 125 20E
Chang Jiang (Yangtze) r. China 59 D3 30 00N 116 00E
Changsha China 59 C2 28 10N 113 00E
Channel Islands British Isles 41 E2 49 30N 2 30W
Channel Tunnel United Kingdom/France 39 F1/2
   5 00N 1 30E
Chard England 41 E3 50 53N 2 58W
Chardzhev Turkmenistan 56 G1 39 09N 63 34E
Chari r. Chad/Sudan 66 D4 11 00N 16 00E
Charleroi Belgium 49 C4 50 25N 4 27E
Charlestown of Aberlour Scotland 31 F2 57 28N
   3 14W
Charleville Australia 72 E3 26 24S 146 14E
Charleville France 48 F4 49 46N 4 43E
Charlotte USA 79 L4 35 03N 80 50W
Charters Towers Australia 72 E3 20 04S 146 16E
Chartres France 48 D4 48 27N 1 30E
Châteauroux France 48 D3 46 49N 1 41E
Chatham England 39 E2 51 23N 0 32E
Cheadle England 34 C2 53 24N 2 13W
Cheb Czech Republic 49 G4 50 08N 12 28E
Cheboksary Russia 56 E3 56 08N 47 12E
Chelmsford England 39 E2 51 44N 2 04W
Cheltenham England 38 B2 51 54N 2 04W
Chelyabinsk Russia 56 G3 55 12N 61 25E
Chemnitz Germany 49 G4 50 50N 12 55E
Chengdu China 59 B3 30 37N 104 06E
Chennai (Madras) India 58 D2 13 05N 80 18E
Chepstow Wales 37 E1 51 39N 2 41W
Cher r. France 48 D3 47 15N 1 30E
Cherbourg France 41 F2 49 38N 1 37W
Chernivtsi Ukraine 42 M5 48 19N 25 52E
Cherwell r. England 38 C2 51 55N 1 20W
Cheshire co. England 34 C2 53 20N 2 30W
Cheshunt England 38 D2 51 43N 0 02W
Chester England 34 C2 53 12N 2 54W
Chesterfield England 37 F3 53 15N 1 25W
Chester-le-Street England 34 D3 54 52N 1 34W
Cheviot Hills England/Scotland 33 G3 55 25 N2 20W
Cheviot, The sum. England 33 G3 55 29N 2 20W
Cheyenne USA 79 J4 41 08N 104 50W
Chiang Mai Thailand 60 A4 18 48N 98 59E
Chiba Japan 59 N2 35 38N 140 07E
Chicago USA 79 L5 41 50N 87 45W
Chichester England 38 D1 50 50N 0 48W
Chiclayo Peru 84 B7 6 47S 79 47W
Chicoutimi Canada 79 M5 48 26N 71 06W
Chieti Italy 51 E5 42 21N 14 10E
Chihuahua Mexico 79 J3 28 40N 106 06W
CHILE 84/85 B6/C2
Chillán Chile 85 B4 36 37S 72 10W
Chiloé Island Chile 85 B3 42 30S 74 00W
Chiltern Hills England 38 C2/D2 51 40N 1 00W
Chimbote Peru 84 B7 9 04S 78 34W
CHINA 59
Chippenham England 38 B2 51 28N 2 07W
Chipping Norton England 38 C2 51 56N 1 32W
Chipping Sodbury England 38 B2 51 33N 2 24W
Chişinău Moldova 42 M5 47 00N 28 50E
Chita Russia 57 M3 52 03N 113 35E
Chittagong Bangladesh 58 E3 22 20N 91 48E
Cholet France 48 C3 47 04N 0 53W
Chongjin North Korea 59 D4 41 50N 129 55E
Chongqing China 59 B2 29 30N 106 35E
Chorley England 34 C2 53 40N 2 38W
Christchurch England 41 F3 50 44N 1 45W
Christchurch New Zealand 73 C2 43 32S 172 38E
Christmas Island Indian Ocean 60 B1 10 28S 105 35E
Churchill Canada 78 K6 58 45N 94 00W
Churchill Falls tn. Canada 78 N6 53 35N 64 00W
Cincinnati USA 79 L4 39 10N 83 30W
Cirencester England 38 C2 51 44N 1 59W
Citlaltépetl mt. Mexico 79 K2 19 00N 97 18W
City of Edinburgh u.a. Scotland 33 F3 55 55N 3 15W
City of Kingston upon Hull u.a. England 35 E2
   53 45N 0 20W
Ciudad Bolívar Venezuela 84 C8 8 06N 63 36W
Ciudadela Balearic Islands 50 G3 40 00N 3 50E
Ciudad Guayana Venezuela 84 C8 8 22N 62 37W
Ciudad Juárez Mexico 79 J4 31 42N 106 29W
Ciudad Obregón Mexico 79 J3 27 28N 109 59W
Ciudad Rodrigo Spain 50 B4 40 36N 6 33W
Clachan Scotland 32 D3 55 45N 5 34W
Clackmannanshire u.a. England 33 F4 56 10N 3 40W
Clacton on Sea England 39 F2 51 48N 1 09E
Claonaig Scotland 32 D3 55 46N 5 22W
Cleethorpes England 35 E2 53 34N 0 02W
Clermont-Ferrand France 48 E2 45 47N 3 05E
Clevedon England 38 B2 51 27N 2 51W

Cleveland Hills England 35 D3 54 25N 1 15W
Clisham mt. Scotland 30 C2 57 58N 6 50W
Clitheroe England 34 C2 53 53N 2 23W
Clones Republic of Ireland 32 B2 54 11N 7 15W
Cluj-Napoca Romania 42 L5 46 47N 23 37E
Clutha r. New Zealand 73 B1 46 00S 169 30E
Clwyd r. Wales 36 D3 53 15N 3 25W
Clyde r. Scotland 33 F3 55 45N 3 55W
Clydebank Scotland 33 E3 55 54N 4 24W
Coalisland Northern Ireland 32 C2 54 32N 6 42W
Coalville England 37 F2 52 44N 1 20W
Coast Mountains Canada 78 G6 58 10N 132 40W
Coatbridge Scotland 33 E3 55 52N 4 01W
Coburg Germany 49 F4 50 15N 10 58E
Cochabamba Bolivia 84 C6 17 26S 66 10W
Cochin India 58 C1 9 56N 76 15E
Cockermouth England 34 B3 54 40N 3 21W
Cognac France 48 C2 45 42N 0 19W
Coimbatore India 58 C1 11 00N 76 57E
Coimbra Portugal 50 A4 40 12N 8 25W
Colchester England 39 E2 51 54N 0 54E
Coldstream tn. Scotland 33 G3 55 39N 2 15W
Coleraine Northern Ireland 32 C3 55 08N 6 40W
Coleraine district Northern Ireland 32 C3 55 00N
   6 40W
Coll i. Scotland 30 C1 56 40N 6 35W
Colmar France 48 G4 48 05N 7 21E
Colne England 34 C2 53 52N 2 09W
Colne r. England 39 E2 51 53N 0 45E
Cologne Germany 49 D4 50 56N 6 57E
COLOMBIA 84 B8
Colombo Sri Lanka 58 C1 6 55N 79 52E
Colonsay i. Scotland 32 C4 56 05N 6 15W
Colorado r. Argentina 85 C4 37 30S 69 00W
Colorado r. USA/Mexico 79 J4 38 00N 109 00W
Colorado state USA 79 J4 39 00N 106 00W
Columbia USA 79 L4 34 00N 81 00W
Columbia r. Canada/USA 78 H6 50 30N 119 00W
Columbus USA 79 L4 39 59N 83 03W
Colwyn Bay tn. Wales 36 D3 53 18N 3 43W
Communism Peak Tajikistan 56 H1 38 59N 72 01E
Como Italy 51 B6 45 48N 9 05E
Comodoro Rivadavia Argentina 85 C3 45 50S 67 30W
Como, Lake Italy 51 B6/7 46 00N 9 00E
COMOROS 67 E3
Conakry Guinea 66 A3 9 30N 13 43W
Concepción Chile 85 B4 36 50S 73 03W
Conejara i. Balearic Islands 50 G3 39 11N 2 58E
CONGO 66 D2
Congo r. Africa 67 B4 3 00S 16 00E
CONGO DEMOCRATIC REPUBLIC 67 C4
Coniston Water l. England 34 B3 54 20N 3 05W
Connecticut state USA 79 M5 41 00N 73 00W
Consett England 34 D3 54 51N 1 49W
Constance, Lake Europe 49 E2 47 40N 9 30E
Constanţa Romania 42 M4 44 12N 28 40E
Constantine Algeria 66 C6 36 22N 6 40E
Conwy Wales 36 D3 53 17N 3 50W
Conwy r. Wales 36 D3 53 20N 3 55W
Conwy u.a. Wales 36 D3 53 10N 3 50W
Cook Islands Pacific Ocean 4 19 30S 159 50W
Cook, Mount New Zealand 73 C2 43 36S 170 09E
Cookstown Northern Ireland 32 C2 54 39N 6 45W
Cookstown district Northern Ireland 32 C2 54 35N
   6 55W
Cook Strait New Zealand 73 C2 41 24S 174 36E
Cooktown Australia 72 E4 15 28S 145 15E
Cooper Creek Australia 72 E3 26 10S 142 20E
Copenhagen Denmark 42 J7 55 43N 12 34E
Coquet r. England 33 H3 55 20N 1 50W
Coral Sea Pacific Ocean 72 F4 15 00S 154 00E
Corby England 38 D2 52 49N 0 32W
Córdoba Argentina 85 C4 31 25S 64 11W
Córdoba Spain 50 C2 37 53N 4 46W
Corfu i. Greece 42 K3 39 00N 19 00E
Cornwall co. England 40 B3/C3 50 25N 4 50W
Corpus Christi USA 79 K3 27 47N 97 26W
Corrientes Argentina 85 D5 27 30S 58 48W
Corsewall Point Scotland 32 D2 55 00N 5 10W
Corsica i. France 51 B5 42 00N 9 00E
Cosenza Italy 51 F3 39 17N 16 16E
Costa Brava geog. reg. Spain 50 G4/5 41 40N 3 50E
Costa del Sol geog. reg. Spain 50 C2/D2 36 40N
   4 40W
COSTA RICA 79 L1
CÔTE D'IVOIRE 66 B3
Cotonou Benin 66 C3 6 24N 2 31E
Cotopaxi vol. Ecuador 84 B7 0 40S 78 28W
Cotswold Hills England 38 B2/C2 51 40N 2 10W
Cottbus Germany 49 H4 51 43N 14 21E
Coupar Angus Scotland 31 F1 56 33N 3 17W
Coutainville France 41 F2 49 03N 1 34W
Coutances France 41 F2 49 03N 1 29W
Coventry England 37 F2 52 25N 1 30W
Cowes England 38 C1 50 45N 1 18W
Craigavon Northern Ireland 32 C2 54 28N 6 25W
Craigavon district Northern Ireland 32 C2 54 30N
   6 30W
Craighouse Scotland 32 D3 55 51N 5 57W
Craignure Scotland 30 D1 56 28N 5 42W
Crail Scotland 33 G4 56 16N 2 38W
Craiova Romania 42 L4 44 18N 23 47E
Cramlington England 33 H3 55 05N 1 35W
Crawley England 38 D2 51 07N 0 12W
Crediton England 40 D3 50 47N 3 39W
Cree r. Scotland 33 E3 55 00N 4 30W
Creeslough Republic of Ireland 32 B3 55 07N 7 55W
Cremona Italy 51 C6 45 08N 10 01E
Crete i. Greece 42 M3 35 00N 25 00E
Crewe England 34 C2 53 05N 2 27W
Crewkerne England 41 E3 50 53N 2 48W
Crianlarich Scotland 31 E1 56 23N 4 37W
Crieff Scotland 31 F1 56 23N 3 52W
Crimea p. Ukraine 43 N5 46 00N 34 00E
CROATIA 42 K5
Cromarty Scotland 31 E2 57 40N 4 02W
Cromarty Firth est. Scotland 31 E2 57 40N 4 20W
Cromer England 39 F3 52 56N 1 18E
Cross Fell sum. England 34 C3 54 43N 2 29W
Crossmaglen Northern Ireland 32 C2 54 05N 6 37W

Crotone Italy 51 F3 39 05N 17 08E
Croydon England 38 D2 51 23N 0 06W
Crumlin Northern Ireland 32 C2 54 37N 6 14W
Cruzeiro do Sul Brazil 84 B7 7 40S 72 39W
Cuanza r. Angola 67 B4 9 40S 15 00E
CUBA 79 M3
Cubango r. Southern Africa 67 B3 17 00S 18 00E
Cúcuta Colombia 84 B8 7 55N 73 31W
Cuenca Ecuador 84 B7 2 54S 79 00W
Cuiabá Brazil 84 D6 15 32S 56 05W
Cuillin Hills Scotland 30 C2 57 15N 6 15W
Culiacán Mexico 79 J3 24 50N 107 23W
Cullen Scotland 31 G2 57 41N 2 49W
Cullompton England 40 D3 50 52N 3 24W
Cumaná Venezuela 84 C9 10 29N 64 12W
Cumbernauld Scotland 33 F3 55 57N 4 00W
Cumbria co. England 34 B3/C3 54 30N 2 50W
Cumnock Scotland 33 E3 55 27N 4 16W
Cunene r. Angola/Namibia 67 B3 17 00S 15 00E
Cuneo Italy 51 A6 44 24N 7 33E
Cunnamulla Australia 72 E3 28 03S 145 43E
Cupar Scotland 33 F4 56 19N 3 01W
Curaçao i. Lesser Antilles 79 N2 12 20N 68 20W
Curitiba Brazil 85 E5 25 25S 49 25W
Cuttack India 58 D3 20 26N 85 56E
Cuzco Peru 84 B6 13 32S 1 57W
Cwmbran Wales 36 D1 51 39N 3 00W
Cyclades is. Greece 42 L3/L4 36 00N 25 00E
CYPRUS 43 N2
CZECH REPUBLIC 42 K5
Częstochowa Poland 42 K6 50 49N 19 07E

D

Daer Reservoir Scotland 33 F3 55 25N 3 30W
Dakar Senegal 66 A4 14 38N 17 27W
Dalbeattie Scotland 33 F2 54 56N 3 49W
Dalian China 59 D3 38 53N 121 37E
Dallas USA 79 K4 32 47N 96 48W
Dalmally Scotland 31 E1 56 24N 4 58W
Dalton-in-Furness England 34 B3 54 09N 3 11W
Daly r. Australia 72 D4 13 30S 130 30E
Damascus Syria 61 D4 33 30N 36 19E
Dammam Saudi Arabia 61 F3 26 25N 50 06E
Da Nang Vietnam 60 B4 16 04N 108 14E
Danube r. Europe 42 L4 44 00N 25 00E
Dar es Salaam Tanzania 67 D4 6 51S 39 18E
Darfur mts. Sudan 61 C2 12 40N 24 20E
Dargaville New Zealand 73 C3 35 56S 173 52E
Darling r. Australia 72 E3 31 00S 144 00E
Darlington England 34 D3 54 31N 1 34W
Darlington u.a. England 34 D3 54 35N 1 34W
Darmstadt Germany 49 E3 49 52N 8 39E
Darnah Libya 42 L2 32 46N 22 39E
Dart r. England 40 D3 50 30N 3 50W
Dartford England 39 E2 51 27N 0 13E
Dartmoor geog. reg. England 40 D3 50 35N 3 50W
Dartmouth England 40 D3 50 21N 3 35W
Darvel Scotland 33 E3 55 37N 4 18W
Darwin Australia 72 D4 12 24S 130 52E
Daugava r. Belarus 42 M7 55 00N 29 00E
Daugavpils Latvia 42 M7 55 52N 26 31E
Dauphiné geog. reg. France 48 F2 45 00N 5 00E
Davao The Philippines 60 D3 7 05N 125 38E
Daventry England 38 C2 52 16N 1 09W
Dawlish England 40 D3 50 35N 3 28W
Dawson Canada 78 F7 64 04N 139 24W
Deal England 39 F2 51 14N 1 24E
Debrecen Hungary 42 L5 47 30N 21 37E
Deccan plat. India 58 C2 18 00N 78 00E
Dee r. Aberdeenshire/AberdeenCity Scotland
   31 G2 57 05N 2 30W
Dee r. Dumfries and Galloway Scotland 33 E2/F2
   54 55N 4 00W
Dee r. England/Wales 36 D3 53 20N 3 10W
Deeps, The b. Scotland 29 D3 60 10N 1 25W
Delaware state USA 79 M4 39 00N 75 00W
Delhi India 58 C3 28 40N 77 14E
Demavand, Mount Iran 61 F4 35 47N 52 08E
Denbigh Wales 36 D3 53 11N 3 25W
Denbighshire u.a. Wales 36 D3 53 10N 3 10W
DENMARK 42 H7
Denver USA 79 J4 39 45N 105 00W
De Panne Belgium 39 F2 51 06N 2 35E
Derby Australia 72 C4 17 18S 123 37E
Derby England 37 F2 52 55N 1 30W
Derby City u.a. England 37 F2 52 53N 1 30W
Derbyshire co. England 37 F3 52 55N 1 30W
Derg r. Northern Ireland 32 B2 54 40N 7 45E
Derwent r. Cumbria England 34 B3 54 40N 3 30W
Derwent r. Derbyshire England 37 F3 53 20N 1 40W
Derwent r. Northumberland/Durham/Tyne and
   Wear England 34 D3 54 50N 2 05W
Derwent r. North Yorkshire/York/East Riding of
   Yorkshire England 35 E2 53 50N 0 55W
Derwent Water l. England 34 B3 54 35N 3 09W
Des Moines USA 79 K5 41 35N 93 35W
Dessau Germany 49 G4 51 51N 12 15E
Detroit USA 79 L5 42 23N 83 05W
Deveron r. Scotland 31 G2 57 35N 2 40W
Devizes England 38 C2 51 21N 1 59W
Devon co. England 40 C3/D3 50 45N 3 50W
Devon Island Canada 78 L8 75 47N 88 00W
Dewsbury England 35 D2 53 42N 1 37W
Dezful Iran 61 E4 32 23N 48 28E
Dhaka Bangladesh 58 E3 23 42N 90 22E
Dibrugarh India 58 E3 27 29N 94 56E
Didcot England 38 C2 51 37N 1 15W
Dieppe France 48 D4 49 55N 1 05E
Dijon France 48 F3 47 20N 5 02E
Dili East Timor 60 D2 8 33S 125 34E
Dingwall Scotland 31 E2 57 35N 4 29W
Dire Dawa Ethiopia 61 E1 9 35N 41 50E
Diss England 39 F3 52 23N 1 06W
Diyarbakir Turkey 43 Q3 37 55N 40 14E
Djelfa Algeria 42 G2 34 43N 3 14E
DJIBOUTI 61 E2
Djibouti Djibouti 61 E2 11 35N 43 11E
Dnieper r. Ukraine/Belarus 56 D3 51 00N 30 00E
Dniester r. Europe 42 M5 48 00N 27 00E

Dnipropetrovsk Ukraine 56 D2 48 29N 35 00E
Dodoma Tanzania 67 D4 6 10S 35 40E
Doha Qatar 61 F3 25 15N 51 36E
Dolgellau Wales 36 D2 52 44N 3 53W
Dolomites *mts.* Italy 49 F2 46 00N 12 00E
DOMINICA 79 N2
DOMINICAN REPUBLIC 79 M2
Don *r.* Russia 56 E3 50 00N 40 30E
Don *r.* Scotland 31 G2 57 15N 2 10W
Donaghadee Northern Ireland 32 D2 54 39N 5 33W
Doncaster England 35 D2 53 32N 1 07W
Donegal Republic of Ireland 32 A2 54 39N 8 07W
Donegal *co.* Republic of Ireland 32 A2/B2 54 55N 8 00W
Donetsk Ukraine 56 D2 48 00N 37 50E
Dongting Hu *l.* China 59 C2 29 00N 113 30E
Doon *r.* Scotland 33 E3 55 20N 4 30W
Dorchester England 41 E2 50 43N 2 26W
Dordogne *r.* France 48 D2 45 00N 1 30E
Dordrecht Netherlands 49 C4 51 48N 4 40E
Dorking England 38 D2 51 14N 0 20W
Dornoch Scotland 31 E2 57 52N 4 02W
Dornoch Firth *est.* Scotland 31 E2 57 55N 3 55W
Dorset *co.* England 41 E3 50 50N 2 20W
Dortmund Germany 49 D4 51 32N 7 27E
Douai France 48 E5 50 22N 3 05E
Douala Cameroon 66 C3 4 04N 9 43E
Douglas Isle of Man British Isles 33 E2 54 09N 4 29W
Douro *r.* Spain/Portugal 50 B4 41 30N 6 30W
Dove *r.* England 37 F3 53 10N 1 50W
Dover England 39 F2 51 08N 1 19E
Dover, Strait of English Channel 39 F1/2 51 00N 1 20W
Down *district* Northern Ireland 32 D2 54 25N 5 55W
Downham Market England 39 E3 52 36N 0 22E
Downpatrick Northern Ireland 32 D2 54 20N 5 43W
Drakensberg *mts.* Republic of South Africa 67 C2 30 00S 28 00E
Drava *r.* Europe 49 G2 46 45N 13 30E
Dresden Germany 49 G4 51 03N 13 45E
Droitwich England 37 E2 52 16N 2 09W
Dromore Northern Ireland 32 C2 54 25N 6 09W
Dronning Maud Land *geog. reg.* Antarctica 86 73 00S 10 00E
Drummore Scotland 32 E2 54 42N 4 54W
Drumnadrochit Scotland 31 E2 57 20N 4 30W
Dubai United Arab Emirates 61 F3 25 14N 55 17E
Dubbo Australia 72 E2 32 15S 148 38E
Dublin Republic of Ireland 36 A3 53 20N 6 15W
Dudley England 37 E2 52 30N 2 05W
Dufftown Scotland 31 F2 57 26N 3 08W
Duisburg Germany 49 D4 51 26N 6 45E
Duluth USA 79 K5 46 45N 92 10W
Dumbarton Scotland 33 E3 55 57N 4 35W
Dumfries Scotland 33 F3 55 04N 3 37W
Dumfries and Galloway *u.a.* Scotland 33 E3/F3 55 10N 4 00W
Dunbar Scotland 33 G4 56 00N 2 31W
Dunblane Scotland 33 F4 56 12N 3 59W
Duncansby Head *c.* Scotland 29 B1 58 39N 3 02W
Dundalk Republic of Ireland 32 C2 54 01N 6 25W
Dundee Scotland 31 G1 56 28N 3 00W
Dundee City *u.a.* Scotland 31 F1/G1 56 30N 2 55W
Dunedin New Zealand 73 B1 45 53S 170 30E
Dunfermline Scotland 33 F4 56 04N 3 29W
Dungannon Northern Ireland 32 C2 54 31N 6 46W
Dungannon *district* Northern Ireland 32 B2/C2 54 30N 7 00W
Dungeness *c.* England 39 E1 50 55N 0 58E
Dungiven Northern Ireland 32 C2 54 56N 6 55W
Dunkerque France 48 E5 51 02N 2 23E
Dunkery Beacon *sum.* England 40 D3 51 11N 3 35W
Dún Laoghaire Republic of Ireland 36 A3 53 17N 6 08W
Dunnet Head Scotland 29 B1 58 40N 3 25W
Dunoon Scotland 32 E3 55 57N 4 56W
Duns Scotland 33 G3 55 47N 2 20W
Dunstable England 38 D2 51 53N 0 32W
Dunvegan Scotland 30 C2 57 26N 6 35W
Durance *r.* France 48 F1 43 50N 5 15E
Durango Mexico 79 J3 24 01N 104 40W
Durban Republic of South Africa 67 D2 29 53S 31 00E
Durham England 34 D2 54 47N 1 34W
Durham *co.* England 34 C3/D3 54 40N 2 00W
Dursley England 37 E1 51 42N 2 21W
Dushanbe Tajikistan 56 G1 38 38N 68 51E
Düsseldorf Germany 49 D4 51 13N 6 47E
Dyce Scotland 31 G2 57 12N 2 11W
Dyfi *r.* Wales 36 D2 52 38N 3 50W

E

Ealing England 38 D2 51 31N 0 18W
Earn *r.* Scotland 31 F1 56 15N 3 40W
East Ayrshire *u.a.* Scotland 33 E3 55 35N 4 15W
Eastbourne England 39 E1 50 46N 0 17E
East Cape New Zealand 73 D3 37 41S 178 33E
East Dereham England 39 E3 52 41N 0 56E
East Dunbartonshire *u.a.* Scotland 33 E3 55 55N 4 15W
Eastern Rift Valley East Africa 67 D4/5 4 00N 36 00E
East Friesian Islands Netherlands 49 D5 53 00N 7 00E
East Kilbride Scotland 33 E3 55 46N 4 10W
Eastleigh England 38 C1 50 58N 1 22W
East London Republic of South Africa 67 C1 33 00S 27 54E
East Lothian *u.a.* Scotland 33 G3 55 56N 2 42W
East Renfrewshire *u.a.* Scotland 33 E3 55 45N 4 25E
East Riding of Yorkshire *u.a.* England 35 E2 53 54N 0 40W
East Sussex *co.* England 39 E1 50 55N 0 10E
EAST TIMOR 60 D2
Ebbw Vale Wales 36 D1 51 47N 3 12W
Ebro *r.* Spain 50 E4 42 00N 1 15W
Ech Cheliff Algeria 42 G3 36 05N 1 15E
ECUADOR 84 B7
Eday *i.* Scotland 29 C2 59 11N 2 47W
Eddrachillis Bay Scotland 30 D3 58 25N 5 15W

Eden *r.* Cumbria England 34 C3 54 45N 2 40W
Eden *r.* Surrey/Kent England 39 E2 51 10N 0 05E
Edinburgh Scotland 33 F3 55 57N 3 13W
Edmonton Canada 78 H6 53 34N 113 25W
Edward, Lake Congo Dem. Rep./Uganda 67 C4 0 30S 30 00E
EGYPT 61 C3
Eigg *i.* Scotland 30 C1 56 55N 6 10W
Eindhoven Netherlands 49 C4 51 26N 5 30E
Elba *i.* Italy 51 C5 42 00N 10 00E
El Bayadh Algeria 42 G2 33 40N 1 00E
Elbe *r.* Europe 49 F5 53 15N 11 00E
Elbrus, Mount Russia 43 Q4 43 21N 42 29E
Elche Spain 50 E3 38 16N 0 41W
Eleuthera *i.* The Bahamas 79 M3 25 05N 76 30W
El Faiyum Egypt 61 D3 29 19N 30 50E
El Fasher Sudan 61 C2 13 37N 25 22E
Elgin Scotland 31 F2 57 39N 3 20W
El Giza Egypt 61 D4 30 01N 31 12E
Elgol Scotland 30 C2 57 09N 6 06W
El Kharga Egypt 61 D3 25 27N 30 32E
Ellen *r.* England 34 B3 54 45N 3 30W
Ellesmere Island Canada 78 L8 77 30N 82 30W
Ellesmere Port England 34 C2 53 17N 2 54W
Ellon Scotland 31 G2 57 22N 2 05W
Ellsworth Land *geog. reg.* Antarctica 86 75 00S 80 00W
El Minya Egypt 61 D3 28 06N 30 45E
El Paso USA 79 J4 31 45N 106 30W
EL SALVADOR 79 L2
Elvas Portugal 50 B3 38 53N 7 10W
Ely England 39 E3 52 24N 0 16E
Emden Germany 49 D5 53 23N 7 13E
Emi Koussi *mt.* Chad 66 D4 19 52N 18 31E
Ems *r.* Germany 49 D5 53 00N 7 00E
Enard Bay Scotland 30 D3 58 10N 5 25W
Enfield England 38 D2 51 39N 0 05W
Enggano *i.* Indonesia 60 B2 5 20S 102 20E
England *country* United Kingdom 28 53 00N 2 00W
English Channel United Kingdom/France 28 50 00N 2 00W
Enniskillen Northern Ireland 32 B2 54 21N 7 38W
Enschede Netherlands 49 D5 52 13N 6 55E
Entebbe Uganda 67 D5 0 04N 32 27E
Épinal France 48 G4 48 10N 6 28E
Epsom England 38 D2 51 20N 0 16W
EQUATORIAL GUINEA 66 D3
Erebus, Mount Antarctica 86 77 40S 167 20E
Erfurt Germany 49 F4 50 58N 11 02E
Erie, Lake Canada/USA 79 L5 42 15N 81 00W
Eriskay *i.* Scotland 30 B2 57 05N 7 10W
Erlangen Germany 49 F3 49 36N 11 02E
Erne *r.* Northern Ireland/Republic of Ireland 32 B2 54 10N 7 30W
Errigal Mountain Republic of Ireland 32 A3 55 02N 8 07W
Erzurum Turkey 43 Q3 39 57N 41 17E
Esfahan Iran 61 F4 32 41N 51 41E
Esha Ness *pt.* Scotland 29 D3 60 29N 1 37W
Esk *r.* England 35 E3 54 30N 0 45W
Esk *r.* Scotland/England 33 F3 55 15N 3 05W
Eskisehir Turkey 43 N3 39 46N 30 30E
Esperance Australia 72 C2 33 51S 121 54E
Esquel Argentina 85 B3 42 55S 71 20W
Essen Germany 49 D4 51 27N 6 57E
Essex *co.* England 39 E2 51 46N 0 30E
ESTONIA 42 M7
ETHIOPIA 61 E1
Ethiopian Highlands Africa 61 D1 8 00N 37 00E
Etna, Mount Italy 51 E2 37 45N 15 00E
Etosha Pan *salt l.* Namibia 67 B3 18 30S 16 30E
Eyre, Lake Australia 72 D3 28 43S 137 11E
Euphrates *r.* Iraq/Syria/Turkey 61 D4/E4 35 00N 40 00E
Europa *i.* Mozambique Channel 67 E2 22 20S 40 20E
Everest, Mount China/Nepal 58 D3 27 59N 86 56E
Evesham England 37 F2 52 06N 1 56W
Evreux France 48 D4 49 03N 1 11E
Evvoia *i.* Greece 42 L3 38 00N 24 00E
Exe *r.* England 40 D4 51 10N 3 35W
Exeter England 40 D3 50 43N 3 31W
Exmoor *geog. reg.* England 40 D4 51 08N 3 40W
Exmouth England 40 D3 50 37N 3 25W
Eyemouth Scotland 33 G3 55 25N 2 06W
Eye Peninsula Scotland 30 C3 58 10N 6 10W

F

Faroe Islands Atlantic Ocean 42 E8 62 00N 7 00W
Fairbanks USA 78 E7 64 50N 147 50W
Fair Head *c.* Northern Ireland 32 C3 55 15N 6 10W
Fair Isle *i.* Shetland Islands Scotland 29 D2 59 32N 1 38W
Faisalabad Pakistan 58 C4 31 25N 73 09E
Fakenham England 39 E3 52 50N 0 51E
Fal *r.* England 40 C3 50 15N 4 55W
Falkirk Scotland 33 F3 55 59N 3 48W
Falkirk *u.a.* Scotland 33 F3/4 56 05N 3 53W
Falkland Islands South Atlantic Ocean 85 D2 52 30S 60 00W
Falmouth England 40 B3 50 08N 5 04W
Falster *i.* Denmark 49 F6/G6 54 00N 12 00E
Fareham England 38 C1 50 51N 1 10W
Farewell, Cape Greenland 78 Q6 60 00N 44 00W
Farewell, Cape New Zealand 73 C2 40 30S 172 41E
Faringdon England 38 C2 51 40N 1 35W
Farnborough England 38 D2 51 17N 0 46W
Farnham England 38 D2 51 13N 0 49W
Faro Portugal 50 B2 37 01N 7 56W
Fawley England 38 C1 50 49N 1 20W
Fens, The *geog. reg.* England 35 E1/F1 52 45N 0 05E
Fergana Uzbekistan 56 H2 40 23N 71 19E
Fermanagh *district* Northern Ireland 32 B2 54 25N 7 45W

Ferrara Italy 51 C6 44 50N 11 38E
Fès Morocco 66 B4 34 05N 5 00W
Fethaland, Point of Scotland 29 D3 60 35N 1 18W
Fetlar *i.* Scotland 29 E3 60 37N 0 52W
Fife *u.a.* Scotland 33 F4/G4 56 10N 3 00W
FIJI 5
Filchner Ice Shelf Antarctica 86 80 00S 37 00W
Finke *r.* Australia 72 D3 25 00S 135 00E
FINLAND 42 M8
Finland, Gulf of Finland/Russia 42 L7 59 40N 23 30E
Finn *r.* Northern Ireland/Republic of Ireland 32 B2 54 50N 7 50W
Fionnphort Scotland 30 C1 56 19N 6 23W
Firth of Clyde *est.* Scotland 32 E3 55 45N 5 00W
Firth of Forth *est.* Scotland 33 F4 56 06N 3 00W
Firth of Lorn *est.* Scotland 30 D1 56 15N 6 00W
Firth of Tay *est.* Scotland 31 F1 56 25N 3 00W
Fishguard Wales 36 C1 51 59N 4 59W
Fitzroy *r.* Australia 72 C4 17 00S 126 00E
Flamborough Head *c.* England 35 D3 54 06N 0 04W
Fleetwood England 34 B2 53 56N 3 01W
Flinders *r.* Australia 72 E3/4 20 00S 142 00E
Flinders Range Australia 72 D2 31 20S 138 45E
Flint Wales 36 D3 53 15N 3 07W
Flintshire *u.a.* Wales 36 D3 53 26S 3 10W
Florence Italy 51 C5 43 47N 11 15E
Flores *i.* Indonesia 60 D2 8 30S 121 00E
Flores Sea Indonesia 60 D2 7 00S 119 00E
Florianópolis Brazil 85 E5 27 35S 48 31W
Florida *state* USA 79 L2 28 00N 82 00W
Florida, Straits of *sd.* Cuba/USA 79 L3 24 00N 81 00W
Fly *r.* Papua New Guinea 72 E5 8 00S 142 00E
Fochabers Scotland 31 F2 57 37N 3 05W
Fóggia Italy 51 E4 41 28N 15 33E
Folkestone England 39 F2 51 05N 1 11E
Fontainebleau France 48 E4 48 24N 2 42E
Forel, Mount Greenland 86 67 00N 37 00W
Forest of Bowland *hills* England 34 C2 54 00N 2 35W
Forfar Scotland 31 G1 56 38N 2 54W
Forli Italy 51 D6 44 13N 12 02E
Formby England 34 B2 53 34N 3 05W
Formentera *i.* Balearic Islands 50 F3 38 41N 1 30E
Fornells Balearic Islands 50 H3 40 04N 4 07E
Forres Scotland 31 F2 57 37N 3 38W
Fortaleza Brazil 84 F7 3 45S 38 35W
Fort Augustus Scotland 31 E2 57 09N 4 41W
Forth *r.* Scotland 33 E4 56 10N 4 00W
Fort McMurray Canada 78 H6 56 45N 111 27W
Fort Peck Reservoir USA 79 J5 48 01N 106 28W
Fort Simpson Canada 78 G7 61 46N 121 15W
Fort William Scotland 31 D1 56 49N 5 07W
Fort Worth USA 79 K4 32 45N 97 20W
Foula *i.* Scotland 29 C3 60 08N 2 05W
Foveaux Strait New Zealand 73 B1 46 42S 167 59E
Fowey England 40 C3 50 20N 4 38W
Fowey *r.* England 40 C3 50 25N 4 30W
Foyle *r.* Northern Ireland/Republic of Ireland 32 B2 54 58N 7 35W
FRANCE 48
Frankfurt Germany 49 E4 50 06N 8 41E
Franz Josef Land *is.* Russia 57 G6 80 00N 50 00E
Fraser *r.* Canada 78 G6 52 00N 122 00W
Fraserburgh Scotland 31 G2 57 42N 2 00W
Freetown Sierra Leone 66 A3 8 30N 13 17W
Freiburg Germany 49 D3 48 00N 7 52E
Fréjus France 48 G1 43 26N 6 44E
Fremantle Australia 72 B2 32 03S 115 46E
French Guiana *territory* France 84 D8 5 00N 53 00W
French Polynesia *is.* Pacific Ocean 4 21 00S 150 00W
Fresno USA 79 H4 36 41N 119 47W
Frome England 41 E2 51 14N 2 20W
Frome *r.* England 41 E2 50 40N 2 20W
Fuji, Mount Japan 59 M2 35 23N 138 42E
Fukui Japan 59 M2 36 04N 136 12E
Fukuoka Japan 59 L1 33 39N 130 21E
Fukushima Japan 59 N2 37 44N 140 28E
Fukuyama Japan 59 L1 34 29N 133 21E
Furnace Scotland 32 D4 56 09N 5 12W
Fushun China 59 D4 41 50N 123 54E
Fuzhou China 59 C2 26 09N 119 17E
Fyn *i.* Denmark 49 F6 55 30N 10 00E
FYROM *see* MACEDONIA, FORMER YUGOSLAV REPUBLIC OF

G

Gabès Tunisia 42 J2 33 52N 10 06E
GABON 66 D2
Gaborone Botswana 67 C2 24 45S 25 55E
Gafsa Tunisia 42 H2 34 28N 8 43E
Gainsborough England 35 E2 53 24N 0 48W
Gairloch *tn.* Scotland 30 D2 57 42N 5 40W
Galapagos Islands Pacific Ocean 4 12 00S 87 00W
Galashiels Scotland 33 G3 55 37N 2 49W
Galați Romania 42 M5 45 27N 28 02E
Gallipoli Italy 51 G4 40 03N 17 59E
GAMBIA, THE 66 A4
Gäncä Azerbaijan 56 F2 40 39N 46 20E
Gander Canada 79 P5 49 00N 54 15W
Ganges *r.* India/Bangladesh 58 D3 24 00N 88 00E
Gap France 48 G2 44 33N 6 05E
Garda, Lake Italy 51 C6 45 00N 10 40E
Garelochhead Scotland 33 E4 56 05N 4 50W
Garonne *r.* France 48 D2 44 45N 0 15E
Gatehouse of Fleet Scotland 33 E2 54 53N 4 11W
Gateshead England 34 D3 54 58N 1 35W
Gaziantep Turkey 43 P3 37 04N 37 21E
Gdańsk Poland 42 K6 54 22N 18 41E
Gdynia Poland 42 K6 54 31N 18 30E
Geelong Australia 72 D2 38 08S 144 20E
Gelsenkirchen Germany 49 D4 51 30N 7 05E
Geneva Switzerland 49 D2 46 13N 6 09E
Geneva, Lake France/Switzerland 49 D2 46 20N 6 20E
Genoa Italy 51 B6 44 24N 8 56E
Gent Belgium 49 B4 51 02N 3 42E
Georgetown Guyana 84 D8 6 46N 58 10W
George Town Malaysia 60 B3 5 25N 100 20E
GEORGIA 56 E2
Georgia *state* USA 79 L4 33 00N 83 00W
Gera Germany 49 G4 50 51N 12 11E

Geraldton Australia 72 B3 28 46S 114 36E
GERMANY 49
GHANA 66 B3
Gibraltar *territory* UK 50 C2 36 09N 5 21W
Gibraltar, Strait of Spain/Morocco 50 C1 35 58N 5 30W
Gibson Desert Australia 72 C3 24 00S 122 00E
Giessen Germany 49 E4 50 35N 8 42E
Gifu Japan 59 M2 35 27N 136 46E
Gigha *i.* Scotland 32 D3 55 40N 5 45W
Gijón Spain 50 C5 43 32N 5 40W
Gillingham England 39 E2 51 24N 0 33E
Gironde *r.* France 48 C2 45 30N 1 00W
Girvan Scotland 32 E3 55 15N 4 51W
Gisborne New Zealand 73 D3 38 40S 178 01E
Glasgow Scotland 33 E3 55 53N 4 15W
Glasgow City *u.a.* Scotland 33 E3 55 50N 4 20W
Glastonbury England 41 E2 51 09N 2 43W
Glenluce Scotland 32 E2 54 53N 4 49W
Glenrothes Scotland 33 F4 56 12N 3 10W
Gloucester England 38 B2 51 53N 2 14W
Gloucestershire *co.* England 38 B2 51 50N 2 20W
Goat Fell *mt.* Scotland 32 D3 55 38N 5 11W
Gobi Desert Mongolia 57 L2 43 30N 100 00E
Godavari *r.* India 58 C2/D2 19 00N 80 00E
Godthåb *see* Nuuk
Goiânia Brazil 84 E6 16 43S 49 18W
Gold Coast *tn.* Australia 72 E2 28 04S 153 25E
Gongga Shan *mt.* China 59 B2 29 34N 101 53E
Good Hope, Cape of Republic of South Africa 67 34 30S 19 00E
Goole England 35 E2 53 42N 0 52W
Gore New Zealand 73 B1 46 06S 168 56E
Goroka Papua New Guinea 72 E5 6 02S 145 22E
Göteborg Sweden 42 J7 57 45N 12 00E
Gotland *i.* Sweden 42 K7 57 30N 18 40E
Göttingen Germany 49 E4 51 32N 9 57E
Governador Valadares Brazil 84 E6 18 51S 41 57W
Gower *p.* Wales 36 C1 51 35N 4 10W
Grafton Australia 72 E3 29 40S 152 58E
Grampian Mountains Scotland 31 E1/F1 56 45N 4 00W
Granada Spain 50 D2 37 10N 3 35W
Grand Bahama *i.* The Bahamas 79 M3 27 00N 78 00W
Grand Canyon USA 79 H4 36 04N 112 07W
Grand Rapids *tn.* USA 79 L5 42 57N 86 40W
Grangemouth Scotland 33 F4 56 01N 3 44W
Grantham England 35 E1 52 55N 0 39W
Grantown-on-Spey Scotland 31 F2 57 20N 3 36W
Grays England 39 E2 51 27N 0 24E
Graz Austria 42 K5 47 05N 15 22E
Great Abaco *i.* The Bahamas 79 M3 26 40N 77 00W
Great Australian Bight *b.* Australia 72 C2 32 31S 130 00E
Great Barrier Island New Zealand 73 D3 36 13S 175 30E
Great Barrier Reef Australia 72 E4/5 15 00S 146 00E
Great Bear Lake Canada 78 H7 66 00N 120 00W
Great Dividing Range *mts.* Australia 72 E2/E3 35 00N 148 00E
Great Driffield England 35 E3 54 01N 0 26W
Greater Antilles *is.* West Indies 79 M2/N2 19 00N 78 00W
Greater London *co.* England 38 D2 51 30N 0 10W
Greater Manchester *co.* England 34 C2 53 30N 2 15W
Great Inagua *i.* The Bahamas 79 M3 21 40N 73 00W
Great Karoo *mts.* Republic of South Africa 67 C1 32 22 30E
Great Malvern England 37 E2 52 07N 2 19W
Great Ouse *r.* England 39 E3 52 40N 0 20E
Great St. Bernard Pass France/Italy 48 G2 45 50N 7 10E
Great Salt Lake USA 79 H5 41 10N 112 40W
Great Sandy Desert Australia 72 C3 21 00S 121 00E
Great Slave Lake Canada 78 H7 62 00N 114 00W
Great Stour *r.* England 39 F2 51 20N 1 10E
Great Torrington England 40 C3 51 57N 4 09W
Great Victoria Desert Australia 72 C3/D3 28 00S 129 00E
Great Wall China 59 B3 39 00N 109 00E
Great Whernside *sum.* England 34 D3 54 10N 1 59W
Great Yarmouth England 39 F3 52 37N 1 44E
GREECE 42 L3
GREENLAND 78 Q8
Greenock Scotland 33 E3 55 57N 4 45W
Greenwich England 38 D2 51 29N 0 00
GRENADA 79 N2
Grenoble France 48 F2 45 11N 5 43E
Greta *r.* England 34 C3 54 10N 2 30W
Greymouth New Zealand 73 C2 42 27S 171 12E
Grimsby England 35 E2 53 35N 0 05W
Groningen Netherlands 49 D5 53 13N 6 35E
Grosseto Italy 51 C5 42 46N 11 07E
Gross Glockner *mt.* Austria 49 G2 47 05N 12 44E
Groznyy Russia 56 E2 43 21N 45 42E
Guadalajara Mexico 79 J3 20 40N 103 20W
Guadalquivir *r.* Spain 50 C2 37 45N 5 30W
Guadalupe *i.* Mexico 79 H3 29 00N 118 24W
Guadeloupe *i.* Lesser Antilles 79 N2 16 30N 61 30W
Guadiana *r.* Spain/Portugal 50 C3 39 00N 5 30W
GUAM 5
Guangzhou China 59 C2 23 08N 113 20E
Guantánamo Cuba 79 M3 20 09N 75 14W
Guarda Portugal 50 B4 40 32N 7 17W
GUATEMALA 79 K2
Guatemala Guatemala 79 K2 14 38N 90 22W
Guayaquil Ecuador 84 B7 2 13S 79 54W
Guernsey *i.* Channel Islands British Isles 41 E2 46 2 35W
Guildford England 38 D2 51 14N 0 35W
GUINEA 66 A4
GUINEA-BISSAU 66 A4
Guinea, Gulf of Atlantic Ocean 66 C3 2 00N 2 30E
Guisborough England 35 D3 54 32N 1 04W
Guiyang China 59 B2 26 35N 106 40E
Gulf, The Middle East 61 F3 27 20N 51 00E
Guwahati India 58 E3 26 10N 91 45E

YANA 84 D8
vadar Pakistan 58 B3 25 07N 62 19E
valior India 58 C3 26 12N 78 09E
vynedd u.a. Wales 36 D2 52 45N 3 55W

arlem Netherlands 49 C5 52 23N 4 39E
chinohe Japan 59 N3 40 30N 141 30E
ifa Israel 61 D4 32 49N 34 59E
il Saudi Arabia 61 E3 27 31N 41 45E
inan i. China 59 B1 18 50N 109 50E
i Phong Vietnam 60 B5 20 50N 106 41E
ITI 79 M2
kodate Japan 59 N3 41 46N 140 44E
lesowen England 37 E2 52 26N 2 05W
lifax Canada 79 N5 44 38N 63 35W
lifax England 34 D2 53 44N 1 52W
lkirk Scotland 31 F3 58 30N 3 30W
lle Germany 49 F4 51 28N 11 58E
lmahera i. Indonesia 60 D3 0 30S 127 00E
lton England 38 D2 51 09N 2 40W
ltwhistle England 34 C3 54 58N 2 27W
madan Iran 61 E4 34 46N 48 35E
mah Syria 43 P3 35 10N 36 45E
mamatsu Japan 59 M1 34 42N 137 42E
mburg Germany 49 F5 53 33N 10 00E
mersley Range Australia 72 B3 22 04S 117 37E
mi China 58 E5 42 37N 93 32E
milton Canada 79 M5 43 15N 79 50W
milton New Zealand 73 D3 37 47S 175 17E
milton Scotland 33 E3 55 47N 4 03W
mm Germany 49 D4 51 40N 7 49E
mpshire co. England 38 C2 51 10N 1 15W
mpshire Downs hills England 38 C2 51 15N 1 10W
ngzhou China 59 D3 30 18N 120 07E
nnover Germany 49 E5 52 23N 9 44E
noi Vietnam 60 B5 21 01N 105 52E
rad Saudi Arabia 61 E3 24 12N 49 12E
rare Zimbabwe 67 D3 17 50S 31 03E
rbin China 59 D4 45 45N 126 41E
rgeysa Somalia 67 E5 9 31N 44 02E
rlech Wales 36 C2 52 52N 4 07W
rlow England 39 E2 51 47N 0 08E
roldswick Scotland 29 E3 60 47N 0 50W
rris i. Scotland 30 C2 57 50N 6 55W
rris, Sound of Scotland 30 B2 57 45N 7 10W
rrogate England 34 D2 54 00N 1 33W
rrow England 38 D2 51 34N 0 20W
rtland Point England 40 C4 51 02N 4 31W
rtlepool England 35 D3 54 41N 1 13W
rtlepool u.a. England 35 D3 54 41N 1 13W
rwich England 39 F2 51 57N 1 17E
rz mts. Europe 49 F4 52 00N 10 00E
slemere England 38 D2 51 06N 0 43W
stings England 39 E1 50 51N 0 36E
stings New Zealand 73 D3 39 39S 176 51E
therleigh England 40 C3 50 49N 4 04W
uraki Gulf New Zealand 73 D3 36 38S 175 04E
vana Cuba 79 L3 23 07N 82 25W
vant England 38 D1 50 51N 0 59W
verfordwest Wales 36 C1 51 49N 4 58W
verhill England 39 E3 52 06N 0 26E
vering England 39 E2 51 34N 0 14E
waiian Islands Pacific Ocean 4 20 00N 156 00W
wera New Zealand 73 D3 39 35S 174 17E
wick Scotland 33 G3 55 25N 2 47W
wke Bay New Zealand 73 D3 39 23S 177 12E
y-on-Wye Wales 36 D2 52 04N 3 07W
y River tn. Canada 78 H7 60 51N 115 42W
aywards Heath England 38 D2 51 00N 0 06W
efei China 59 C3 31 55N 117 18E
agang China 59 E4 47 36N 130 30E
eidelberg Germany 49 E3 49 25N 8 42E
eilbronn Germany 49 E3 49 08N 9 14E
elensburgh Scotland 33 E4 56 01N 4 44W
elmsdale Scotland 31 F3 58 07N 3 40W
elmsdale r. Scotland 31 F3 58 10N 3 50W
elsinki Finland 42 L8 60 08N 25 00E
elvellyn mt. England 34 B3 54 32N 3 02W
emel Hempstead England 38 D2 51 46N 0 28W
emsworth England 35 D2 53 38N 1 21W
engelo Netherlands 49 D5 52 16N 6 46E
enley-on-Thames England 38 D2 51 32N 0 56W
erat Afghanistan 58 B4 34 20N 62 12E
ereford England 37 E2 52 04N 2 43W
erefordshire u.a. England 37 E2 52 12N 2 40W
erma Ness c. Scotland 29 E3 60 50N 0 54W
ermosillo Mexico 79 H3 29 15N 110 59W
ertford England 38 D2 51 48N 0 05W
exham England 34 C3 54 58N 2 06W
eysham England 34 C3 54 02N 2 54W
ghland u.a. Scotland 30/31 D2/E2 57 00N 5 00W
gh Wycombe England 38 D2 51 38N 0 46W
lla Iraq 61 E4 32 28N 44 29E
llingdon England 38 D2 51 32N 0 27W
lversum Netherlands 49 C5 52 14N 5 10E
malayas mts. Asia 58 28 00N 85 00E
meji Japan 59 L1 34 50N 134 40E
nckley England 37 F2 52 33N 1 21W
ndu Kush mts. Afghanistan 58 B4 35 00N 70 00E
roshima Japan 59 L1 34 23N 132 27E
tchin England 38 D2 51 57N 0 17W
obart Australia 72 D4 42 53S 147 19E
o Chi Minh City Vietnam 60 B4 10 46N 106 43E
odeida Yemen Republic 61 E2 14 50N 42 58E
ófn Iceland 42 C8 64 16N 15 10W
oggar mts. Algeria 66 C5 23 50N 6 00E
ohhot China 59 C4 40 49N 117 37E
okkaido i. Japan 59 N3 43 00N 143 00E
olderness p. England 35 E2 53 45N 0 05W
olguín Cuba 79 L4 20 54N 76 15W
olyhead Wales 36 C3 53 19N 4 38W

Holy Island England 33 H3 55 41N 1 48W
Holy Island Wales 36 C3 53 16N 4 39W
Homs Syria 61 D4 34 42N 36 40E
Homyel' Belarus 56 D3 52 25N 31 00E
HONDURAS 79 L2
Hong Kong China 59 C2 23 00N 114 00E
Honiara Solomon Islands 72 F5 9 28S 159 57E
Honiton England 41 D3 50 48N 3 13W
Honshu i. Japan 59 M2 37 15N 139 00E
Horn, Cape Chile 85 C2 56 00S 67 15W
Horncastle England 35 E2 53 13N 0 07W
Hornsea England 35 E2 53 55N 0 10W
Horsham England 38 D2 51 28N 0 21W
Hospitalet Spain 50 G4 41 21N 2 06E
Hounslow England 38 D2 51 28N 0 21W
Houston USA 79 K3 29 45N 95 25W
Hove England 38 D1 50 50N 0 10W
Howe, Cape Australia 72 E2 37 29S 149 59E
Howth Republic of Ireland 36 A3 53 23N 6 04W
Hoy i. Scotland 29 B1 58 48N 3 20W
Huainan China 59 C3 32 41N 117 06E
Huambo Angola 67 B3 12 44S 15 47E
Huancayo Peru 84 B6 12 05S 75 12W
Huang He r. China 59 C3 36 00N 116 00E
Hubli India 58 C2 15 20N 75 14E
Huddersfield England 34 D2 53 39N 1 47W
Hudson r. USA 79 M5 43 20N 73 50W
Hudson Bay Canada 78 L6/7 60 00N 89 00W
Hue Vietnam 60 B4 16 28N 107 35E
Huelva Spain 50 B2 37 15N 6 56W
Hufuf Saudi Arabia 61 E3 25 20N 49 34E
Hugh Town England 40 A2 49 55N 6 19W
Hull r. England 35 E2 53 50N 0 25W
Humber r. England 35 E2 53 40N 0 10W
HUNGARY 42 K5
Hungnam North Korea 59 D3 39 49N 127 40E
Hunstanton England 39 E3 52 57N 0 30E
Huntingdon England 38 D3 52 20N 0 12W
Huntly Scotland 31 G2 57 27N 2 47W
Huron, Lake Canada/USA 79 L5 45 00N 83 00W
Hyderabad India 58 C2 17 22N 78 26E
Hyderabad Pakistan 58 B3 25 22N 68 22E

Iaşi Romania 42 M5 47 09N 27 38E
Ibadan Nigeria 66 C3 7 23N 3 56E
Ibagué Colombia 84 B8 4 25N 75 20W
Ibiza Balearic Islands 50 F3 38 54N 1 26E
Ibiza i. Balearic Islands 50 F3 39 00N 1 20E
ICELAND 42 C9
Idaho state USA 79 H5 44 00N 115 00W
Ieper (Ypres) Belgium 39 G1 50 51N 2 53E
IJsselmeer l. Netherlands 49 C5 52 45N 5 15E
Ilchester England 41 E3 51 01N 2 41W
Ilebo Congo Dem. Rep. 67 C4 4 20S 20 35E
Ilfracombe England 40 C4 51 13N 4 08W
Ilhéus Brazil 84 F6 14 50S 39 06W
Ilkeston England 37 F2 52 59N 1 18W
Ilkley England 35 D2 53 55N 1 50W
Illinois state USA 79 L5 40 00N 89 00W
Ilminster England 41 E3 50 56N 2 56W
Immingham England 35 E2 53 36N 0 11W
Imphal India 58 E3 24 47N 93 55E
Inca Balearic Islands 50 G3 39 43N 2 54E
Inchon South Korea 59 D3 37 30N 126 38E
INDIA 58 C3
Indiana state USA 79 L5 40 00N 86 00W
Indianapolis USA 79 L5 39 45N 86 10W
Indian Ocean 7
INDONESIA 60 A3/D2
Indore India 58 C3 22 42N 75 54E
Indus r. Asia 58 B3 27 00N 68 00E
Ingleborough sum. England 34 C3 54 10N 2 23W
Ingolstadt Germany 49 F3 48 46N 11 27E
Inishowen Peninsula Republic of Ireland 32 B3 55 15N 7 15W
Inland Sea sd. Japan 59 L1 34 00N 132 30E
Inn r. Europe 49 G3 48 15N 12 30E
Inner Hebrides is. Scotland 30 C1/2 56 45N 6 45W
Innerleithen Scotland 33 F3 55 38N 3 05W
Inner Sound Scotland 30 D2 57 25N 5 55W
Innsbruck Austria 49 J5 47 17N 11 25E
Inuvik Canada 78 F7 68 16N 133 40W
Inveraray Scotland 32 D4 56 13N 5 05W
Inverbervie Scotland 31 G1 56 51N 2 17W
Invercargill New Zealand 73 B1 46 25S 168 22E
Inverclyde u.a. Scotland 33 E3 55 50N 4 45W
Invergarry Scotland 31 E2 57 02N 4 47W
Invergordon Scotland 31 E2 57 42N 4 10W
Inverkeithing Scotland 33 F4 56 02N 3 25W
Invermoriston Scotland 31 E2 57 13N 4 38W
Inverness Scotland 31 E2 57 27N 4 15W
Inverurie Scotland 31 G2 57 17N 2 23W
Iona i. Scotland 30 C1 56 19N 6 25W
Ionian Island Greece 43 J3 39 40N 20 51E
Ionian Sea Mediterranean Sea 42 K3 38 00N 27 00E
Iowa state USA 79 K5 42 00N 94 00W
Ipoh Malaysia 60 B3 4 36N 101 05E
Ipswich England 39 F3 52 04N 1 10E
Iquique Chile 84 B5 20 15S 70 08W
Iquitos Peru 84 B7 3 51S 73 13W
Iraklion Greece 42 M3 35 20N 25 08E
IRAN 61 F4
IRAQ 61 E4
Irbid Jordan 43 P2 32 33N 35 51E
Irian Jaya admin. Indonesia 72 D5 3 00S 133 00E
Irish Sea British Isles 28 53 30N 5 30W
Irkutsk Russia 57 L3 52 18N 104 15E
Irrawaddy r. Myanmar 60 A4 16 00N 97 30E
Irthing r. England 34 C3 55 00N 2 40W
Irtysh r. Russia 56 H3 57 30N 72 30E
Irvine Scotland 33 E3 55 37N 4 40W
Isafjördour Iceland 42 B9 66 05N 23 08W
Ishikari r. Japan 59 N3 43 20N 141 20E
Isigny-sur-Mer France 41 F2 49 18N 1 06W
Isla r. Scotland 31 F1 56 40N 3 15W
Islamabad Pakistan 58 C4 33 42N 73 10E

Island Magee p. Northern Ireland 32 D2 53 45N 5 45W
Islay i. Scotland 32 C3 55 48N 6 12W
Isle of Anglesey u.a. Wales 36 C3 53 18N 4 25W
Isle of Man British Isles 33 C2 54 15N 4 30W
Isle of Wight u.a. England 38 C1 50 40N 1 20W
ISRAEL 61 D4
Istanbul Turkey 42 M4 41 02N 28 57E
Istria p. Croatia 49 G1 45 00N 14 00E
Itabuna Brazil 84 F6 14 48S 39 18W
ITALY 51
Itchen r. England 38 C2 51 05N 1 15W
Ivanovo Russia 56 E3 57 00N 41 00E
Iwaki Japan 59 N2 37 03N 140 58E
Izhevsk Russia 43 S7 56 49N 53 11E
Izmir Turkey 42 M3 38 25N 27 10E
Izu Islands Japan 59 M1 34 20N 139 20E

Jabalpur India 58 C3 23 10N 79 59E
Jackson USA 79 K4 32 20N 90 11W
Jacksonville USA 79 L4 30 20N 81 40W
Jaffna Sri Lanka 58 D1 9 40N 80 01E
Jaipur India 58 C3 26 53N 75 50E
Jakarta Indonesia 60 B2 6 08S 106 45E
JAMAICA 79 M2
Jambi Indonesia 60 B2 1 34S 103 37E
James Bay Canada 78 L6 53 45N 81 00W
Jammu & Kashmir state Southern Asia 58 C4 29 40N 76 30E
Jamshedpur India 58 D3 22 47N 86 12E
JAPAN 59
Japan, Sea of Pacific Ocean 59 M3 39 00N 137 00E
Jauf Saudi Arabia 61 D3 29 49N 39 52E
Java i. Indonesia 60 B2/C2 7 00S 110 00E
Javalambre mt. Spain 50 E4 40 05N 1 02W
Java Peak Indonesia 60 C2 5 00S 137 09E
Java Sea Indonesia 60 C2 5 00S 112 00E
Jedburgh Scotland 33 G3 55 29N 2 34W
Jedda Saudi Arabia 61 D3 21 30N 39 10E
Jena Germany 49 F4 50 56N 11 35E
Jerez de la Frontera Spain 50 B2 36 41N 6 08W
Jersey i. Channel Islands British Isles 41 E2 49 13N 2 07W
Jerusalem Israel/Jordan 61 D4 31 47N 35 13E
Jiamusi China 59 E4 46 59N 130 29E
Jiayuguan China 59 A4 39 47N 98 14E
Jilin China 59 D4 43 53N 126 35E
Jinan China 59 C3 36 41N 117 00E
Jinsha Jiang (Yangtze) r. China 59 B2 27 30N 103 00E
Jixi China 59 E4 45 17N 131 00E
Jizan Saudi Arabia 61 E2 16 56N 42 33E
João Pessoa Brazil 84 F7 7 06S 34 53W
Johannesburg Republic of South Africa 67 C2 26 10S 28 02E
John o'Groats Scotland 31 F3 58 38N 3 05W
Johnstone Scotland 33 E3 55 50N 4 31W
Johor Bahru Malaysia 60 B3 1 27N 103 45E
Joinville Brazil 85 E5 26 20S 48 55W
Jönköping Sweden 42 J7 57 45N 14 10E
JORDAN 61 D4
Jos Plateau Nigeria 66 C3/4 9 30N 8 55E
Juan Fernández Islands Chile 85 B4 33 30S 80 00W
Juba Sudan 61 D1 4 50N 31 35E
Juba r. Somalia/Ethiopia 67 E5 0 00N 41 00E
Juiz de Fora Brazil 84 E5 21 47S 43 23W
Jungfrau mt. Switzerland 49 D2 46 33N 7 58E
Jura i. Scotland 32 D3/D4 55 55N 6 00W
Jura mts. France/Switzerland 48 F3 46 30N 6 00E
Jura, Sound of Scotland 32 D3/4 56 00N 5 45W
Jutland p. Denmark 49 E6 55 00N 9 00E

Kabul Afghanistan 58 B4 34 30N 70 00E
Kabwe Zambia 67 C3 14 29S 28 25E
Kaduna Nigeria 66 C4 10 28N 7 25E
Kaesong South Korea 59 D3 37 59N 126 30E
Kagoshima Japan 59 L1 31 37N 130 32E
Kainji Reservoir Nigeria 66 C4 10 25N 4 56E
Kaipara Harbour New Zealand 73 C3 36 12S 174 06E
Kaiserslautern Germany 49 D3 49 27N 7 47E
Kalahari Desert Southern Africa 67 C2 23 30S 23 00E
Kalemie Congo Dem. Rep. 67 C4 5 57S 29 10E
Kalgoorlie Australia 72 C2 30 49S 121 29E
Kaliningrad Russia 56 C3 54 40N 20 30E
Kamchatka Peninsula Russia 57 R3 57 30N 160 00E
Kampala Uganda 67 D5 0 19N 32 35E
Kananga Congo Dem. Rep. 67 C4 5 53S 22 26E
Kanazawa Japan 59 M2 36 35N 136 38E
Kandahar Afghanistan 58 B4 31 35N 65 45E
Kandalaksha Russia 42 N9 67 09N 32 31E
Kandla India 58 C3 23 03N 70 11E
Kandy Sri Lanka 58 D1 7 17N 80 40E
Kankan Guinea 66 B4 10 22N 9 11W
Kano Nigeria 66 C4 12 00N 8 31E
Kanpur India 58 D3 26 27N 80 14E
Kansas state USA 79 K4 38 00N 98 00W
Kansas City USA 79 K4 39 02N 94 33W
Kaohsiung Taiwan 59 D2 22 36N 120 17E
Kapuas r. Indonesia 60 C2 0 30N 112 00E
Karachi Pakistan 58 B3 24 52N 67 03E
Karaganda Kazakhstan 56 H2 49 53N 73 07E
Karbala Iraq 61 E4 32 37N 44 03E
Kariba, Lake Zambia/Zimbabwe 67 C3 17 00S 28 00E
Karlovac Croatia 51 E6 45 30N 15 34E
Karlsruhe Germany 49 E3 49 00N 8 24E
Karun r. Iran 61 E4 32 00N 48 00E
Kasai r. Angola/Congo Dem. Rep. 67 B4 4 00S 19 00E
Kashi China 58 C4 39 29N 76 02E
Kassala Sudan 61 D2 15 24N 36 30E
Kassel Germany 49 E4 51 18N 9 30E
Kasserine Tunisia 51 D5 35 11N 8 48E
Katherine Australia 72 D4 14 27S 132 15E
Kathmandu Nepal 58 D3 27 42N 85 19E
Katowice Poland 42 K6 50 15N 18 59E

Kaunas Lithuania 42 L6 54 52N 23 55E
Kayes Mali 66 A4 14 26N 11 28W
Kayseri Turkey 43 P3 38 42N 35 28E
KAZAKHSTAN 56 G2
Kazan' Russia 56 E3 55 45N 49 10E
Keady Northern Ireland 32 C2 54 15N 6 42W
Keighley England 34 D2 53 52N 1 54W
Keith Scotland 31 G2 57 32N 2 57W
Kelso Scotland 33 G3 55 36N 2 25W
Kemerovo Russia 56 J3 55 25N 86 05E
Kendal England 34 C3 54 20N 2 45W
Kenilworth England 37 E2 52 21N 1 34W
Kenitra Morocco 66 B6 34 20N 6 34W
Kennet r. England 38 C2 51 28N 1 45W
Kent co. England 39 E2 51 15N 0 09E
Kentucky state USA 79 L4 37 00N 85 00W
KENYA 67 D5
Kenya, Mount Kenya 67 D4 0 10S 37 19E
Kerema Papua New Guinea 72 E5 7 59S 145 46E
Kerguelen is. Indian Ocean 5 49 15N 69 10E
Kerman Iran 61 F4 30 18N 57 05E
Kermanshah Iran 61 E4 34 19N 47 04E
Kerrera i. Scotland 32 D1 56 24N 5 33W
Keswick England 34 B3 54 37N 3 08W
Kettering England 38 D3 52 24N 0 44W
Keynsham England 38 B2 51 26N 2 30W
Khabarovsk Russia 57 P2 48 32N 135 08E
Khaniá Greece 42 L3 35 31N 24 01E
Khanka, Lake Asia 57 P2 45 00N 132 30E
Kharkiv Ukraine 56 D2 50 00N 36 15E
Khartoum Sudan 61 D2 15 33N 32 35E
Kherson Ukraine 56 D2 46 39N 32 38E
Khulna Bangladesh 58 D3 22 49N 89 34E
Khyber Pass Afghanistan/Pakistan 58 C4 34 06N 71 05E
Kidderminster England 37 E2 52 23N 2 14W
Kidsgrove England 37 E3 53 05N 2 14W
Kidwelly Wales 36 C1 51 45N 4 18W
Kiel Germany 49 F6 54 20N 10 08E
Kielder Water res. England 33 G3 55 10N 2 30W
Kiev Ukraine 56 D3 50 25N 30 30E
Kigali Rwanda 67 D4 1 56S 30 04E
Kigoma Tanzania 67 C4 4 52S 29 36E
Kikwit Congo Dem. Rep. 67 B4 5 02S 18 51E
Kilbrannan Sound Scotland 32 D3 55 30N 5 30W
Kilimanjaro, Mount Tanzania 67 D4 3 04S 37 22E
Kilkeel Northern Ireland 32 C2 54 04N 6 00W
Kilmacrenan Republic of Ireland 32 B3 55 02N 7 47W
Kilmaluag Scotland 30 C2 57 41N 6 17W
Kilmarnock Scotland 33 E3 55 36N 4 30W
Kilmory Scotland 32 D3 55 55N 5 40W
Kimberley Republic of South Africa 67 C2 28 45S 24 46E
Kinabalu, Mount Malaysia 60 C3 6 03N 116 32E
Kinbrace Scotland 31 F3 58 15N 3 56W
Kingsbridge England 40 D3 50 17N 3 46W
King's Lynn England 39 E3 52 45N 0 24E
Kingston Jamaica 79 M2 17 58N 76 48W
Kingston upon Hull England 35 E2 53 45N 0 20W
Kingston upon Thames England 38 D2 51 25N 0 18W
Kingswood England 38 B2 51 28N 2 30W
Kington England 36 D2 52 12N 3 01W
Kingussie Scotland 31 E2 57 05N 4 03W
Kinloch Scotland 30 C2 57 01N 6 17W
Kinross Scotland 31 F1 56 13N 3 27W
Kinshasa Congo Dem. Rep. 67 B4 4 18S 15 18E
Kintyre p. Scotland 32 D3 55 30N 5 35W
KIRIBATI 4/5
Kirkbean Scotland 33 F2 54 55N 3 36W
Kirkby England 34 C2 53 29N 2 54W
Kirkby Stephen England 34 C3 54 28N 2 20W
Kirkcaldy Scotland 33 F4 56 07N 3 10W
Kirkcudbright Scotland 33 E2 54 50N 4 03W
Kirkintilloch Scotland 33 E3 55 57N 4 10W
Kirk Michael Isle of Man British Isles 33 C2 54 17N 4 35W
Kirkpatrick, Mount Antarctica 86 84 25S 165 30E
Kirkuk Iraq 61 E4 35 28N 44 26E
Kirkwall Scotland 29 C1 58 59N 2 58W
Kirov Russia 56 E3 58 00N 49 38E
Kirriemuir Scotland 31 F1 56 41N 3 01W
Kisangani Congo Dem. Rep. 67 C5 0 33N 25 14E
Kisumu Kenya 67 D4 0 08S 34 47E
Kitakami r. Japan 59 N2 39 00N 141 20E
Kita Kyushu Japan 59 L1 33 52N 130 49E
Kitwe Zambia 67 C3 0 08S 30 30E
Kitzbühel Austria 51 D7 47 27N 12 23E
Kivu, Lake Congo Dem. Rep./Rwanda 67 C4 2 00S 29 00E
Klagenfurt Austria 49 H2 46 38N 14 20E
Klaipėda Lithuania 42 L7 55 43N 21 07E
Knaresborough England 35 D3 54 00N 1 27W
Knighton England 36 D2 52 21N 3 03W
Kobe Japan 59 M1 34 40N 135 12E
Koblenz Germany 49 D4 50 21N 7 36E
Kochi Japan 59 L1 33 33N 133 32E
Kodiak Island USA 78 D6 57 30N 153 40W
Kokand Uzbekistan 56 H2 40 33N 70 55E
Kola Peninsula Russia 42 P9 67 00N 39 00E
Kolhapur India 58 C2 16 40N 74 20E
Kolkata (Calcutta) India 58 D3 22 30N 88 20E
Kolyma r. Russia 57 R4 68 00N 152 00E
Komsomolsk-on-Amur Russia 57 P3 50 32N 136 59E
Konya Turkey 59 N2 37 03N 140 52E
Koriyama Japan 59 N2 37 23N 140 22E
Kosciusko, Mount Australia 72 E2 36 27S 148 17E
Kota Bharu Malaysia 60 B3 6 08N 102 14E
Kota Kinabalu Malaysia 60 C3 5 59N 116 04E
Kotlas Russia 43 R8 61 15N 46 35E
Kragujevac Serbia and Montenegro 42 L4 44 01N 20 55E
Kra, Isthmus of Myanmar/Thailand 60 A4 10 20N 99 00E
Kraków Poland 42 K6 50 03N 19 55E
Kranj Slovenia 51 E7 46 15N 14 20E
Krasnodar Russia 56 D2 45 02N 39 00E
Krasnovodsk Turkmenistan 56 F2 40 01N 53 00E
Krasnoyarsk Russia 57 K3 56 05N 92 46E
Kratie Cambodia 60 B4 12 30N 106 03E

Krefeld Germany **49** D4 51 20N 6 32E
Krishna r. India **58** C2 16 00N 79 00E
Kryvyy Rih Ukraine **56** D2 47 55N 33 24E
Kuala Lumpur Malaysia **60** B3 3 09N 101 42E
Kuala Terengganu Malaysia **60** B3 5 20N 103 09E
Kuantan Malaysia **60** B3 3 48N 103 19E
Kuching Malaysia **60** C3 1 35N 110 21E
Kuh-e-Hazaran mt. Iran **61** F3 29 35N 57 20E
Kumamoto Japan **59** L1 32 50N 130 42E
Kumasi Ghana **66** B3 6 45N 1 35W
Kunlun Shan mts. China **58** D4 36 30N 85 00E
Kunming China **59** B2 25 04N 102 41E
Kupang Indonesia **60** D1 10 13S 123 38E
Kurgan Russia **56** G3 55 30N 65 20E
Kuril Islands Russia **57** R2 50 00N 155 00E
Kursk Russia **56** D3 51 45N 36 14E
Kushiro Japan **59** N3 42 58N 144 24E
Kutaisi Georgia **43** Q4 42 15N 42 44E
KUWAIT 61 E3
Kuwait Kuwait **61** E3 29 20N 48 00E
Kwangju South Korea **59** D3 35 07N 126 52E
Kyle of Lochalsh Scotland **30** D2 57 17N 5 43W
Kyoga, Lake Uganda **67** D5 2 00N 34 00E
Kyoto Japan **59** M2 35 02N 135 45E
KYRGYZSTAN 56 H2
Kyushu i. Japan **59** L1 32 20N 131 00E

L

Laâyoune Western Sahara **66** A5 27 10N 13 11W
La Coruña Spain **50** A5 43 22N 8 24W
Ladoga, Lake Russia **56** D4 61 00N 30 00E
Lae Papua New Guinea **72** E5 6 45S 147 00E
Lagos Nigeria **66** C3 6 27N 3 28E
La Grande Rivière r. Canada **78** L6 53 34N 74 36W
Lahore Pakistan **58** C4 31 35N 74 18E
Lairg Scotland **31** E3 58 01N 4 25W
Lake District geog. reg. England **34** B3/C3 54 30N 3 00W
Lakshadweep (Laccadive Islands) India **58** C2 9 30N 73 00E
Lambert Glacier Antarctica **86** 73 00S 70 00E
Lambourn r. England **38** C2 51 30N 1 30W
Lammermuir Hills Scotland **33** G3 55 50N 2 45W
Lampedusa i. Italy **51** D1 35 00N 12 00E
Lampeter Wales **36** C2 52 07N 4 05W
Lanark Scotland **33** F3 55 41N 3 48W
Lancang Jiang (Mekong) r. China/Myanmar/Laos/Cambodia **43** A3 32 00N 98 00E
Lancashire co. England **34** C2 53 50N 2 30W
Lancaster England **34** C3 54 03N 2 48W
Land's End c. England **40** B3 50 03N 5 44W
Langholm Scotland **33** G3 55 09N 3 00W
Languedoc geog. reg. France **48** E1/F2 44 00N 4 00E
Lanzhou China **59** B3 36 01N 103 45E
LAOS 60 B4
La Paz Bolivia **84** C6 16 30S 68 10W
La Plata Argentina **85** D4 34 52S 57 55W
La Puebla Balearic Islands **50** H3 39 46N 3 01E
Largs Scotland **32** E3 55 48N 4 52W
Lárisa Greece **42** L3 39 38N 22 25E
Larne Northern Ireland **32** D2 54 51N 5 49W
Larne district Northern Ireland **32** D2 54 50N 5 50W
la Rochelle France **48** C3 46 10N 1 09W
Larsen Ice Shelf Antarctica **86** 67 00S 62 00W
La Sagra mt. Spain **50** D2 37 57N 2 34W
Las Palmas Canary Islands **66** A5 28 08N 15 27W
Las Vegas USA **79** H4 36 10N 115 10W
Latakia Syria **61** D4 35 31N 35 47E
Latina Italy **51** D4 41 28N 12 53E
LATVIA 42 M7
Launceston Australia **72** E1 41 27S 147 09E
Launceston England **40** C3 50 38N 4 21W
Laurencekirk Scotland **31** G1 56 50N 2 29W
Lausanne Switzerland **49** D2 46 32N 6 39E
Laval France **48** C4 48 04N 0 45W
Leader Water r. Scotland **33** G3 55 45N 2 50W
LEBANON 61 D4
Ledbury England **37** E2 52 02N 2 25W
Leeds England **34** D2 53 50N 1 35W
Leeuwin, Cape Australia **72** B2 34 21S 115 08E
le Havre France **48** D4 49 30N 0 06E
Leicester England **37** F2 52 38N 1 05W
Leicester City u.a. England **37** F2 52 36N 1 08W
Leicestershire co. England **37** F2/G2 52 30N 1 00W
Leiden Netherlands **49** C5 52 10N 4 30E
Leighton Buzzard England **38** D2 51 55N 0 41W
Leipzig Germany **49** G4 51 20N 12 25E
Leith Hill England **38** D2 51 11N 0 23W
Leitrim co. Republic of Ireland **32** A2 54 05N 8 00W
le Mans France **48** D4 48 00N 0 12E
Lena r. Russia **57** N4 64 30N 127 00E
Lens France **48** E5 50 26N 2 50E
Leominster England **37** E2 52 14N 2 45W
León Mexico **79** J3 21 10N 101 42W
León Spain **50** C5 42 35N 5 34W
le Puy France **48** E2 45 03N 3 53E
Lerwick Scotland **29** D3 60 09N 1 09W
LESOTHO 67 C2
Lessay France **41** F2 49 13N 1 32W
Lesser Antilles is. West Indies **79** N2 18 00N 65 00W
Letchworth England **38** D2 51 58N 0 14W
le Touquet-Paris-Plage France **39** F1 50 13N 1 36E
Letterkenny Republic of Ireland **32** B2 54 57N 7 44W
Leverkusen Germany **49** D4 51 02N 6 59E
Levin New Zealand **73** D2 40 37S 175 17E
Lewes England **38** E1 50 52N 0 01E
Lewis i. Scotland **30** C3 58 15N 6 30W
Leyburn England **34** D3 54 19N 1 49W
Leyland England **34** C2 53 42N 2 42W
Leyte i. The Philippines **60** D4 11 00N 125 00E
Lhasa China **58** E3 29 08N 87 43E
Lianyungang China **59** C3 34 37N 119 10E
Liao He r. China **59** D4 42 30N 122 00E
Liard r. Canada **78** G7 61 00N 122 00W
LIBERIA 66 B3
Libreville Gabon **66** C3 0 30N 9 25E
LIBYA 66 D5

Libyan Desert North Africa **61** C3 25 00N 25 00E
Lichfield England **37** F2 52 42N 1 48W
Liddel Water r. England/Scotland **33** G3 55 15N 2 50W
LIECHTENSTEIN 49 E2
Liège Belgium **49** C4 50 38N 5 35E
Liepāja Latvia **42** L7 56 30N 21 00E
Likasi Congo Dem. Rep. **67** C3 10 58S 26 47E
Lille France **48** E5 50 39N 3 05E
Lillers France **39** G1 50 34N 2 29E
Lilongwe Malawi **67** D3 13 58S 33 49E
Lima Peru **84** B6 12 06S 8 40W
Limassol Cyprus **43** N2 34 04N 33 03E
Limavady Northern Ireland **32** C3 55 03N 6 57W
Limavady district Northern Ireland **32** B2/C2 54 50N 7 00W
Limoges France **48** D2 45 50N 1 15E
Limpopo r. Southern Africa **67** C2 22 30S 28 00E
Lincoln England **35** E2 53 14N 0 33W
Lincolnshire co. England **35** E2 53 10N 0 20W
Lincoln Wolds hills England **35** E2 53 25N 0 05W
Lingga i. Indonesia **60** B2 0 10S 104 40E
Linköping Sweden **42** K7 58 25N 15 35E
Linlithgow Scotland **33** F3 55 59N 3 37W
Linz Austria **42** J5 48 19N 14 18E
Lipetsk Russia **56** D3 52 37N 39 36E
Lisbon Portugal **50** A3 38 44N 9 08W
Lisburn Northern Ireland **32** C2 54 31N 6 03W
Lisburn district Northern Ireland **32** C2 54 30N 6 10W
Lisieux France **48** D4 49 09N 0 14E
Liskeard England **40** C3 50 28N 4 28W
Lismore Scotland **30** D1 56 30N 5 30W
LITHUANIA 42 L7
Littlehampton England **38** D1 50 48N 0 33W
Little Minch sd. Scotland **30** C2 57 45N 6 30W
Little Ouse r. England **39** E3 52 30N 0 30E
Little Rock USA **79** K4 34 42N 92 17W
Liuzhou China **59** B2 24 17N 109 15E
Liverpool England **34** C2 53 25N 2 55W
Livingston Scotland **33** F3 55 53N 3 32W
Livorno Italy **51** C5 43 33N 10 18E
Lizard England **40** B2 49 57N 5 13W
Lizard Point England **40** B2 49 56N 5 13W
Ljubljana Slovenia **51** E7 46 04N 14 30E
Llandeilo Wales **36** D1 51 53N 3 59W
Llandovery Wales **36** D1 51 59N 3 48W
Llandrindod Wells Wales **36** D2 52 15N 3 23W
Llandudno Wales **36** D3 53 19N 3 49W
Llanelli Wales **36** C1 51 42N 4 10W
Llangollen Wales **36** D2 52 58N 3 10W
Llanidloes Wales **36** D2 52 27N 3 32W
Lleida Spain **50** F4 41 37N 0 38E
Lleyn Peninsula Wales **36** C2 52 53N 4 30W
Lobito Angola **67** B3 12 20S 13 34E
Lochaline tn. Scotland **30** D1 56 32N 5 47W
Loch Arkaig l. Scotland **30** D1 56 59N 5 10W
Loch Awe l. Scotland **30/31** D1 56 15N 5 17W
Lochdon tn. Scotland **30** D1 56 25N 5 36W
Loch Doon l. Scotland **33** E2 55 26N 4 38W
Loch Earn l. Scotland **31** E1 56 25N 4 10W
Loch Eishort est. Scotland **30** D2 57 08N 6 00W
Loch Eriboll b. Scotland **31** E3 58 31N 4 41W
Loch Ericht l. Scotland **31** E1 56 48N 4 25W
Loch Etive l. Scotland **30/31** D1 56 30N 5 10W
Loch Fyne b. Scotland **30** D4 56 10N 5 05W
Lochgilphead tn. Scotland **32** D4 56 03N 5 26W
Loch Katrine l. Scotland **33** E4 56 16N 4 30W
Loch Ken l. Scotland **33** E2 55 02N 4 07W
Loch Leven l. Scotland **31** F1 56 15N 3 23W
Loch Linnhe b. Scotland **30** D1 56 35N 5 25W
Loch Lochy l. Scotland **31** E1 56 58N 4 55W
Loch Lomond l. Scotland **33** E4 56 10N 4 35W
Loch Long l. Scotland **32/33** E4 56 10N 4 50W
Lochmaben tn. Scotland **33** F3 55 08N 3 27W
Lochmaddy tn. Scotland **30** B2 57 36N 7 08W
Loch Nan Clar l. Scotland **31** E3 58 30N 4 00W
Loch Maree l. Scotland **30** D2 57 40N 5 30W
Loch Mullardoch l. Scotland **31** E2 57 27N 4 58W
Lochnagar mt. Scotland **31** F1 56 57N 3 16W
Loch Ness l. Scotland **31** E2 57 02N 4 30W
Loch Rannoch l. Scotland **31** E1 56 41N 4 18W
Lochranza tn. Scotland **32** D3 55 42N 5 18W
Loch Shiel l. Scotland **30** D1 56 45N 5 35W
Loch Shin l. Scotland **31** E3 58 05N 4 30W
Loch Snizort b. Scotland **30** C2 57 30N 6 30W
Loch Tay l. Scotland **31** E1 56 31N 4 10W
Loch Torridon b. Scotland **30** D2 57 35N 5 46W
Lockerbie Scotland **33** F3 55 07N 3 22W
Łódź Poland **42** K6 51 49N 19 28E
Logan, Mount Canada **78** E7 60 34N 140 25W
Logroño Spain **50** D5 42 28N 2 26W
Loire r. France **48** D3 47 30N 1 00E
Lolland i. Denmark **49** F6 54 45N 12 20E
Lombok i. Indonesia **60** C2 8 30S 116 30E
Lomé Togo **66** C3 6 10N 1 21E
London England **38** D2 51 30N 0 10W
Londonderry Northern Ireland **32** B2 54 59N 7 19W
Londonderry district Northern Ireland **32** B2 54 55N 7 20W
Londrina Brazil **84** D5 23 18S 51 13W
Long Eaton England **37** F2 52 54N 1 15W
Long Island The Bahamas **79** M3 23 20N 75 00W
Long Mynd sum. England **37** E2 52 32N 2 52W
Longreach Australia **72** D3 23 26S 144 15E
Longs Peak USA **79** J5 40 20N 105 50W
Looe England **40** C3 51 21N 4 27W
Lorient France **48** B3 47 45N 3 21W
Los Angeles USA **79** H4 34 00N 118 15W
Lossiemouth Scotland **31** F2 57 43N 3 18W
Lostwithiel England **40** C3 50 25N 4 40W
Lot r. France **48** E2 44 30N 2 15E
Louangphrabang Laos **60** B4 19 53N 102 10E
Lough Allen l. Republic of Ireland **32** A2 54 15N 8 00W
Lough Beg l. Northern Ireland **32** C2 54 48N 6 16W
Loughborough England **37** F2 52 47N 1 11W
Lough Derg l. Republic of Ireland **32** B2 52 55N 8 15W
Lough Foyle est. Northern Ireland/Republic of Ireland **32** B3 55 10N 7 10W

Lough Macnean Lower l. Northern Ireland **32** B2 54 17N 7 50W
Lough Macnean Upper l. Northern Ireland/Republic of Ireland **32** B2 54 18N 7 55W
Lough Melvin l. Northern Ireland/Republic of Ireland **32** A2 54 25N 8 05W
Lough Neagh l. Northern Ireland **32** C2 54 35N 6 30W
Lough Oughter l. Republic of Ireland **32** B2 54 00N 7 30W
Lough Swilly b. Republic of Ireland **32** B3 55 20N 7 35W
Louisiana state USA **79** K4 32 00N 92 00W
Louisville USA **79** L4 38 13N 85 48W
Lourdes France **48** C1 43 06N 0 02W
Louth England **35** E2 53 22N 0 01W
Louth co. Republic of Ireland **32** C1/2 53 55N 6 25W
Lower California p. Mexico **79** H3 27 30N 113 00W
Lower Lough Erne l. Northern Ireland **32** B2 54 25N 7 45W
Lowestoft England **39** F3 52 29N 1 45E
Lowther Hills Scotland **33** F3 55 25N 3 45W
Lualaba r. Congo Dem. Rep. **67** C4 4 00S 26 30E
Luanda Angola **67** B4 8 50S 13 15E
Lubango Angola **67** B3 14 55S 13 30E
Lübeck Germany **49** F5 53 52N 10 40E
Lublin Poland **42** L6 51 18N 22 31E
Lubumbashi Congo Dem. Rep. **67** C3 11 41S 27 29E
Luce Bay Scotland **32/33** E2 54 47N 4 50W
Lucerne Switzerland **49** E2 47 03N 8 17E
Lucknow India **58** D3 26 50N 80 54E
Lüderitz Namibia **67** B2 26 38S 15 10E
Ludhiana India **58** C4 30 56N 75 52E
Ludlow England **37** E2 52 22N 2 43W
Ludwigshafen Germany **49** E3 49 29N 8 27E
Lugano Switzerland **49** E2 46 01N 8 57E
Luhans'k Ukraine **56** D2 48 35N 39 20E
Luleå Sweden **42** L5 65 35N 22 10E
Lundy i. England **40** C4 51 11N 4 40W
Lune r. England **34** C3 54 15N 2 40W
Luoyang China **59** C3 34 47N 112 26E
Lurgan Northern Ireland **32** C2 54 28N 6 20W
Lusaka Zambia **67** C3 15 26S 28 20E
Luton England **38** D2 51 53N 0 25W
Luton u.a. England **38** D2 51 53N 0 30W
LUXEMBOURG 49 C3/D3
Luxembourg Luxembourg **49** D3 49 37N 6 08E
Luxor Egypt **61** D3 25 41N 32 24E
Luzon i. The Philippines **60** D4 15 00N 122 00E
L'viv Ukraine **56** C2 49 50N 24 00E
Lybster Scotland **31** F3 58 18N 3 13W
Lyme Bay England **41** E3 50 40N 2 55W
Lyme Regis England **41** E3 50 44N 2 57W
Lymington England **38** C1 50 46N 1 33W
Lynn Lake tn. Canada **78** J6 56 51N 101 01W
Lynton England **40** D4 51 15N 3 50W
Lyons France **48** F2 45 46N 4 50E
Lys r. France **39** G1 50 40N 2 10E
Lytham St. Anne's England **34** B2 53 45N 3 01W

M

Maas r. Netherlands **49** C4 51 50N 5 45E
Maastricht Netherlands **49** C4 50 51N 5 42E
Mablethorpe England **35** F3 53 21N 0 15E
Macao China **59** C2 22 10N 113 40E
Macapá Brazil **84** D8 0 04N 51 04W
Macclesfield England **34** C2 53 16N 2 07W
Macdonnell Ranges Australia **72** D3 23 42S 128 42E
Macduff Scotland **31** G2 57 40N 2 29W
MACEDONIA, FORMER YUGOSLAV REPUBLIC OF (FYROM) 42 L4
Maceió Brazil **84** F7 9 40S 35 44W
Machynlleth Wales **36** D2 52 35N 3 51W
Mackay, Lake Australia **72** C3 22 25S 128 42E
Mackenzie r. Canada **78** G7 64 00N 123 00W
Mackenzie Mountains Canada **78** G7 66 00N 132 00W
McKinley, Mount USA **78** E7 62 02N 151 01W
Mâcon France **48** F3 46 18N 4 50E
MADAGASCAR 67 E2/3
Madang Papua New Guinea **72** E5 5 14S 145 45E
Madeira r. Brazil **84** C7 6 00S 61 30W
Madeira Islands Atlantic Ocean **5** 32 45N 17 00W
Madras see Chennai
Madrid Spain **50** D4 40 25N 3 43W
Madura i. Indonesia **60** C2 7 00S 113 00E
Madurai India **58** C1 9 55N 78 07E
Maebashi Japan **59** M2 36 24N 139 04E
Magadan Russia **57** R3 59 38N 150 50E
Magdalena r. Colombia **84** B8 3 00N 75 40W
Magdeburg Germany **49** F5 52 08N 11 37E
Maggiore, Lake Italy **51** B6/7 46 00N 8 00E
Maghera Northern Ireland **32** C2 54 51N 6 40W
Magherafelt Northern Ireland **32** C2 54 45N 6 36W
Magherafelt district Northern Ireland **32** C2 54 45N 6 50W
Magnitogorsk Russia **56** F3 53 28N 59 06E
Mahajanga Madagascar **67** E3 15 40S 46 20E
Mahakam r. Indonesia **60** C3 0 30N 116 00E
Mahilyow Belarus **56** C3 53 54N 30 20E
Mahón Balearic Islands **50** H3 39 54N 4 15E
Maidenhead England **38** D2 51 32N 0 44W
Maidstone England **39** E2 51 17N 0 32E
Maiduguri Nigeria **66** D4 11 53N 13 16E
Main r. Germany **49** F4 50 00N 10 30E
Main r. Northern Ireland **32** C2 54 50N 6 25W
Mai-Ndombe, Lake Congo Dem. Rep. **67** B4 2 00S 18 20E
Maine state USA **79** N5 45 00N 70 00W
Mainland i. Orkney Islands Scotland **29** B1/B2 59 00N 3 15W
Mainland i. Shetland Islands Scotland **29** D3 60 15N 1 20W
Mainz Germany **49** D3 50 00N 8 16E
Makassar Strait Indonesia **60** C2 0 00 119 00E
Makeyevka Ukraine **56** D2 48 01N 38 00E
Makhachkala Russia **56** E2 43 00N 47 30E
Malabo Equatorial Guinea **66** C3 3 45N 8 48E
Malacca, Strait of Indonesia **60** B3 4 00N 100 00E
Málaga Spain **50** C2 36 43N 4 25W

Malahide Republic of Ireland **36** A3 53 27N 6 09W
Malakal Sudan **61** D1 9 31N 31 40E
Malang Indonesia **60** C2 7 59S 112 45E
Malanje Angola **67** B4 9 32S 16 20E
Malatya Turkey **43** P3 38 22N 38 18E
MALAWI 67 D3
Malawi, Lake see Nyasa, Lake
Malaya admin. Malaysia **60** B3 5 00N 102 00E
MALAYSIA 60 B3/C3
MALDIVES 58 C1
MALI 66 B4
Malin Head c. Republic of Ireland **32** B3 55 30N 7 20W
Mallaig Scotland **30** D2 57 00N 5 50W
Mallorca i. Balearic Islands **50** G3 39 50N 2 30E
Malmesbury England **38** B2 51 36N 2 06W
Malmö Sweden **42** J7 55 35N 13 00E
MALTA 51 E1
Malton England **35** E3 54 08N 0 48W
Manacor Balearic Islands **50** G3 39 35N 3 12E
Manado Indonesia **60** D3 1 32N 124 55E
Managua Nicaragua **79** L2 12 06N 86 18W
Manaus Brazil **84** D7 3 06S 60 00W
Manawatu r. New Zealand **73** D2 40 30S 176 00E
Manchester England **34** C2 53 30N 2 15W
Mandalay Myanmar **58** E3 21 57N 96 04E
Manfredonia Italy **51** E4 41 37N 15 55E
Mangalore India **58** C2 12 54N 74 51E
Mangotsfield England **38** B2 51 29N 2 31W
Manila The Philippines **60** D4 14 37N 120 58E
Manitoba province Canada **78** K6 55 00N 98 00W
Manizales Colombia **84** B8 5 03N 75 32W
Mannheim Germany **49** E3 49 30N 8 28E
Mansfield England **37** F3 53 09N 1 11W
Manzanares Spain **50** D3 39 00N 3 23W
Maputo Mozambique **67** D2 25 58S 32 35E
Maracaibo Venezuela **84** B9 10 44N 71 37W
Maracaibo, Lake Venezuela **84** B8 9 50N 71 30W
Marañon r. Peru **84** B7 7 00S 77 40W
Marbella Spain **50** C2 36 31N 4 53W
Marble Bar Australia **72** B3 21 10S 119 43E
Mar del Plata Argentina **85** D4 38 00S 57 32W
Marden England **39** E2 51 11N 0 30E
Margarita i. Venezuela **79** N2 11 30N 64 00W
Margate England **39** F2 51 24N 1 24E
Maribor Slovenia **51** E7 46 34N 15 38E
Marie Byrd Land geog. reg. Antarctica **86** 77 00S 130 00W
Mariscal Estigarribia Paraguay **84** C5 22 03S 60 35W
Mariupol Ukraine **56** D2 47 05N 37 34E
Market Drayton England **37** E2 52 54N 2 29W
Market Harborough England **37** G2 52 29N 0 55W
Market Rasen England **35** E2 53 24N 0 21W
Markham, Mount Antarctica **86** 82 45S 160 25E
Marlborough England **38** C2 51 26N 1 43W
Marlow England **38** D2 51 35N 0 48W
Marne r. France **48** E4 49 00N 4 00E
Marrakech Morocco **66** B4 31 49N 8 00W
Marsala Italy **51** D2 37 48N 12 27E
Marseille France **48** F1 43 18N 5 22E
MARSHALL ISLANDS 5
Martinique i. Lesser Antilles **79** N2 14 30N 61 00W
Maryborough Australia **72** E3 25 33S 152 42E
Maryland state USA **79** M4 39 00N 77 00W
Maryport England **34** B3 54 43N 3 30W
Maseru Lesotho **67** C2 29 19S 27 29E
Mashhad Iran **61** F4 36 16N 59 34E
Massachusetts state USA **79** M5 42 00N 72 00W
Massawa Eritrea **61** D2 15 42N 39 25E
Massif Central mts. France **48** E2 45 00N 3 00E
Masterton New Zealand **73** D2 40 57S 175 39E
Matadi Congo Dem. Rep. **67** B4 5 50S 13 32E
Matamoros Mexico **79** K3 25 33N 103 51W
Matlock England **37** F3 53 08N 1 32W
Mato Grosso geog. reg. Brazil **84** D6 14 00S 56 00W
Matsue Japan **59** L2 35 29N 133 04E
Matsuyama Japan **59** L1 33 50N 132 47E
Matterhorn mt. Switzerland **49** D1 45 59N 7 39E
MAURITANIA 66 A5
MAURITIUS 5
Maybole Scotland **33** E3 55 21N 4 41W
Mazatlán Mexico **79** J3 23 11N 106 25W
Mbandaka Congo Dem. Rep. **67** B5 0 03N 18 28E
Mbeya Tanzania **67** D4 8 54S 33 29E
Mbuji-Mayi Congo Dem. Rep. **67** C4 6 10S 23 39E
Mecca Saudi Arabia **61** D3 21 26N 39 49E
Medan Indonesia **60** A3 3 35N 98 39E
Medellín Colombia **84** B8 6 15N 75 36W
Medina Saudi Arabia **61** D3 24 30N 39 35E
Mediterranean Sea Africa/Europe **42/43** 35 00N 15 00E
Medway r. England **39** E2 51 24N 0 30E
Medway u.a. England **39** E2 51 28N 0 35E
Meekatharra Australia **72** B3 26 35S 118 30E
Meerut India **58** C3 29 00N 77 42E
Mega Ethiopia **61** D1 4 02N 38 19E
Meharry, Mount Australia **72** B3 22 58S 118 35E
Meig r. Scotland **31** E2 57 40N 4 50W
Meknes Morocco **66** B4 33 53N 5 37W
Mekong (Lancang Jiang) r. Cambodia/Laos/Myanmar/China **59** B1 15 00N 105 00E
Melbourne Australia **72** E2 37 49S 144 58E
Melrose Scotland **33** G3 55 36N 2 44W
Melton Mowbray England **37** G2 52 46N 0 53W
Melville Island Canada **78** H8 75 30N 112 00W
Memphis USA **79** K4 35 10N 90 00W
Menam r. Thailand **60** B4 15 00N 100 00E
Mendip Hills England **41** E4 51 18N 2 45W
Mendoza Argentina **85** C4 32 48S 68 52W
Menorca i. Balearic Islands **50** H3 39 45N 4 15E
Mentawai Islands Indonesia **60** A2 2 00N 99 00E
Menzies, Mount Antarctica **86** 73 30S 62 00E
Meon r. England **38** C1 50 55N 1 10W
Mere England **38** B2 51 06N 2 16W
Mérida Mexico **79** L3 20 59N 89 39W
Mersey r. England **34** C2 53 20N 2 55W
Merseyside co. England **34** C2 53 30N 3 20W
Mersin Turkey **43** N3 36 47N 34 37E
Merthyr Tydfil Wales **36** D1 51 46N 3 23W
Merthyr Tydfil u.a. Wales **36** D1 51 48N 3 20W
Merton England **38** D2 51 25N 0 12W
Messina Italy **51** E3 38 13N 15 33E

tz France 48 G4 49 07N 6 11E
use r. Belgium/France 49 C4 50 30N 5 00E
xicali Mexico 79 H4 32 36N 115 30W
XICO 79 H4/K2
xico City Mexico 79 K2 19 25N 99 10W
xico, Gulf of Mexico 79 L3 25 00N 90 00W
ami USA 79 L3 25 45N 80 15W
chigan state USA 79 K5 44 00N 85 00W
chigan, Lake Canada/USA 79 L5 45 00N 87 00W
ch, The sd. Scotland 30 C3/D3 58 00N 6 00W
ckle Fell sum. England 34 C3 54 38N 2 18W
ddlesbrough England 35 D3 54 35N 1 14W
ddlesbrough u.a. England 35 D3 54 33N 1 04W
dlothian u.a. Scotland 33 F3 55 50N 3 05W
an Italy 51 B6 45 28N 9 12E
denhall England 39 E3 52 21N 0 24E
dura Australia 72 E2 34 12S 142 09E
ford Haven Wales 36 B1 51 44N 5 02W
ton Sound New Zealand 73 B2 44 41S 167 56E
ton Keynes England 38 D3 52 02N 0 42W
ton Keynes England 38 D3 52 10N 0 40W
ton Ness c. Scotland 31 G1 56 40N 2 20W
waukee USA 79 L5 43 03N 87 56W
ndanao i. The Philippines 60 D3 8 00N 125 00E
ndoro i. The Philippines 60 D4 13 00N 121 00E
nehead England 40 D4 51 13N 3 29W
ngulay i. Scotland 30 B1 56 49N 7 38W
nneapolis USA 79 K5 45 00N 93 15W
nnesota state USA 79 K5 47 00N 95 00W
nsk Belarus 42 M5 53 51N 27 30E
skolc Hungary 42 L5 48 07N 20 47E
sool i. Indonesia 60 E2 1 50S 129 55E
sratah Libya 66 D6 32 23N 15 06E
ssissippi r. USA 79 K4 33 00N 90 30W
ssissippi state USA 79 K4 32 00N 90 00W
ssouri r. USA 79 J5 48 00N 109 00W
ssouri state USA 79 K4 38 00N 93 00W
yazaki Japan 59 L1 31 56N 131 27E
bile USA 79 L4 30 40N 88 00W
cambique Mozambique 67 E3 15 03S 40 45E
dena Italy 51 C6 44 39N 10 55E
ffat Scotland 33 F3 55 20N 3 27W
gadishu Somalia 67 E5 2 02N 45 21E
ld Wales 36 D3 53 10N 3 08W
LDOVA 42 M5
luccas is. Indonesia 60 D3/E2 4 00S 127 00E
lucca Sea Indonesia 60 D2 0 30S 125 30E
mbasa Kenya 67 C4 4 04S 39 40E
NACO 48 G1
nadhliath Mountains Scotland 31 E2 57 10N 00W
naghan Republic of Ireland 32 C2 54 15N 6 58W
naghan co. Republic of Ireland 32 B2/C2 54 10N 00W
nforte Spain 50 B5 42 32N 7 30W
NGOLIA 57 L2
nmouth Wales 37 E1 51 50N 2 43W
nmouthshire u.a. Wales 37 E1 51 47N 2 55W
nrovia Liberia 66 A3 6 20N 10 46W
ntana state USA 79 H5 47 00N 111 00W
ntauban France 48 D2 44 01N 1 20E
ntbéliard France 48 G3 47 31N 6 48E
nt Blanc mt. France/Italy 48 G2 45 50N 6 52E
nte Carlo Monaco 48 G1 43 44N 7 25E
nterrey Mexico 79 J3 25 40N 100 20W
ntes Claros tn. Brazil 84 E6 16 45S 43 52W
ntevideo Uruguay 85 D4 34 55S 56 10W
ntgomery Wales 36 D2 52 34N 3 10W
ntluçon France 48 E3 46 20N 2 36E
ntpellier France 48 E1 43 36N 3 53E
ntréal Canada 79 M5 45 32N 73 36W
ntreux Switzerland 49 D2 46 27N 6 55E
ntrose Scotland 31 G1 56 43N 2 29W
nza Italy 51 B6 45 35N 9 16E
osonee Canada 79 L6 51 18N 80 39W
ray u.a. Scotland 31 F2 57 20N 3 10W
ray Firth est. Scotland 31 F2 57 45N 3 45W
recambe England 34 C3 54 04N 2 53W
recambe Bay England 34 B3/C3 54 00N 3 00W
relia Mexico 79 J2 19 40N 101 11W
reton-in-Marsh England 38 C2 51 59N 1 42W
rioka Japan 59 N2 39 43N 141 08E
rlaix France 48 B4 48 35N 3 50W
ROCCO 66 B6
roni Comoros 67 E3 11 40S 43 16E
rotai i. Indonesia 60 D3 2 30N 128 30E
rven mt. Scotland 31 F3 58 14N 3 42W
scow Russia 56 D3 55 45N 37 42E
sel r. Germany/France 49 D3 50 00N 7 00E
stoles Spain 50 D4 40 19N 3 53W
sul Iraq 61 E4 36 21N 43 08E
therwell Scotland 33 E3 55 48N 3 59W
ulmein Myanmar 58 E2 16 30N 97 38E
unt Hagen tn. Papua New Guinea 72 E5 5 54S 14 13E
unt Isa tn. Australia 72 D3 20 44S 139 29E
unt Magnet tn. Australia 72 B3 28 02S 117 50E
unts Bay England 36 B3 50 05N 5 30W
yale Kenya 66 D5 3 31N 39 04E
yle district Northern Ireland 32 C3 55 10N 6 10W
ZAMBIQUE 67 D3
zambique Channel Mozambique/Madagascar 67 E3 18 00S 42 00E
ck i. Scotland 30 C1 56 50N 6 15W
ckle Roe i. Scotland 29 D3 60 22N 1 26W
danjiang China 59 D4 44 36N 129 42E
kalla Yemen Republic 61 E2 14 34N 49 09E
lhacén mt. Spain 50 D2 37 04N 3 19W
lhouse France 48 G3 47 45N 7 21E
ll i. Scotland 30 C1/D1 56 25N 6 00W
ll Head c. Scotland 32 C2 56 59N 2 58W
llion England 40 B3 50 01N 5 14W
ll of Galloway c. Scotland 32 E2 54 38N 4 50W
ll of Kintyre c. Scotland 32 C3 55 17N 5 55W
ll of Oa c. Scotland 32 C3 55 35N 6 20W
ll, Sound of Scotland 30 C2 56 30N 6 00W
ltan Pakistan 58 C4 30 10N 71 36E
mbai (Bombay) India 58 C2 18 56N 72 51E

München Gladbach Germany 49 D4 51 12N 6 25E
Munich Germany 49 F3 48 08N 11 35E
Münster Germany 49 D4 51 58N 7 37E
Mur r. Europe 49 H2 47 00N 14 00E
Murchison i. Australia 72 B3 26 00S 117 00E
Murcia Spain 50 E2 37 59N 1 08W
Murmansk Russia 56 D4 68 59N 33 08E
Muroran Japan 59 N3 42 21N 140 59E
Murray r. Australia 72 E2 35 40S 144 00E
Murrumbidgee r. Australia 72 E2 35 00S 145 00E
Muscat Oman 61 F3 23 37N 58 38E
Musi r. Indonesia 60 B2 3 00S 104 00E
Musselburgh Scotland 33 F3 55 57N 3 04W
Mwanza Tanzania 67 D4 2 31S 32 56E
Mweru, Lake Congo Dem. Rep./Zambia 67 C4 8 30S 28 30E
MYANMAR (BURMA) 58 E3
Mykolayiv Ukraine 56 D2 46 57N 32 00E
Mynydd Eppynt hills Wales 36 D2 52 02N 3 35W
Mynydd Preseli hills Wales 36 C1 51 58N 4 45W
Mysore India 58 C2 12 18N 76 37E

N

Naberezhnyye Chelny Russia 56 F3 55 42N 52 19E
Nabeul Tunisia 42 J3 36 30N 10 44E
Nador Morocco 50 D1 35 10N 3 00W
Nagano Japan 59 M2 36 39N 138 10E
Nagasaki Japan 59 K1 32 45N 129 52E
Nagoya Japan 59 M2 35 08N 136 53E
Nagpur India 58 C3 21 10N 79 12E
Nairn Scotland 31 F2 57 35N 3 53W
Nairn r. Scotland 31 E2 57 28N 4 10W
Nairobi Kenya 67 D4 1 17S 36 50E
Najran Saudi Arabia 61 E2 17 37N 44 40E
Namangan Uzbekistan 56 H2 40 59N 71 41E
Namib Desert Namibia 67 B2 22 00S 14 00E
NAMIBIA 67 B2
Nampo North Korea 59 D3 38 51N 125 10E
Nampula Mozambique 67 D3 15 09S 39 14E
Namur Belgium 49 C4 50 28N 4 52E
Nanchang China 59 C2 28 33N 115 58E
Nancy France 48 G4 48 42N 6 12E
Nanjing China 59 C3 32 03N 118 47E
Nanning China 59 B2 22 50N 108 19E
Nan Shan mts. China 59 A3 38 00N 99 00E
Nantes France 48 C3 47 14N 1 35W
Napier New Zealand 73 D3 39 30S 176 54E
Naples Italy 51 E4 40 50N 14 15E
Napo r. Ecuador/Peru 84 B7 1 30S 74 30W
Narbonne France 48 E1 43 11N 3 00E
Narmada r. India 58 C3 22 00N 78 00E
Narvik Norway 42 K9 68 26N 17 25E
Nassau The Bahamas 79 M3 25 05N 77 20W
Nasser, Lake Egypt 61 D3 22 35N 31 40E
Natal Brazil 84 F7 5 46S 35 15W
Natuna Islands Indonesia 60 B3 3 40N 108 00E
NAURU 5
Ndjamena Chad 66 D4 12 10N 14 59E
Ndola Zambia 67 C3 13 00S 28 39E
Neath Wales 36 D1 51 40N 3 48W
Neath Port Talbot u.a. Wales 36 D1 51 40N 3 45W
Nebraska state USA 79 J5 42 00N 102 00W
Negro r. Argentina 85 C4 39 39S 67 30W
Negro r. Bolivia/Brazil 84 C7 1 00S 62 20W
Negros i. The Philippines 60 D3 10 00N 123 00E
Neiva Colombia 84 B8 2 58N 75 15W
Nelson England 34 C2 53 51N 2 13W
Nelson New Zealand 73 C2 41 30S 172 30E
Nelson r. Canada 78 K6 57 00N 94 00W
Nemuro Japan 59 P3 43 22N 145 36E
Nene r. England 39 E3 52 45N 0 10E
Nen Jiang r. China 59 D4 45 00N 124 00E
NEPAL 58 D3
NETHERLANDS 49 C5/D5
Nevada state USA 79 H4 39 00N 118 00W
Nevers France 48 E3 47 00N 3 09E
Nevis i. St. Kitts and Nevis 79 N2 17 00N 62 30W
Newark USA 79 M5 40 43N 74 11W
Newark-on-Trent England 37 G3 53 05N 0 49W
New Britain i. Papua New Guinea 72 F5 4 45S 150 30E
New Brunswick province Canada 79 N5 47 30N 66 00W
Newburgh Scotland 33 F4 57 18N 2 00W
Newbury England 38 C2 51 24N 1 19W
New Caledonia i. Pacific Ocean 5 22 00S 165 00E
Newcastle Australia 72 F2 32 57S 151 43E
Newcastle Northern Ireland 32 D2 54 12N 5 54W
Newcastle Emlyn Wales 36 C2 52 02N 4 28W
Newcastle-under-Lyme England 37 E3 53 00N 2 14W
Newcastle upon Tyne England 34 D3 54 59N 1 35W
New Cumnock Scotland 33 E3 55 24N 4 12W
Newfoundland i. Canada 79 P5 53 51N 56 56W
Newfoundland and Labrador province Canada 78 P6 56 00N 60 00W
New Galloway Scotland 33 E3 55 05N 4 10W
New Hampshire state USA 79 M5 43 00N 72 00W
New Ireland i. Papua New Guinea 72 F5 3 15S 152 30E
New Jersey state USA 79 M4 40 00N 75 00W
Newman Australia 72 B3 23 22S 119 43E
Newmarket England 39 E3 52 15N 0 25E
New Mexico state USA 79 J4 35 00N 107 00W
New Orleans USA 79 K3 30 00N 90 03W
New Plymouth New Zealand 73 C3 39 04S 174 04E
Newport Isle of Wight England 38 C1 50 42N 1 18W
Newport Telford and Wrekin England 37 E2 52 47N 2 22W
Newport Wales 36 D1 51 35N 3 00W
Newport u.a. Wales 36 D1 51 33N 3 00W
Newquay England 40 B3 50 25N 5 05W
New Quay Wales 36 C2 52 13N 4 22W
Newry Northern Ireland 32 C2 54 11N 6 20W
Newry and Mourne district Northern Ireland 32 C2 54 10N 6 20W
New Siberian Islands Russia 57 Q5 75 00N 145 00E
New South Wales state Australia 72 E2 32 00S 145 00E
Newton Abbot England 40 D3 50 32N 3 36W
Newton Aycliffe England 34 D3 54 37N 1 34W

Newtonmore Scotland 31 E2 57 04N 4 08W
Newton Stewart Scotland 33 E2 54 57N 4 29W
Newtown Wales 36 D2 52 32N 3 19W
Newtownabbey Northern Ireland 32 D2 54 40N 5 54W
Newtownabbey district Northern Ireland 32 D2 54 45N 5 55W
Newtownards Northern Ireland 32 D2 54 36N 5 41W
Newtownhamilton Northern Ireland 32 C2 54 12N 6 35W
Newtownstewart Northern Ireland 32 B2 54 43N 7 24W
New York USA 79 M5 40 40N 73 50W
New York state USA 79 M5 43 00N 76 00W
NEW ZEALAND 73
Ngaoundéré Cameroon 66 D3 7 20N 13 35E
Nguru Nigeria 66 D4 12 53N 10 30E
Nha-Trang Vietnam 60 B4 12 15N 109 10E
Niamey Niger 66 C4 13 32N 2 05E
Nias i. Indonesia 60 A3 1 00N 97 30E
NICARAGUA 79 L2
Nicaragua, Lake Nicaragua 79 L2 11 50N 86 00W
Nice France 48 G1 43 42N 7 16E
Nicobar Islands India 58 E1 8 30N 94 00E
Nicosia Cyprus 60 N1 35 11N 33 23E
Nidd r. England 34 D3 54 05N 1 40W
Nieuwpoort Belgium 39 G2 51 08N 2 45E
NIGER 66 C4
Niger r. Africa 66 B4 11 00N 5 00W
NIGERIA 66 C3
Niigata Japan 59 M2 37 58N 139 02E
Nijmegen Netherlands 49 C4 51 50N 5 52E
Nile r. Sudan/Egypt 61 D3 28 00N 31 00E
Nimba, Mount Guinea/Liberia 66 B3 7 39N 8 30W
Nîmes France 48 F1 43 50N 4 21E
Niort France 48 C3 46 19N 0 27W
Niš Serbia and Montenegro 42 L4 43 20N 21 54E
Niterói Brazil 84 E5 22 54S 43 06W
Nith r. Scotland 33 F3 55 15N 3 50W
Nizhniy Novgorod Russia 56 F3 56 20N 44 00E
Nizhniy Tagil Russia 56 F3 58 00N 59 58E
Norfolk USA 79 M4 36 54N 76 18W
Norfolk co. England 39 E3/F3 52 45N 1 00E
Norfolk Broads geog. reg. England 39 F3 52 45N 1 30E
Norilsk Russia 57 J4 69 21N 88 02E
Normandy geog. reg. France 48 C4/D4 49 00N 0 00
Norrköping Sweden 42 K7 58 35N 16 10E
Northallerton England 35 D3 54 20N 1 26W
Northampton England 38 D3 52 14N 0 54W
Northamptonshire co. England 38 C3/D3 52 20N 1 00W
North Ayrshire u.a. Scotland 32/33 D3/E3 55 30N 5 05W
North Berwick Scotland 33 G4 56 04N 2 44W
North Cape New Zealand 73 C4 34 25S 173 03E
North Carolina state USA 79 M4 36 00N 80 00W
North Channel British Isles 32 D2/3 55 20N 5 50W
North Dakota state USA 79 J5 47 00N 102 00W
North Down district Northern Ireland 32 D2 54 35N 5 50W
North Downs hills England 38/39 D2/E2 51 15N 0 30E
North Dvina r. Russia 56 E4 63 00N 43 00E
North East Lincolnshire u.a. England 35 E2 53 30N 0 10W
Northern Ireland province United Kingdom 32 B2 54 40N 7 00W
NORTHERN MARIANAS 5
Northern Territory Australia 72 D4 19 00S 132 00E
North Esk r. Scotland 31 G1 56 50N 2 50W
North Foreland c. England 39 F2 51 23N 1 27E
North Friesian Islands Germany 49 E6 54 00N 8 00E
North Island New Zealand 73 D3 39 00N 176 00E
NORTH KOREA 59 D4
North Lanarkshire u.a. Scotland 33 F3 55 50N 3 55W
North Lincolnshire u.a. England 35 E2 53 40N 0 40W
North Pole Arctic Ocean 86 90 00N
North Ronaldsay i. Scotland 29 C2 59 23N 2 26W
North Sea Atlantic Ocean 42 G7 57 00N 4 00E
North Shields England 35 D4 55 01N 1 26W
North Uist i. Scotland 30 B2 57 04N 7 15W
Northumberland co. England 33 G3/H3 55 10N 2 00W
Northwest Highlands Scotland 30/31 D2/E3 58 00N 5 00W
North West Somerset u.a. England 38 B2 51 25N 2 50W
Northwest Territories territory Canada 78 H7 64 00N 110 30W
Northwich England 34 C2 53 16N 2 32W
North York Moors England 35 E3 55 22N 0 45W
North Yorkshire co. England 34/35 D3/E3 54 05N 1 20W
Norton England 35 E3 54 08N 0 48W
NORWAY 42 H7/M9
Norwich England 39 F3 52 38N 1 18E
Nottingham England 37 F2 52 58N 1 10W
Nottingham City u.a. England 37 F2 52 58N 1 10W
Nottinghamshire co. England 37 F3/G3 53 20N 1 00W
Nouadhibou Mauritania 66 A5 20 54N 17 01W
Nouakchott Mauritania 66 A4 18 09N 15 58W
Novara Italy 51 B6 45 27N 8 37E
Nova Scotia province Canada 79 N5 45 30N 63 00W
Novaya Zemlya is. Russia 56 F5 74 00N 55 00E
Novgorod Russia 42 N7 58 30N 31 20E
Novokuznetsk Russia 57 J3 53 45N 87 12E
Novosibirsk Russia 56 J3 55 04N 83 05E
Nuevo Laredo Mexico 79 K3 27 39N 99 30W
Nu Jiang (Salween) r. China/Myanmar 58 E4 31 30N 94 00E
Nullarbor Plain Australia 72 C2 30 30S 129 00E
Nunavut territory Canada 78 K7 67 30N 95 30W
Nuneaton England 37 F2 52 32N 1 28W
Nunivak i. USA 78 C6 60 00N 166 00W
Nuremberg Germany 49 F3 49 27N 11 05E
Nuuk (Godthåb) Greenland 78 P7 64 10N 51 40W
Nyala Sudan 61 C2 12 01N 24 50E
Nyasa, Lake (Lake Malawi) Malawi/Mozambique 67 D3 12 00S 35 00E

O

Oahe, Lake USA 79 J5 45 00N 100 00W
Oamaru New Zealand 73 C1 45 06S 170 58E
Ob r. Russia 56 G4 64 00N 65 00E
Oban Scotland 30 D1 56 25N 5 29W
Oberammergau Germany 49 F2 47 35N 11 07E
Obihiro Japan 59 N3 42 56N 143 10E
Obi Islands i. Indonesia 60 D2 1 30S 127 30E
Ochil Hills Scotland 31 F1 56 15N 3 30W
Odense Denmark 42 J7 55 24N 10 25E
Oder r. Europe 49 H5 53 00N 14 30E
Odessa Ukraine 56 D2 46 30N 30 46E
Ogbomoso Nigeria 66 C3 8 05N 4 11E
Ohio r. USA 79 L4 37 07N 89 10W
Ohio state USA 79 L5 40 00N 83 00W
Oiapoque Brazil 84 D8 3 54N 51 46W
Oise r. France 48 E4 49 30N 3 00E
Oita Japan 59 L1 33 15N 131 36E
Okavango Swamp Botswana 67 C3 19 00S 23 00E
Okayama Japan 59 L1 34 40N 133 54E
Okehampton England 40 C3 50 44N 4 00W
Okhotsk, Sea of Russia 57 Q3 56 00N 145 00E
Oki Islands Japan 59 L2 36 05N 133 00E
Oklahoma state USA 79 K4 36 00N 98 00W
Oklahoma City USA 79 K4 35 28N 97 33W
Öland i. Sweden 42 K7 56 45N 51 50E
Olbia Italy 51 B4 40 56N 9 30E
Oldenburg Germany 49 E5 53 08N 8 13E
Oldham England 34 C2 53 33N 2 07W
Oldmeldrum Scotland 31 G2 57 20N 2 20W
Olongapo The Philippines 60 D4 14 49N 120 17E
Olympus, Mt. Greece 42 L4 40 05N 22 21E
Omagh Northern Ireland 32 B2 54 36N 7 18W
Omagh district Northern Ireland 32 B2 54 30N 7 30W
Omaha USA 79 K5 41 15N 96 00W
OMAN 61 F3
Oman, Gulf of Iran/Oman 61 F3 24 30N 58 30E
Omdurman Sudan 61 D2 15 37N 32 29E
Omsk Russia 56 H3 55 00N 73 22E
Onega, Lake l. Russia 56 D4 62 00N 40 00E
Onitsha Nigeria 66 C3 6 10N 6 47E
Ontario province Canada 79 L6 57 00N 85 00W
Ontario, Lake Canada/USA 79 M5 43 45N 78 00W
Oostende Belgium 49 B4 51 13N 2 55E
Oporto Portugal 50 A4 41 09N 8 37W
Oran Algeria 66 B6 35 45N 0 38W
Orange France 48 F2 44 08N 4 48E
Orange r. Southern Africa 67 B2 29 00S 19 00E
Ord r. Australia 72 C4 15 00S 129 00E
Örebro Sweden 42 K7 59 17N 15 13E
Oregon state USA 79 G5 44 00N 120 00W
Orel Russia 56 D3 52 58N 36 04E
Orenburg Russia 56 F3 51 50N 55 00E
Orford Ness c. England 39 F3 52 05N 1 34E
Orinoco r. Venezuela/Colombia 84 C8 6 40N 64 30W
Oristano Italy 51 B3 39 54N 8 36E
Orkney Islands u.a. Scotland 29 B1/C2 59 00N 3 00W
Orléans France 48 D3 47 54N 1 54E
Orne r. France 41 G1/2 49 00N 1 30W
Oronsay i. Scotland 32 C4 56 00N 6 15W
Orsk Russia 56 F3 51 13N 58 35E
Ortles mt. Italy 51 F2 46 31N 10 33E
Oruro Bolivia 84 C6 17 59S 67 08W
Osaka Japan 59 M1 34 40N 135 30E
Osh Kyrgyzstan 56 H2 40 37N 72 49E
Oslo Norway 42 J7 59 56N 10 45E
Osnabrück Germany 49 E5 52 17N 8 03E
Osorno Chile 85 B3 40 35S 73 14W
Ostrava Czech Republic 42 K5 49 50N 18 15E
Osumi Islands Japan 59 L1 30 30N 130 30E
Oswestry England 36 D2 52 52N 3 03W
Otranto Italy 51 G4 40 08N 18 30E
Ottawa Canada 79 M5 45 00N 77 00W
Ouagadougou Burkina 66 B4 12 20N 1 40W
Oubangui r. Central Africa 67 C5 4 00N 21 00E
Oujda Morocco 66 B6 34 41N 1 45W
Oulu Finland 42 M9 65 02N 25 27E
Oundle England 38 D3 52 29N 0 29W
Ouse r. England 35 E2 53 42N 0 41W
Outer Hebrides is. Scotland 30 B1/C3 58 00N 7 00W
Out Skerries is. Scotland 29 E3 60 25N 0 46W
Oviedo Spain 50 C5 43 21N 7 18W
Oxford England 38 C2 51 46N 1 15W
Oxfordshire co. England 38 C2 51 50N 1 25W

P

Pabbay i. Scotland 30 B2 57 47N 7 14W
Pacific Ocean 79 J2
Padang Indonesia 60 B2 1 00S 100 21E
Paderborn Germany 49 E4 51 43N 8 44E
Padstow England 40 C3 50 33N 4 56W
Padua Italy 51 C6 45 24N 11 53E
Paisley Scotland 33 E3 55 50N 4 26W
Pakanbaru Indonesia 60 B3 0 33N 101 30E
PAKISTAN 58 B3
Palau Islands Pacific Ocean 60 E3 7 30N 134 30E
Palawan i. The Philippines 60 C3 10 00N 119 00E
Palembang Indonesia 60 B2 2 59S 104 45E
Palermo Italy 51 D3 38 08N 13 23E
Palma Balearic Islands 50 G3 39 35N 2 39E
Palmerston North New Zealand 73 D2 40 22S 175 37E
Pamirs mts. Asia 58 C4 38 00N 74 00E
Pamplona Spain 50 E5 42 49N 1 39W
PANAMA 79 L1
Panamá Panama 79 M1 8 57N 19 30W
Panama Canal Panama 79 L1 9 00N 80 00W
Panay i. The Philippines 60 D4 11 00N 122 00E
Pantelleria i. Italy 51 D2 36 00N 12 00E
Papa Stour i. Scotland 29 D2 60 20N 1 42W
Papa Westray i. Scotland 29 C2 59 22N 2 54W
PAPUA NEW GUINEA 72 E5
PARAGUAY 84 D5
Paraguay r. South America 84 D5 21 20S 58 20W
Paramaribo Suriname 84 D8 5 52N 55 14W

Paraná Argentina 85 C4 31 45S 60 30W
Paraná r. South America 85 D5 30 00S 59 50W
Paris France 48 E4 48 52N 2 20E
Parma Italy 51 C6 44 48N 10 19E
Parnaíba Brazil 84 E7 2 58S 41 46W
Parrett r. England 41 E4 51 05N 2 55W
Parry Islands Canada 78 J5 75 15N 109 00W
Pasto Colombia 84 B8 1 12N 77 17W
Patagonia geog. reg. Argentina 85 C3 48 00S 70 00W
Patna India 58 D3 25 37N 85 12E
Patra Greece 42 L3 38 14N 21 44E
Pau France 48 C1 43 18N 0 22W
Peace r. Canada 78 H6 57 30N 117 00W
Pechora Russia 43 T9 65 14N 57 18E
Pechora r. Russia 43 S9 66 00N 53 00E
Peebles Scotland 33 F3 55 39N 3 12W
Peel Isle of Man British Isles 33 E2 54 14N 4 42W
Peel Fell sum. Scotland/England 33 G3 55 17N 2 35W
Pegasus Bay New Zealand 73 C2 43 22S 172 55E
Pegu Myanmar 58 E2 17 18N 96 31E
Peipus, Lake Estonia/Russia 42 M7 58 00N 27 45E
Peloponnese geog. reg. Greece 42 L3 37 00N 22 00E
Pelotas Brazil 85 D4 31 45S 52 20W
Pematangsiantar Indonesia 60 A3 2 59N 99 01E
Pembroke Wales 36 C1 51 41N 4 55W
Pembrokeshire u.a. Wales 36 B1/C1 51 50N 5 00W
Peñalara mt. Spain 50 D4 40 51N 3 58W
Penicuik Scotland 33 F3 55 50N 3 14W
Pennines hills England 34 C3 54 30N 2 10W
Pennsylvania state USA 79 M5 41 00N 78 00W
Penrith England 34 C3 54 40N 2 44W
Penryn England 40 B3 50 09N 5 06W
Pentland Firth sd. Scotland 29 B1 58 45N 3 10W
Pentland Hills Scotland 33 F3 55 45N 3 30W
Pen-y-ghent sum. England 34 C3 54 10N 2 14W
Penza Russia 56 E3 53 11N 45 00E
Penzance England 40 B3 50 07N 5 33W
Perm Russia 56 F3 58 01N 56 10E
Perpignan France 48 E1 42 42N 2 54E
Perth Australia 72 B2 31 57S 115 52E
Perth Scotland 31 F1 56 42N 3 28W
Perth and Kinross u.a. Scotland 31 E1/F1 56 45N 3 50W
PERU 84 B6
Perugia Italy 51 D5 43 07N 12 23E
Pescara Italy 51 E5 42 27N 14 13E
Peshawar Pakistan 58 C4 34 01N 71 33E
Peterborough England 38 D3 52 35N 0 15W
Peterborough u.a. England 38 D3 52 40N 0 15W
Peterhead Scotland 31 H2 57 30N 1 46W
Peterlee England 35 D3 54 46N 1 19W
Petersfield England 38 D2 51 00N 0 56W
Petropavlovsk Kazakhstan 56 G3 54 53N 69 13E
Petropavlovsk-Kamchatskiy Russia 57 R3 53 03N 158 43E
Petrozavodsk Russia 42 N8 61 46N 34 19E
Pforzheim Germany 49 E3 48 53N 8 41E
Philadelphia USA 79 M4 40 00N 75 10W
PHILIPPINES 60 D3/4
Phnom Penh Cambodia 60 B4 11 35N 104 55E
Phoenix USA 79 H4 33 30N 112 03W
Piacenza Italy 51 B6 45 03N 9 41E
Pickering England 35 E3 54 14N 0 46W
Pickering, Vale of England 35 E3 54 10N 0 45W
Pietermaritzburg Republic of South Africa 67 D2 29 36S 30 24E
Pilcomayo r. South America 84 C5 24 00S 61 00W
Piraeus Greece 42 L3 37 57N 23 42E
Pisa Italy 51 C5 43 43N 10 24E
Pitcairn Islands Pacific Ocean 4 25 04S 130 06W
Pitlochry Scotland 31 F1 56 43N 3 45W
Piura Peru 84 A7 5 15S 80 38W
Plenty, Bay of New Zealand 73 D3 37 48S 177 12E
Ploieşti Romania 42 M4 44 57N 26 01E
Plovdiv Bulgaria 42 L4 42 08N 24 45E
Plymouth England 40 C3 50 23N 4 10W
Plymouth u.a. England 40 C3 50 24N 4 10W
Plynlimon mt. Wales 36 D2 52 28N 3 47W
Po r. Italy 51 C6/D6 45 00N 12 00E
Pobeda Peak Kyrgyzstan 56 J2 42 25N 80 15E
Pointe Noire tn. Congo 66 D2 4 46S 11 53E
Poitiers France 48 D3 46 35N 0 20E
POLAND 42 K6
Ponta Grossa Brazil 85 D5 25 07S 50 09W
Pontardulais Wales 36 C1 51 43N 4 02W
Pontefract England 35 D2 53 42N 1 18W
Pontianak Indonesia 60 B2 0 05S 109 16E
Pontypool Wales 36 D1 51 43N 3 02W
Pontypridd Wales 36 D1 51 37N 3 22W
Poole England 41 F3 50 43N 1 59W
Poole u.a. England 41 F3 50 45N 1 58W
Poolewe Scotland 30 D2 57 45N 5 37W
Poopo, Lake Bolivia 84 C4 18 30S 67 20W
Popocatepetl vol. Mexico 79 K2 19 02N 98 38W
Porbandar India 58 B3 21 04N 69 40E
Port Askaig Scotland 32 C3 55 51N 6 07W
Port Augusta Australia 72 D2 32 30S 137 48E
Port-au-Prince Haiti 79 M2 18 33N 72 20W
Port Elizabeth Republic of South Africa 67 C1 33 58S 25 36E
Port Ellen Scotland 32 C3 55 39N 6 12W
Port Gentil Gabon 66 C2 0 40S 8 50E
Port Glasgow Scotland 33 E3 55 56N 4 41W
Port Harcourt Nigeria 66 C3 4 43N 7 05E
Port Hedland Australia 72 B3 20 18S 118 35E
Porthmadog Wales 36 C2 52 55N 4 08W
Portknockie Scotland 31 G2 57 42N 2 52W
Portland USA 78 G5 45 32N 122 40W
Portland Bill c. England 41 E3 50 31N 2 27W
Port Lincoln Australia 72 D2 34 44S 135 52E
Port Moresby Papua New Guinea 72 E5 9 30S 147 07E
Portnahaven Scotland 32 C3 55 41N 6 31W
Pôrto Alegre Brazil 85 D4 30 03S 51 10W
Port of Ness Scotland 30 C3 58 29N 6 13W
Port of Spain Trinidad and Tobago 79 N2 10 38N 61 31W

Porto Novo Benin 66 C3 6 30N 2 47E
Pôrto Velho Brazil 84 C7 8 45S 63 54W
Portpatrick Scotland 32 D2 54 51N 5 07W
Port Pirie Australia 72 D2 33 10S 138 02E
Portree Scotland 30 C2 57 24N 6 12W
Port Said Egypt 61 D4 31 17N 32 18E
Portsmouth England 38 C1 50 48N 1 05W
Portsmouth u.a. England 38 C1 50 50N 1 04W
Portsoy Scotland 31 G2 57 41N 2 41W
Port Sudan Sudan 61 D2 19 38N 37 07E
Port Talbot Wales 36 D1 51 36N 3 47W
PORTUGAL 50 A3
Potenza Italy 51 E4 40 38N 15 48E
Potsdam Germany 49 G5 52 24N 13 04E
Powys u.a. Wales 36 D2 52 10N 3 30W
Poyang Hu l. China 59 C2 29 00N 116 30E
Poznań Poland 42 K6 52 25N 16 53E
Prague Czech Republic 42 J6 50 06N 14 26E
Prato Italy 51 C5 43 53N 11 06E
Preston England 34 C2 53 46N 2 42W
Prestwick Scotland 33 E3 55 30N 4 37W
Pretoria Republic of South Africa 67 C2 25 45S 28 12E
Prijedor Bosnia-Herzegovina 51 F6 45 00N 16 41E
Prince Edward Island province Canada 79 N5 46 30N 63 00W
Prince Rupert Canada 78 F6 54 09N 130 20W
Principe i. Gulf of Guinea 66 C3 1 37N 7 27E
Pripet r. Belarus 42 M6 52 00N 28 00E
Provence geog. reg. France 48 F1/G1 44 00N 6 00E
Providence USA 79 M5 41 50N 71 28W
Providence, Cape New Zealand 73 B1 46 01S 166 28E
Prudhoe Bay tn. USA 78 E7 70 05N 148 20W
Pskov Russia 42 M7 57 48N 28 26E
Pucallpa Peru 84 B7 8 21S 74 33W
Puebla Mexico 79 K2 19 03N 98 10W
Puerto Montt Chile 85 B3 41 28S 73 00W
PUERTO RICO 79 N2
Puig Mayor mt. Balearic Islands 50 G3 39 49N 2 47E
Pukekohe New Zealand 73 C3 37 12S 174 54E
Pune India 58 C2 18 34N 73 58E
Punta Arenas Chile 85 B2 53 10S 70 56W
Pusan South Korea 59 D3 35 05N 129 02E
Puy de Sancy mt. France 48 E2 45 32N 2 48E
Pwllheli Wales 36 C2 52 53N 4 25W
Pyongyang North Korea 59 D3 39 00N 125 47E
Pyrénées mts. France/Spain 50 F5 42 50N 0 30E

Q

Qaidam Pendi (Qaidam Basin) China 59 A4 37 30N 94 00E
QATAR 61 F3
Qattara Depression Egypt 61 C3 24 00N 27 30E
Qazvin Iran 61 E4 36 16N 50 00E
Qingdao China 59 D3 36 04N 120 22E
Qinghai Hu l. China 59 B3 37 00N 100 00E
Qiqihar China 59 D4 47 23N 124 00E
Qizil r. Iran 61 E4 36 00N 48 00E
Qom Iran 61 F4 34 39N 50 57E
Quantock Hills England 41 D4 51 05N 3 15W
Québec Canada 79 M5 46 50N 71 15W
Québec province Canada 79 M6 51 00N 75 00W
Queen Charlotte Islands Canada 78 F6 53 30N 131 50W
Queen Elizabeth Islands Canada 78 J8 77 30N 105 00W
Queensland state Australia 72 E3 22 00S 143 00E
Queenstown New Zealand 73 B1 45 02S 168 40E
Quetta Pakistan 58 B4 30 12N 67 00E
Quezon City The Philippines 60 D4 14 39N 121 02E
Qui Nhon Vietnam 60 B4 13 47N 109 11E
Quito Ecuador 84 B7 0 14S 78 30W

R

Raasay i. Scotland 30 C2 57 25N 6 05W
Rabat-Salé Morocco 66 B6 34 02N 6 51W
Rainier, Mount USA 78 G5 46 52N 121 45W
Raipur India 58 D3 21 16N 81 42E
Rajang r. Malaysia 60 C3 2 00N 114 00E
Rakaia r. New Zealand 73 C2 43 00S 172 00E
Ramsey Isle of Man British Isles 33 E2 54 19N 4 23W
Ramsgate England 39 F2 51 20N 1 25E
Randalstown Northern Ireland 32 C2 54 45N 6 19W
Rangitaiki r. New Zealand 73 D3 38 45S 177 00E
Ras Dashen mt. Ethiopia 61 D2 13 15N 38 27E
Rasht Iran 61 E4 37 18N 49 38E
Rathlin Island Northern Ireland 32 C3 55 20N 6 10W
Rathlin Sound Northern Ireland 32 C3 55 20N 6 25W
Rattray Scotland 31 F1 56 36N 3 20W
Ravenna Italy 51 D6 44 25N 12 12E
Rawalpindi Pakistan 58 C4 33 36N 73 04E
Reading England 38 D2 51 28N 0 59W
Reading u.a. England 38 D2 51 27N 0 59W
Recife Brazil 84 F7 8 06S 34 53W
Recklinghausen Germany 49 D4 51 37N 7 11E
Redbridge England 39 E2 51 34N 0 05E
Redcar England 35 D3 54 37N 1 04W
Redcar and Cleveland u.a. England 35 D3/E3 54 30N 1 00W
Redditch England 37 F2 52 19N 1 56W
Rede r. England 33 G3 55 15N 2 20W
Redhill tn. England 38 D2 51 14N 0 11W
Redruth England 40 B3 50 13N 5 14W
Red Sea Middle East 61 D3 25 00N 35 00E
Regensburg Germany 49 G3 49 01N 12 07E
Reggio di Calabria Italy 51 E3 38 06N 15 39E
Reggio nell'Emilia Italy 51 C6 44 42N 10 37E
Regina Canada 78 J6 50 30N 104 38W
Reigate England 38 D2 51 14N 0 13W
Reims France 48 F4 49 15N 4 02E
Remscheid Germany 49 D4 51 10N 7 11E
Renfrewshire u.a. Scotland 33 E3 55 50N 4 40W
Rennes France 48 C4 48 06N 1 40W
Reno USA 79 H4 39 32N 119 49W

REPUBLIC OF IRELAND 28
REPUBLIC OF SOUTH AFRICA 67 C2
Resistencia Argentina 85 D5 27 28S 59 00W
Reutlingen Germany 49 E3 48 30N 9 13E
Reykjavik Iceland 42 B4 64 09N 21 58W
Rhayader Wales 36 D2 52 18N 3 30W
Rhine r. Europe 49 D4 50 30N 7 30E
Rhode Island state USA 79 M5 41 00N 71 00W
Rhodes i. Greece 42 M3 36 00N 28 00E
Rhondda Wales 36 D1 51 40N 3 30W
Rhondda Cynon Taff u.a. Wales 36 D1 51 40N 3 30W
Rhône r. Switzerland/France 48 F2 45 00N 4 50E
Rhum i. Scotland 30 C1/2 57 00N 6 20W
Rhyl Wales 36 D3 53 19N 3 29W
Ribble r. England 34 C2 53 45N 2 30W
Ribeirão Preto Brazil 84 E5 21 09S 47 48W
Richmond England 34 D3 54 24N 1 44W
Richmond USA 79 M4 37 34N 77 27W
Richmond upon Thames England 38 D2 51 28N 0 19W
Riga Latvia 42 L7 56 53N 24 08E
Rimini Italy 51 D6 44 03N 12 34E
Ringwood England 38 C1 50 51N 1 47W
Rio Branco tn. Brazil 84 C7 9 59S 67 49W
Rio de Janeiro tn. Brazil 84 E5 22 53S 43 17W
Rio Grande r. Mexico/USA 79 J3 29 30N 105 00W
Rio Grande tn. Brazil 85 D4 32 03S 52 08W
Ripon England 34 D3 54 08N 1 31W
River Plate Estuary Uruguay/Argentina 85 D4 35 00S 57 00W
Riyadh Saudi Arabia 61 E3 24 39N 46 46E
Roanne France 48 F3 46 02N 4 05E
Robson, Mount Canada 78 H6 53 08N 118 18W
Rochdale England 34 C2 53 38N 2 09W
Rochester England 39 E2 51 24N 0 30E
Rochester USA 79 M5 43 12N 77 37W
Rockhampton Australia 72 F3 23 22S 150 30E
Rocky Mountains Canada/USA 78/79 F7/J4 46 00N 110 00W
Roebourne Australia 72 B3 20 45S 117 08E
ROMANIA 42 L5
Rome Italy 51 D4 41 53N 12 30E
Romsey England 38 C1 50 59N 1 30W
Ronne Ice Shelf Antarctica 86 77 00S 60 00W
Rora Head Scotland 29 B1 58 52N 3 26W
Roraima mt. Guyana 84 C8 5 14N 60 44W
Rosario Argentina 85 C4 33 00S 60 40W
Rosehearty Scotland 31 G2 57 42N 2 07W
Rosenheim Germany 51 D7 47 51N 12 09E
Rossano Italy 51 F3 39 35N 16 38E
Ross Ice Shelf Antarctica 86 80 00S 180 00
Ross of Mull p. Scotland 30 C1 56 20N 6 10W
Ross-on-Wye England 37 E1 51 55N 2 35W
Ross Sea Antarctica 86 75 00S 180 00
Rostock Germany 49 G6 54 06N 12 09E
Rostov-on-Don Russia 56 D2 47 15N 39 45E
Rotherham England 35 D2 53 26N 1 20W
Rothes Scotland 31 F2 57 31N 3 13W
Rothesay Scotland 32 D3 55 51N 5 03W
Rotorua New Zealand 73 D3 38 08S 176 14E
Rotterdam Netherlands 49 C4 51 54N 4 28E
Rouen France 48 D4 49 26N 1 05E
Rousay i. Scotland 29 B2 59 10N 3 00W
Royal Leamington Spa England 37 F2 52 18N 1 31W
Royal Tunbridge Wells England 39 E2 51 08N 0 16E
Royston England 38 D3 52 03N 0 01W
Ruapehu mt. New Zealand 73 D3 39 18S 175 34E
Rubha Hunish c. Scotland 30 C2 57 40N 6 20W
Rugby England 37 F2 52 23N 1 15W
Rugeley England 37 F2 52 46N 1 55W
Rügen i. Germany 49 G6 54 00N 14 00E
Rukwa, Lake Tanzania 67 D4 8 00S 33 00E
Runcorn England 34 C2 53 20N 2 44W
RUSSIA see RUSSIAN FEDERATION
RUSSIAN FEDERATION (RUSSIA) 56/57
Rutland u.a. England 38 D3 52 42N 0 35W
Rutland Water l. England 38 D3 52 40N 0 37W
Ruvuma r. Tanzania/Mozambique 67 D3 11 00S 39 00E
Ruwenzori, Mount Congo Dem. Rep./Uganda 67 C5 0 23N 29 54E
RWANDA 67 C4
Ryazan Russia 56 D3 54 37N 39 43E
Rybinsk Russia 56 D3 58 03N 38 50E
Rybinsk Reservoir Russia 43 P7 59 00N 38 00E
Ryde England 38 C1 50 44N 1 10W
Rye England 39 E1 50 57N 0 44E
Ryukyu Islands Japan 59 D2 27 30N 127 30E

S

Saale r. Germany 49 F4 51 15N 12 00E
Saar r. Germany/France 49 D3 49 15N 6 30E
Saarbrücken Germany 49 D3 49 15N 6 58E
Sabadell Spain 50 G4 41 33N 2 07E
Sabah admin. Malaysia 60 C3 5 00N 115 00E
Sabhā Libya 66 D5 27 02N 14 26E
Sacramento USA 79 G4 38 32N 121 30W
Sado i. Japan 59 M2 38 20N 138 30E
Saffron Walden England 39 E3 52 01N 0 15E
Safi Morocco 66 B6 32 20N 9 17W
Sahara Desert North Africa 66 A5/E5 22 50N 0 00
St. Abb's Head c. Scotland 33 G3 55 55N 2 09W
St. Agnes England 40 B3 50 18N 5 13W
St. Albans England 38 D2 51 46N 0 21W
St. Albans Head c. England 41 E3 50 34N 2 04W
St. Andrews Scotland 31 G2 56 20N 2 48W
St. Anton Austria 49 F2 47 09N 10 17E
St. Austell England 40 C3 50 20N 4 48W
St. Bees Head c. England 34 B3 54 31N 3 39W
St. Bride's Bay Wales 36 B1 51 50N 5 15W
St. Brieuc France 48 B4 48 31N 2 45W
St. Catherine's Point England 38 C1 50 34N 1 18W
St. David's Wales 36 B1 51 53N 5 16W
St. David's Head Wales 36 B1 51 55N 5 19W
St-Denis France 48 E4 48 57N 2 22E
St-Dizier France 48 F4 48 38N 4 58E

Saintes France 48 C2 45 44N 0 38W
St-Étienne France 48 F2 45 26N 4 23E
St. Gallen Switzerland 51 B7 47 25N 9 23E
St. George's Channel British Isles 36 A1/B2 52 00 6 00W
St. Germain France 48 E4 48 55N 2 08E
St. Gotthard Pass Switzerland 49 E2 46 34N 8 3
St. Helena i. Atlantic Ocean 5 15 58S 5 43W
St. Helens England 34 C2 53 28N 2 44W
St. Helier Jersey Channel Islands 41 E2 49 12N 2 07W
St. Ives Cambridgeshire England 38 D3 52 20N 0 05W
St. Ives Cornwall England 40 B3 50 12N 5 29W
Saint John Canada 79 N5 45 16N 66 03W
St. John's Canada 79 P5 47 34N 52 41W
St. John's Point Northern Ireland 32 D2 54 15N 5 40W
St. John's Town of Dalry Scotland 33 E3 55 07N 4 10W
St. Just England 40 B3 50 07N 5 41W
St. Kilda i. Scotland 30 A2 57 49N 8 34W
ST. KITTS AND NEVIS 79 N2
St. Lawrence i. Alaska 78 C7 63 15N 169 50W
St. Lawrence r. Canada 79 N5 47 30N 70 0
St. Lawrence, Gulf of Canada 79 N5 49 00N 62 30W
St-Lô France 41 F2 49 07N 1 05W
St. Louis Senegal 66 A4 16 01N 16 30W
St. Louis USA 79 K4 38 40N 90 15W
ST. LUCIA 79 N2
St. Magnus Bay Scotland 29 D3 60 25N 1 35W
St-Malo France 48 C4 48 39N 2 00W
St. Martin's i. England 40 A2 49 58N 6 17W
St. Mary's i. England 40 A2 49 55N 6 18W
St. Mary's Loch l. Scotland 33 F3 55 29N 3 12W
St. Matthew i. USA 78 B7 60 30N 172 30W
St. Moritz Switzerland 49 F2 46 30N 9 51E
St-Nazaire France 48 B3 47 17N 2 12W
St. Neots England 38 D3 52 14N 0 17W
St-Omer France 39 G1 50 45N 2 15E
St. Paul USA 79 K5 45 00N 93 10W
St. Peter-Port Guernsey Channel Islands 41 E2 49 27N 3 32W
St. Petersburg Russia 56 D3 59 55N 30 25E
Saint Pierre & Miquelon is. Atlantic Ocean 79 P5 47 00N 56 20W
St-Quentin France 48 E4 49 51N 3 17E
St-Tropez France 48 G1 43 16N 6 39E
ST. VINCENT AND THE GRENADINES 79 N2
Sakhalin i. Russia 57 S3 50 00N 143 00E
Salado r. Argentina 85 C5 28 30S 62 30W
Salalah Oman 61 F2 17 00N 54 04E
Salamanca Spain 50 C4 40 58N 5 40W
Salcombe England 40 D3 50 13N 3 47W
Sale England 34 C2 53 26N 2 19W
Salem India 58 C2 11 38N 78 08E
Salerno Italy 51 E4 40 40N 14 46E
Salford England 34 C2 53 30N 2 16W
Salisbury England 38 C2 51 05N 1 48W
Salisbury Plain England 38 C2 51 10N 1 55W
Salta Argentina 84 C5 24 46S 65 28W
Saltash England 40 C3 50 24N 4 12W
Saltcoats Scotland 33 E3 55 38N 4 47W
Saltillo Mexico 79 J3 25 30N 101 00W
Salt Lake City USA 79 H5 40 45N 111 55W
Salvador Brazil 84 F6 12 58S 38 29W
Salween r. see Nu Jiang
Salzburg Austria 42 J5 47 48N 13 03E
Salzgitter Germany 49 F5 52 13N 10 20E
Samar i. The Philippines 60 D4 12 00N 125 00E
Samara Russia 56 F3 53 10N 50 10E
Samarinda Indonesia 60 C2 0 30S 117 09E
Samarkand Uzbekistan 56 G1 39 40N 66 57E
Sambre r. France 48 E5 50 15N 3 50E
SAMOA 4/5
Samsun Turkey 43 P4 41 17N 36 22E
Sana Yemen Republic 61 E2 15 23N 44 14E
Sanaga r. Cameroon 66 D3 5 00N 14 00E
San Antonio r. USA 79 K3 29 00N 97 00W
San Antonio Abad Balearic Islands 50 F3 38 59N 1 19E
San Benito Islands Mexico 79 H3 28 00N 115 00
San Cristobal Venezuela 84 B8 7 46N 72 15W
Sandakan Malaysia 60 C3 5 52N 118 04E
Sanday i. Scotland 29 C2 59 15N 2 30W
San Diego USA 79 H4 32 45N 117 10W
Sandown England 38 C1 50 39N 1 09W
San Francisco USA 79 G4 37 45N 122 27W
San Francisco Javier Balearic Islands 50 F3 38 43 1 26E
San José Costa Rica 79 L1 9 59N 84 04W
San Juan Argentina 85 C4 31 33S 68 31W
San Juan Puerto Rico 79 N2 18 29N 66 08W
Sanliurfa Turkey 43 P3 37 09N 38 49E
San Luis Potosí Mexico 79 J3 22 10N 101 00W
SAN MARINO 51 D5
San Miguel de Tucumán Argentina 85 C5 26 47S 65 15W
San Pedro Sula Honduras 79 L2 15 26N 88 01W
Sanquhar Scotland 33 F3 55 22N 3 56W
San Salvador El Salvador 79 L2 13 40N 89 10W
San Sebastián Spain 50 E5 43 19N 1 59W
Santa Clara Cuba 79 M3 22 25N 79 58W
Santa Cruz Bolivia 84 C6 17 50S 63 10W
Santa Fé Argentina 85 C4 31 00S 60 50W
Santa Marta Colombia 84 B9 11 18N 74 10W
Santander Spain 50 D5 43 28N 3 48W
Santañy Balearic Islands 50 G3 39 22N 3 07E
Santarém Brazil 84 D7 2 26S 54 41W
Santarém Portugal 50 A3 39 14N 8 40W
Santiago Chile 85 B4 33 30S 70 40W
Santiago r. Mexico 79 J3 104 00N 21 30N
Santiago de Cuba Cuba 79 M3 20 00N 75 49W
Santiago del Estero Argentina 85 C5 27 47S 64 15W
Santo Domingo Dominican Republic 79 N2 18 30 69 57W
Santos Brazil 84 E5 23 56S 46 22W
São Francisco r. Brazil 84 E6 13 40S 44 00W

Index 95

Luís Brazil **84 E7** 2 34S 44 16W
...**ne** r. France **48 F3** 47 30N 5 30E
...**Paulo** Brazil **84 E5** 23 33S 46 39W
...**Tomé** i. Gulf of Guinea **66 C3** 0 25N 6 35E
...**O TOMÉ AND PRINCIPE 66 C3**
...**poro** Japan **59 N3** 43 05N 141 21E
...**atov** Russia **56 E3** 51 30N 45 55E
...**awak** admin. Malaysia **60 C3** 1 00N 111 00E
...**dinia** i. Italy **51 B4** 40 00N 9 00E
...**k** Chad **66 D3** 9 08N 18 22E
...**k** i. Channel Islands British Isles **41 E2** 49 26N 2 22W
...**katchewan** province Canada **78 J6** 55 00N 105 00W
...**katchewan** r. Canada **78 J6** 53 30N 105 00W
...**katoon** Canada **78 J6** 52 10N 106 40W
...**ssari** Italy **51 B4** 40 43N 8 34E
...**UDI ARABIA 61 E3**
...**amur** France **48 C3** 47 16N 0 05W
...**va** r. Europe **51 F6** 45 45N 16 15E
...**vel** mt. Northern Ireland **32 B2** 54 49N 7 02W
...**y'un** Yemen Republic **61 E2** 15 59N 48 44E
...**fell Pike** mt. England **34 B3** 54 27N 3 14W
...**lasaig** Scotland **32 C4** 56 04N 6 12W
...**lloway** Scotland **29 D3** 60 08N 1 17W
...**lpay** i. Highland Scotland **30 D2** 57 15N 6 00W
...**lpay** i. Western Isles Scotland **30 C2** 57 15N 6 00W
...**apa** Scotland **29 C1** 58 58N 2 59W
...**apa Flow** sd. Scotland **29 B1** 58 55N 3 00W
...**rba** i. Scotland **32 D4** 56 45N 5 50W
...**rborough** England **35 E3** 54 17N 0 24W
...**arp** i. Scotland **30 B3** 58 02N 7 00W
...**efferville** Canada **78 N6** 54 50N 67 00W
...**elde** r. Netherlands **49 B4/C4** 51 00N 4 00E
...**werin** Germany **49 F5** 53 38N 11 25E
...**lly, Isles of** England **40 A2** 49 56N 6 20W
...**tland** country United Kingdom **28** 56 10N 4 00W
...**ttish Borders** u.a. Scotland **33 F3/G3** 55 30N 2 30W
...**nthorpe** England **35 E2** 53 35N 0 39W
...**ascale** England **34 B3** 54 24N 3 29W
...**ton** England **41 D3** 50 43N 3 05W
...**ttle** USA **78 G5** 47 35N 122 20W
...**dan** France **48 F4** 49 42N 4 57E
...**ne** r. France **48 D4** 49 15N 1 15E
...**kondi Takoradi** Ghana **66 B3** 4 59N 1 43W
...**by** England **35 D2** 53 48N 1 04W
...**kirk** Scotland **33 G3** 55 33N 2 50W
...**lsey Bill** p. England **38 D1** 50 43N 0 48W
...**vas** geog. reg. South America **84 C7** 7 00S 65 00W
...**marang** Indonesia **60 C2** 6 58S 110 29E
...**mipalatinsk** Kazakhstan **56 J3** 50 26N 80 16E
...**ndai** Japan **59 N2** 38 16N 140 52E
...**NEGAL 66 A4**
...**negal** r. Senegal/Mauritania **66 A4** 16 00N 16 00W
...**nnar** Sudan **61 D2** 13 31N 33 38E
...**nnen** England **40 B3** 50 03N 5 42W
...**oul** South Korea **59 D3** 37 32N 127 00E
...**ram** i. Indonesia **60 D2** 3 30S 129 30E
...**ram Sea** Indonesia **60 D2** 3 30S 130 00E
...**RBIA AND MONTENEGRO 42 L4**
...**remban** Malaysia **60 B3** 2 43N 102 57E
...**rov** Russia **56 G3** 59 42N 60 32E
...**tif** Algeria **42 H3** 36 11N 5 24E
...**túbal** Portugal **50 A3** 38 31N 8 54W
...**vastopol** Ukraine **56 D2** 44 36N 33 31E
...**venoaks** England **39 E2** 51 16N 0 12E
...**vern** r. England **37 E1** 51 30N 2 30W
...**verodvinsk** Russia **43 R8** 64 35N 39 50E
...**ville** Spain **50 C2** 37 24N 5 59W
...**ward** USA **78 E7** 60 05N 149 34W
...**YCHELLES 5**
...**ax** Tunisia **66 D6** 34 45N 10 43E
...**urr Mór** r. Scotland **31 D2** 57 42N 5 03W
...**aftesbury** England **41 E4** 51 01N 2 12W
...**akhty** Russia **43 Q5** 47 43N 40 16E
...**anghai** China **59 D3** 31 06N 121 22E
...**anklin** England **38 C1** 50 38N 1 10W
...**annon** r. Republic of Ireland **32 B2** 54 15N 8 00W
...**apinsay** i. Scotland **29 C2** 59 03N 2 51W
...**eerness** England **39 E2** 51 27N 0 45E
...**effield** England **35 D2** 53 23N 1 30W
...**epton Mallet** England **41 E4** 51 12N 2 33W
...**erborne** England **41 E3** 50 57N 2 31W
...**erbrooke** Canada **79 M5** 45 24N 71 54W
...**eringham** England **39 F2** 52 57N 1 12E
...**etland Islands** u.a. Scotland **29 D3** 60 00N 1 15W
...**iant Islands** Scotland **30 C2** 57 55N 6 20W
...**iel** r. Scotland **30 D2** 57 09N 5 25E
...**ijiazhuang** China **59 C3** 38 04N 114 28E
...**ikoku** i. Japan **59 L3** 33 40N 134 00E
...**imonoseki** Japan **59 L3** 33 59N 130 58E
...**ilka** r. Russia **57 M3** 52 00N 118 00E
...**izuoka** Japan **59 M1** 34 59N 138 24E
...**iraz** Iran **61 F3** 29 38N 52 34E
...**rewsbury** England **37 E2** 52 43N 2 45W
...**ropshire** co. England **37 E2** 52 35N 2 25W
...**ymkent** Kazakhstan **56 J2** 42 16N 69 05E
...**berian Lowland** Russia **56 H4** 60 00N 75 00E
...**bu** Malaysia **60 C3** 2 19N 111 50E
...**chuan Basin** see Sichuan Pendi
...**chuan Pendi** (Sichuan Basin) China **59 B3** 32 00N 107 00E
...**cily** i. Italy **51 E2** 37 00N 14 00E
...**di-Bel-Abbès** Algeria **42 F3** 35 15N 0 39W
...**dlaw Hills** Scotland **31 F1/G1** 56 30N 3 10W
...**dmouth** England **41 D3** 50 41N 3 15W
...**egen** Germany **49 E4** 50 52N 8 02E
...**ena** Italy **51 C5** 43 19N 11 19E
...**ERRA LEONE 66 A3**

Sierra Madre mts. Mexico **79 J3** 26 00N 108 00W
Sierra Nevada mts. Spain **50 D3** 37 00N 3 20W
Sierra Nevada mts. USA **79 H4** 37 00N 119 00W
Simferopol Ukraine **56 D2** 44 57N 34 05E
Simplon Pass Europe **49 E2** 46 15N 8 03E
Simpson Desert Australia **72 D3** 25 00S 137 00E
Sinai, Mount Egypt **61 D3** 28 32N 33 59E
SINGAPORE 60 B3
Singkep i. Indonesia **60 B2** 0 20S 104 30E
Sinuiju North Korea **59 D4** 40 04N 124 25E
Siracusa Italy **51 E2** 37 04N 15 19E
Sirte Libya **42 K2** 31 13N 16 35E
Sivas Turkey **43 P3** 39 44N 37 01E
Skegness England **35 F2** 53 10N 0 21E
Skelmersdale England **34 C2** 53 33N 2 48W
Skiddaw mt. England **34 B3** 54 40N 3 08W
Skikda Algeria **42 H3** 36 53N 6 54E
Skipton England **34 C2** 53 58N 2 01W
Skopje FYROM **42 L4** 42 00N 21 28E
Skye i. Scotland **30 C2** 57 20N 6 15W
Sleaford England **35 E1** 53 00N 0 24W
Sleat, Sound of Scotland **30 D2** 57 00N 5 55W
Slieve Donard mt. Northern Ireland **32 D2** 54 11N 5 55W
Slieve Snaght sum. Republic of Ireland **32 B3** 55 12N 7 20W
Slough England **38 D2** 51 31N 0 36W
Slough u.a. England **38 D2** 51 31N 0 36W
SLOVAKIA 42 K5
SLOVENIA 51 E7
Smallwood Reservoir Canada **78 N6** 54 10N 63 50W
Smolensk Russia **56 D3** 54 49N 32 04E
Snaefell mt. Isle of Man British Isles **33 E2** 54 16N 4 28W
Snake r. USA **79 H5** 43 00N 114 00W
Snowdon mt. Wales **36 C3** 53 04N 4 05W
Snowy Mountains Australia **72 E2** 36 24S 148 28E
Soar r. England **37 F2** 52 40N 1 10W
Soay i. Scotland **30 C2** 57 08N 6 14W
Sochi Russia **43 P4** 43 35N 39 46E
Socotra i. Yemen Republic **61 F2** 12 05N 54 10E
Sofia Bulgaria **42 L4** 42 40N 23 18E
Sokhumi Georgia **43 Q4** 43 01N 41 01E
Sokoto Nigeria **66 C4** 13 02N 5 15E
Solapur India **58 C2** 17 43N 75 56E
Solihull England **37 F2** 52 25N 1 45W
Sóller Balearic Islands **50 G3** 39 46N 2 42E
SOLOMON ISLANDS 72 F5
Solway Firth est. Scotland/England **34 B3** 54 40N 3 40W
SOMALIA 67 E5
Somerset co. England **41 D4/E4** 51 10N 3 00W
Somme r. France **48 E4** 49 45N 2 30E
Songhua Hu res. China **59 D4** 43 30N 126 51E
Songhua Jiang r. China **59 D4** 46 30N 129 00E
Songkhla Thailand **60 B3** 7 12N 100 35E
Song-koi r. China/Vietnam **58 B2** 23 00N 102 00E
Sousse Tunisia **66 D6** 35 50N 10 38E
Southampton England **38 C1** 50 55N 1 25W
Southampton u.a. England **38 C1** 50 54N 1 27W
Southampton Island Canada **78 L7** 64 50N 85 00W
South Australia state Australia **72 D3** 27 00S 135 00E
South Ayrshire u.a. Scotland **32/33 D2/E3** 55 20N 4 40W
South Barrule hill Isle of Man British Isles **33 E2** 54 09N 4 40W
South Benfleet England **39 E2** 51 33N 0 34E
South Carolina state USA **79 L4** 34 00N 81 00W
South China Sea Pacific Ocean **60 C4** 15 00N 110 00E
South Dakota state USA **79 J5** 45 00N 102 00W
South Downs hills England **38/39 D1/E** 150 50N 0 45W
Southend Scotland **32 D3** 55 20N 5 38W
Southend u.a. England **39 E2** 51 33N 0 45E
Southend-on-Sea England **39 E2** 51 33N 0 43E
Southern Alps mts. New Zealand **73 C2** 43 07S 171 13E
Southern Ocean 86
Southern Uplands Scotland **33 E3/G3** 55 30N 3 30W
South Esk r. Scotland **31 G1** 56 40N 2 40W
South Georgia i. South Atlantic Ocean **85 F2** 54 00S 36 00W
South Gloucestershire u.a. England **38 B2** 51 30N 2 30W
South Island New Zealand **73 C2** 42 30S 172 00E
SOUTH KOREA 59 D3
South Lanarkshire u.a. Scotland **33 E3/F3** 55 35N 3 55W
South Molton England **40 D4** 51 01N 3 50W
South Orkney Islands Southern Ocean **85 E1** 60 00S 45 00W
South Pole Antarctica **86** 90 00S
Southport England **34 B2** 53 39N 3 01W
South Ronaldsay i. Scotland **29 C1** 58 47N 2 56W
South Shields England **35 D3** 54 59N 1 26W
South Uist i. Scotland **30 B2** 57 20N 7 15W
Southwest Cape New Zealand **73 B1** 48 00S 168 00E
Southwold England **39 F3** 52 20N 1 40E
South Yorkshire co. England **34/35 D2** 53 30N 1 30W
Sovetskaya Gavan Russia **57 Q2** 48 57N 140 16E
SPAIN 50 C3
Spalding England **35 E1** 52 47N 0 10W
Spencer Gulf Australia **72 D2** 34 30S 136 53E
Spennymoor tn. England **34 D3** 54 42N 1 35W
Spey r. Scotland **31 F2** 57 40N 3 10W
Spilsby England **35 F2** 53 11N 0 06E
Spitsbergen i. Arctic Ocean **86** 79 00N 15 00E
Split Croatia **42 K4** 43 31N 16 28E
Spokane USA **78 H5** 47 40N 117 25W
Spurn Head England **35 F2** 53 36N 0 07E
SRI LANKA 58 D1
Srinagar Jammu & Kashmir **58 C4** 34 08N 74 50E
Stafford England **37 E2** 52 48N 2 07W
Staffordshire co. England **37 E2/F2** 52 50N 2 00W

Staines England **38 D2** 51 26N 0 30W
Stamford England **35 E1** 52 39N 0 29W
Stanley Falkland Islands **85 D2** 51 45S 57 56W
Start Bay England **40 D3** 50 16N 3 35W
Start Point England **40 D3** 50 13N 3 38W
Stavanger Norway **42 H7** 58 58N 5 45E
Stavropol Russia **43 Q5** 45 03N 41 59E
Stevenage England **38 D2** 51 55N 0 14W
Stewart Island New Zealand **73 B1** 46 55S 167 55E
Stinchar r. Scotland **32 D3** 55 10N 4 45W
Stirling Scotland **33 F4** 56 07N 3 57W
Stirling u.a. Scotland **33 E4** 56 10N 4 15W
Stockbridge England **38 C2** 51 07N 1 29W
Stockholm Sweden **42 K7** 59 20N 18 05E
Stockport England **34 C2** 53 25N 2 10W
Stockton-on-Tees England **35 D3** 54 34N 1 19W
Stockton-on-Tees u.a. England **35 D3** 54 33N 1 24W
Stoke-on-Trent England **37 E3** 53 00N 2 10W
Stoke-on-Trent u.a. England **37 E3** 53 02N 2 10W
Stonehaven Scotland **31 G1** 56 58N 2 13W
Stornoway Scotland **30 C3** 58 12N 6 23W
Storr, The mt. Scotland **30 C2** 57 30N 6 11W
Stour r. Dorset England **41 E3** 50 50N 2 10W
Stour r. Suffolk/Essex England **39 E2/F2** 51 55N 0 55E
Stourbridge England **37 E2** 52 27N 2 09W
Stourport-on-Severn England **37 E2** 52 21N 2 16W
Stowmarket England **39 F3** 52 11N 1 00E
Stow-on-the-Wold England **38 C2** 51 56N 1 44W
Strabane Northern Ireland **32 B2** 54 49N 7 27W
Strabane district Northern Ireland **32 B2** 54 45N 7 30W
Stralsund Germany **49 G6** 54 18N 13 06E
Strangford Lough inlet Northern Ireland **32 D2** 54 25N 5 45W
Stranraer Scotland **32 D2** 54 55N 5 02W
Strasbourg France **48 G4** 48 35N 7 45E
Stratford-upon-Avon England **37 F2** 52 12N 1 41W
Strathy Point Scotland **31 E3** 58 35N 4 02W
Stroma i. Scotland **31 F3** 58 40N 3 08W
Stromness Scotland **29 B1** 58 57N 3 18W
Stronsay i. Scotland **29 C2** 59 07N 2 37W
Stronsay Firth sd Scotland **29 C2** 59 00N 2 55W
Stroud England **38 B2** 51 45N 2 12W
Strumble Head c. Wales **36 B2** 52 02N 5 04W
Sturt Desert Australia **72 E3** 27 00S 139 00E
Stuttgart Germany **49 E3** 48 47N 9 12E
Sucre Bolivia **84 C6** 19 05S 65 15W
SUDAN 61 C2
Sudbury Canada **79 L5** 46 30N 81 01W
Sudbury England **39 E2** 52 02N 0 44E
Suez Egypt **61 D3** 29 59N 32 33E
Suez Canal Egypt **61 D3** 30 40N 32 20E
Suffolk co. England **39 E3/F3** 52 10N 1 00E
Sula Islands Indonesia **60 D2** 1 50S 124 50E
Sulawesi i. Indonesia **60 D2** 2 00S 120 00E
Sullom Voe inlet Scotland **29 D3** 60 27N 1 20W
Sulu Sea The Philippines/Malaysia **60 D3** 8 00N 120 00E
Sumatra i. Indonesia **60 A3/B2** 0 00 100 00E
Sumba i. Indonesia **60 C2** 10 00S 120 00E
Sumbawa i. Indonesia **60 C2** 8 00S 118 00E
Sumburgh Head Scotland **29 D2** 59 51N 1 16W
Sunda Strait Indonesia **60 B2** 5 50S 105 30E
Sunderland England **35 D3** 54 55N 1 23W
Superior, Lake Canada/USA **79 L5** 48 00N 88 00W
Surabaya Indonesia **60 C2** 7 14S 112 45E
Surakarta Indonesia **60 C2** 7 32S 110 50E
Surat India **58 C3** 21 10N 72 54E
SURINAME 84 D8
Surrey co. England **38 D2** 51 25N 0 14W
Sutton England **38 D2** 51 22N 0 12W
Sutton Coldfield England **37 F2** 52 34N 1 48W
Sutton in Ashfield England **37 F3** 53 08N 1 15W
Suzhou China **59 D3** 31 21N 120 40E
Sverdrup Islands Canada **78 K8** 79 00N 96 00W
Swaffham England **39 E3** 52 39N 0 41E
Swale r. England **34 D3** 54 30N 2 00W
Swanage England **41 F3** 50 37N 1 58W
Swansea Wales **36 D1** 51 38N 3 57W
Swansea u.a. Wales **36 C1** 51 40N 4 05W
SWAZILAND 67 D2
SWEDEN 42 J7/L9
Swilly r. Republic of Ireland **32 B3** 55 00N 7 30W
Swindon England **38 C2** 51 34N 1 47W
Swindon u.a. England **38 C2** 51 32N 1 46W
SWITZERLAND 49 D2/E2
Sydney Australia **72 F2** 33 52S 151 13E
Sydney Canada **79 N5** 46 10N 60 10W
Syktyvkar Russia **43 S8** 61 42N 50 45E
Symbister Scotland **29 D3** 60 21N 1 02W
Syr Darya r. Asia **56 G2** 45 00N 66 00E
SYRIA 61 D4
Szczecin Poland **42 J6** 53 25N 14 32E
Szeged Hungary **42 L5** 46 15N 20 09E

T

Tabora Tanzania **67 D4** 5 01S 32 48E
Tabriz Iran **61 E4** 38 05N 46 18E
Tabuk Saudi Arabia **61 D3** 28 33N 36 36E
Tacoma USA **78 G5** 47 16N 122 30W
Tadcaster England **35 D2** 53 53N 1 16W
Taegu South Korea **59 D3** 35 52N 128 36E
Taejon South Korea **59 D3** 36 20N 127 26E
Tagus r. Spain/Portugal **50 B3** 39 30N 7 00W
Tahat, Mount Algeria **66 C5** 23 18N 5 33E
Taibei Taiwan **59 D2** 25 03N 121 30E
Taif Saudi Arabia **61 E3** 21 15N 40 21E
Tai Hu l. China **59 D3** 31 15N 120 10E
Tain Scotland **31 E2** 57 48N 4 04W
TAIWAN 59 D2
Taiyuan China **59 C3** 37 50N 112 30E
Ta'izz Yemen Republic **61 E2** 13 35N 44 02E
TAJIKISTAN 56 H1
Takamatsu Japan **59 L1** 34 20N 134 01E
Takazze r. Africa **61 D2** 14 00N 38 00E
Talaud Islands Indonesia **60 D3** 4 00N 127 00E
Talca Chile **85 B4** 35 28S 71 40W

Talcahuano Chile **85 B4** 36 40S 73 10W
Tamanrasset Algeria **66 C5** 22 50N 5 28E
Tamar r. England **40 C3** 50 35N 4 15W
Tambov Russia **43 Q6** 52 44N 41 28E
Tampa USA **79 L3** 27 58N 82 38W
Tampere Finland **42 L8** 61 32N 23 45E
Tampico Mexico **79 K3** 22 18N 97 52W
Tamworth England **37 F2** 52 39N 1 40W
Tana, Lake Ethiopia **61 D2** 12 00N 37 20E
Tanga Tanzania **67 D4** 5 07S 39 05E
Tanganyika, Lake East Africa **67 C4** 7 00S 30 00E
Tangier Morocco **50 C2** 35 48N 5 45W
Tangshan China **59 C3** 39 37N 118 05E
Tanimbar Islands Indonesia **60 E2** 7 30S 131 30E
Tanjungkarang Indonesia **60 B2** 5 28S 105 16E
TANZANIA 67 D4
Tapajós r. Brazil **84 D7** 9 10S 56 20W
Taransay i. Scotland **30 B2** 57 55N 7 00W
Táranto Italy **51 F4** 40 28N 17 15E
Tarbat Ness c. Scotland **31 F2** 57 50N 3 45W
Tarbert Argyll and Bute Scotland **32 D3** 55 52N 5 26W
Tarbert Western Isles Scotland **30 C2** 57 54N 6 49W
Tarbes France **48 D1** 43 14N 0 05E
Tarbet Scotland **33 E4** 56 12N 4 43W
Tarim Basin see Tarim Pendi
Tarim He r. China **58 D4** 38 00N 77 00E
Tarim Pendi (Tarim Basin) China **58 D4/5** 39 00N 84 00E
Tarn r. France **48 E1** 44 00N 2 15E
Tarragona Spain **50 F4** 41 07N 1 15E
Tashkent Uzbekistan **56 G2** 41 16N 69 13E
Tasman Bay New Zealand **73 C2** 41 00S 173 14E
Tasmania state Australia **72 E1** 42 00S 143 00E
Tasman Sea Pacific Ocean **7** 39 00S 155 00E
Taunton England **41 D4** 51 01N 3 06W
Taupo New Zealand **73 D3** 38 42S 176 05E
Taupo, Lake New Zealand **73 D3** 38 55S 175 49E
Tauranga New Zealand **73 D3** 37 41S 176 10E
Tavistock England **40 C3** 50 33N 4 08W
Tavy r. England **40 C3** 50 33N 4 05W
Taw r. England **40 C3** 51 00N 4 00W
Tay r. Scotland **31 F1** 56 30N 3 30W
T'bilisi Georgia **56 E2** 41 43N 44 48E
Te Anau, Lake New Zealand **73 B1** 45 13S 167 45E
Tébessa Algeria **42 H3** 35 21N 8 06E
Tees r. England **35 D3** 54 34N 1 22W
Tegucigalpa Honduras **79 L2** 14 05N 87 14W
Tehran Iran **61 F4** 35 40N 51 26E
Teifi r. Wales **36 C2** 52 03N 4 30W
Teign r. England **40 D3** 50 33N 3 40W
Teignmouth England **40 D3** 50 33N 3 29W
Tel Aviv-Yafo Israel **61 D4** 32 05N 34 46E
Telford England **37 E2** 52 42N 2 28W
Telford and Wrekin u.a. England **37 E2** 52 45N 2 30W
Teme r. England **37 E2** 52 20N 2 30W
Temuco Chile **85 B4** 38 45S 72 40W
Tenby Wales **36 C1** 51 41N 4 43W
Tenerife i. Canary Islands **66 A5** 28 15N 16 35W
Tennant Creek tn. Australia **72 D4** 19 38S 134 12E
Tennessee r. USA **79 L4** 36 00N 89 00W
Tennessee state USA **79 L4** 35 00N 87 00W
Teramo Italy **51 D5** 42 40N 13 43E
Teresina Brazil **84 E7** 5 09S 42 46W
Terni Italy **51 D5** 42 34N 12 39E
Terracina Italy **51 D4** 41 17N 13 15E
Test r. England **38 C1** 51 10N 1 30W
Tétouan Morocco **66 B6** 35 34N 5 22W
Teviot r. Scotland **33 G3** 55 30N 2 45W
Tewkesbury England **38 B2** 51 59N 2 09W
Texas state USA **79 K4** 31 00N 100 00W
THAILAND 60 B4
Thailand, Gulf of Asia **60 B4** 10 50N 101 00E
Thame England **38 D2** 51 45N 0 59W
Thame r. England **38 D2** 51 45N 1 00W
Thames r. England **38 D2** 51 30N 0 05E
Thar Desert India **58 C3** 27 30N 72 00E
The Hague Netherlands **49 C5** 52 05N 4 16E
The Needles rocks England **38 C1** 50 39N 1 35W
The Peak mt. England **37 F3** 53 24N 1 51W
The Solent sd. England **38 C1** 50 45N 1 25W
Thessaloníki Greece **42 L4** 40 38N 22 58E
Thetford England **39 E3** 52 25N 0 45E
The Vale of Glamorgan u.a. Wales **36 D1** 52 30N 3 30W
The Wrekin pk. England **37 E2** 52 41N 2 32W
Thimphu Bhutan **58 D3** 27 32N 89 43E
Thionville France **48 G4** 49 22N 6 11E
Thirsk England **35 D3** 54 14N 1 20W
Thornaby-on-Tees England **35 D3** 54 34N 1 18W
Thornhill Scotland **33 F3** 55 15N 3 46W
Three Kings Islands New Zealand **73 C4** 34 10S 172 07E
Thunder Bay tn. Canada **79 L5** 48 27N 89 12W
Thurrock England **39 E2** 51 28N 0 20E
Thurrock u.a. England **39 E2** 51 30N 0 23E
Thurso Scotland **31 F3** 58 35N 3 32W
Thurso r. Scotland **31 F3** 58 35N 3 35W
Tianjin China **59 C3** 39 08N 117 12E
Tibetan Plateau Tibet **58 D4** 33 00N 85 00E
Tibesti mts. Chad **66 D5** 21 00N 17 00E
Tien Shan mts. China **58 C5/D5** 41 00N 76 00E
Tierra del Fuego i. Chile/Argentina **85 C2** 54 00S 67 30W
Tighnabruaich Scotland **32 D3** 55 56N 5 14W
Tigris r. Iraq **61 E4** 34 00N 42 00E
Tijuana Mexico **79 H4** 32 29N 117 10W
Tilburg Netherlands **49 D4** 51 34N 5 05E
Timaru New Zealand **73 C2** 44 24S 171 15E
Timișoara Romania **42 L5** 45 45N 21 15E
Timor i. Indonesia **60 D2** 9 00S 125 00E
Timor Sea Australia **72 C4** 12 30S 127 00E
Tiranë Albania **42 K4** 41 20N 19 49E
Tiree i. Scotland **30 C1** 56 30N 6 55W
Titicaca, Lake Peru/Bolivia **84 C6** 16 00S 69 30W
Tiverton England **40 D3** 50 55N 3 29W
Tivoli Italy **51 D4** 41 58N 12 48E
Tizi Ouzou Algeria **50 H2** 36 44N 4 05E
Toamasina Madagascar **67 E3** 18 10S 49 23E

Tobago i. Trinidad and Tobago 84 C9 11 15N 60 40W
Tobermory Scotland 30 C1 56 37N 6 05W
Tobol r. Russia 56 G3 56 00N 66 00E
Tocantins r. Brazil 84 E7 8 40S 48 00W
TOGO 66 C3
Tokoroa New Zealand 73 D3 38 14S 175 52E
Tokyo Japan 59 M2 35 40N 139 45E
Toledo USA 79 L5 41 40N 83 35W
Toliara Madagascar 67 E2 23 20S 43 41E
Tol'yatti Russia 56 E3 53 32N 49 24E
Tombouctou Mali 66 B4 16 49N 2 59W
Tomsk Russia 56 J3 56 30N 85 05E
Tonbridge England 39 E2 51 12N 0 16E
Tone r. England 41 D4/E4 51 00N 3 00W
Tone r. Japan 59 N2 36 00N 140 00E
TONGA 5
Toowoomba Australia 72 F3 27 34S 151 58E
Torbay England 40 D3 50 27N 3 30W
Torbay u.a. England 40 D3 50 26N 3 30W
Tordesillas Spain 50 C4 41 30N 5 00W
Torfaen u.a. Wales 36 D1 51 45N 3 03W
Toronto Canada 79 M5 43 42N 79 46W
Toros Dağlari mts. Turkey 43 N3 36 00N 33 00E
Torpoint tn. England 40 C3 50 22N 4 11W
Torre del Greco Italy 51 E4 40 46N 14 22E
Torrens, Lake Australia 72 D2 30 58S 137 52E
Torreón Mexico 79 J3 25 34N 103 25W
Torres Strait Australia 72 E5 9 30S 142 00E
Torridge r. England 40 C3 50 55N 4 15W
Tortosa Spain 50 F4 40 49N 0 31E
Tory Island Republic of Ireland 32 A3 55 16N 8 14W
Tory Sound Republic of Ireland 32 A3 55 15N 8 05W
Totnes England 40 D3 50 25N 3 41W
Totton England 38 C1 50 56N 3 06W1 29W
Tottori Japan 59 L2 35 32N 134 12E
Toubkal, Mount Morocco 66 B6 31 03N 7 57W
Touggourt Algeria 66 C6 33 08N 6 04E
Toulon France 48 F1 43 07N 5 55E
Toulouse France 48 D3 43 33N 1 24E
Tours France 48 D3 47 23N 0 42E
Towcester England 38 D3 52 08N 1 00W
Townsville Australia 72 E4 19 17S 146 48E
Toyama Japan 59 M2 36 42N 137 14E
Trabzon Turkey 43 P4 41 00N 39 43E
Trent r. England 37 G3 53 30N 0 50W
Trento Italy 51 C7 46 04N 11 08E
Tresco i. England 40 A2 49 57N 6 20W
Trevose Head England 40 B3 50 33N 5 01W
Trier Germany 49 D3 49 45N 6 39E
Trieste Italy 51 D6 45 39N 13 47E
Trincomalee Sri Lanka 58 D1 8 34N 81 13E
Trinidad i. Trinidad and Tobago 84 C9 11 00N 61 30W
TRINIDAD AND TOBAGO 79 N2
Tripoli Lebanon 61 D4 34 27N 35 50E
Tripoli Libya 66 D6 32 54N 13 11E
Tristan da Cunha i. Atlantic Ocean 5 37 15S 12 30W
Trivandrum India 58 C1 8 30N 76 57E
Tromsø Norway 42 K9 69 42N 19 00E
Trondheim Norway 42 J8 63 36N 10 23E
Troon Scotland 33 E3 55 32N 4 40W
Trowbridge England 38 B2 51 20N 2 13W
Troyes France 48 F4 48 18N 4 05E
Trujillo Peru 84 B7 8 06S 79 00W
Trujillo Spain 50 C3 39 28N 5 53W
Truro England 40 B3 50 16N 5 03W
Tsimlyansk Reservoir Russia 43 Q5 47 30N 43 00E
Tsugaru Channel Japan 59 N3 41 30N 140 30E
Tubruq Libya 66 E6 32 05N 23 59E
Tucson USA 79 H4 32 15N 110 57W
Tula Russia 56 D3 54 11N 37 38E
Tulsa USA 79 K4 36 07N 95 58W
Tunis Tunisia 66 D6 36 50N 10 13E
TUNISIA 66 C6
Turin Italy 51 A6 45 04N 7 40E
Turkana, Lake Ethiopia/Kenya 67 D5 4 00N 36 00E
TURKEY 43 N3
TURKMENISTAN 56 F1
Turks and Caicos Islands West Indies 79 M3 21 30N 72 00W
Turku Finland 42 L8 60 27N 22 15E
Turpan Depression China 58 D5/E5 42 40N 89 30E
Turriff Scotland 31 G2 57 32N 2 28W
TUVALU 5
Túy Spain 50 A5 42 03N 8 39W
Tver Russia 56 D3 56 49N 35 57E
Tweed r. Scotland/England 33 G3 55 45N 2 10W
Tynda Russia 57 N3 55 10N 124 35E
Tyndrum Scotland 31 E1 57 27N 4 44W
Tyne r. England 34 D2 54 58N 2 00W
Tyne and Wear co. England 35 D2 54 55N 1 20W
Tynemouth England 35 D4 55 01N 1 24W
Tyrrhenian Sea Europe 51 C4/D4 40 00N 12 00E
Tyumen Russia 56 G3 57 11N 65 29E
Tywi r. Wales 36 C1 51 45N 3 20W

U
Uberaba Brazil 84 E6 19 47S 47 57W
Uberlândia Brazil 84 E6 18 57S 48 17W
Ucayali r. Peru 84 B7 7 30S 75 00W
Udine Italy 51 D7 46 04N 13 14E
Uele r. Congo Dem. Rep. 67 C5 4 00N 26 00E
Ufa Russia 56 F3 54 45N 55 58E
UGANDA 67 D5
Ujung Pandang Indonesia 60 C2 5 09S 119 28E
Ukhta Russia 43 S8 63 33N 53 44E
UKRAINE 56 D2
Ulan Bator Mongolia 59 L2 47 54N 106 52E
Ulan-Ude Russia 57 L3 51 55N 107 40E
Ullapool Scotland 30 D2 57 54N 5 10W
Ullswater l. England 34 C3 54 35N 2 55W
Ullung Island South Korea 59 L2 37 30N 132 00E
Ulm Germany 49 F3 48 24N 10 00E
Ulva i. Scotland 30 C1 56 30N 6 15W

Ul'yanovsk Russia 56 E3 54 19N 48 22E
Umeå Sweden 42 L8 63 50N 20 15E
Unimak Island USA 78 C6 55 00N 164 00W
UNITED ARAB EMIRATES 61 F3
UNITED KINGDOM 42 F6
UNITED STATES OF AMERICA (USA) 79
Unst i. Scotland 29 E3 60 45N 0 55W
Upper Lough Erne l. Northern Ireland 32 B2 54 15N 7 30W
Uppsala Sweden 42 K7 59 55N 17 38E
Ural Mountains Russia 56 F3 57 00N 60 00E
Ural'sk Kazakhstan 56 F3 51 19N 51 20E
Ure r. England 34 D3 54 20N 2 00W
Urmia, Lake Iran 61 E4 37 20N 45 55E
URUGUAY 85 D4
Uruguay r. South America 85 D5 28 30S 55 30W
Ürümqi China 58 D5 43 43N 87 38E
Usk Wales 36 D1 51 59N 3 35W
Ustinov Russia 56 F3 54 55N 53 11E
Ust-Kut Russia 57 L3 56 48N 105 42E
Utah state USA 79 H4 39 0N 112 00W
Utrecht Netherlands 49 C5 52 05N 5 07E
Utsunomiya Japan 59 M2 36 33N 139 52E
Uttoxeter England 37 F2 52 54N 1 52W
UZBEKISTAN 56 G2

V
Vaal r. Republic of South Africa 67 C2 27 30S 25 00E
Vaasa Finland 42 L8 63 06N 21 36E
Vadodara India 58 C3 22 19N 73 14E
Vaduz Liechtenstein 49 E2 47 08N 9 32E
Valdepeñas Spain 50 D3 38 46N 3 24W
Valdivia Chile 85 B4 39 46S 73 15W
Valence France 48 F2 44 56N 4 54E
Valencia Spain 50 E3 39 29N 0 24W
Valencia Venezuela 84 C9 10 14N 67 59W
Valenciennes France 48 E5 50 22N 3 32E
Valladolid Spain 50 C4 41 39N 4 45W
Valletta Malta 51 E1 35 54N 14 32E
Valognes France 41 F2 49 31N 1 28W
Valparaíso Chile 85 B4 33 05S 71 40W
Vancouver Canada 78 G5 49 13N 123 06W
Vancouver Island Canada 78 G5 48 55N 124 33W
Vänern, Lake Sweden 42 J7 59 00N 13 30E
Van, Lake Turkey 43 Q3 38 33N 42 46E
Vannes France 48 B3 47 40N 2 44W
Vantaa Finland 42 L8 60 20N 24 50E
VANUATU 5
Varanasi India 58 D3 25 20N 83 00E
Varaždin Croatia 51 F7 46 18N 16 21E
Varna Bulgaria 42 M4 43 12N 27 57E
VENEZUELA 84 C8
Venice Italy 51 D6 45 26N 12 20E
Veracruz Mexico 79 K2 19 11N 96 10W
Verdun France 48 F4 49 10N 5 24E
Verkhoyansk Russia 57 P4 67 35N 133 25E
Vermont state USA 79 M5 44 00N 73 00W
Verona Italy 51 C6 45 26N 11 00E
Versailles France 48 E4 48 48N 2 07E
Vesuvius mt. Italy 51 E4 40 49N 14 26E
Veurne Belgium 39 G2 51 04N 2 40E
Vicenza Italy 51 C6 45 33N 11 32E
Vichy France 48 E3 46 07N 3 25E
Victoria Canada 78 G5 48 26N 123 20W
Victoria r. Australia 72 D4 17 00S 131 00E
Victoria state Australia 72 E2 47 00S 143 00E
Victoria Falls Zambia/Zimbabwe 67 C3 17 55S 25 51E
Victoria Island Canada 78 H8 70 45N 115 00W
Victoria, Lake East Africa 67 D4 2 00S 33 00E
Vienna Austria 42 K5 48 13N 16 22E
Vienne r. France 48 D3 46 30N 0 30E
Vientiane Laos 60 B4 17 59N 102 38E
Vierzon France 48 E3 47 14N 2 03E
VIETNAM 60 B4
Vigo Spain 50 A5 42 15N 8 44W
Vijayawada India 58 D2 16 34N 80 40E
Villach Austria 51 D7 46 37N 13 51E
Vilnius Lithuania 42 M6 54 40N 25 19E
Viña del Mar Chile 85 B4 33 02S 71 35W
Vinh Vietnam 60 B4 18 42N 105 41E
Vinnytsya Ukraine 56 C2 49 11N 28 30E
Vinson Massif mts. Antarctica 86 78 02S 22 00W
Vire r. France 41 F2 49 15N 1 05W
Virginia state USA 79 M4 38 00N 77 00W
Virgin Islands West Indies 79 N2 18 00N 64 30W
Visakhapatnam India 58 D2 17 42N 83 24E
Vitória Brazil 84 E5 20 20S 40 18W
Vitoria Spain 50 D5 42 51N 2 40W
Vitsyebsk Belarus 56 D3 55 10N 30 14E
Vladikavkaz Russia 43 Q4 43 02N 44 43E
Vladimir Russia 56 E3 56 08N 40 25E
Vladivostok Russia 57 P2 43 09N 131 53E
Volga r. Russia 56 E3 51 30N 48 00E
Volgograd Russia 56 E2 48 45N 44 30E
Vologda Russia 56 D3 59 10N 39 55E
Volta, Lake Ghana 66 B3 7 30N 0 30W
Vorkuta Russia 56 G4 67 27N 64 00E
Voronezh Russia 56 D3 51 40N 39 13E
Vosges mts. France 48 G4 48 10N 6 50E
Vyrnwy r. Wales 36 D2 52 45N 3 10W
Vyrnwy, Lake Wales 36 D2 52 47N 3 30W

W
Waal r. Netherlands 49 C4 51 50N 5 00E
Waddington, Mount Canada 78 G6 51 22N 125 14W
Wadebridge England 40 C3 50 32N 4 50W
Wadi Halfa Sudan 61 D3 21 55N 31 20E
Wad Medani Sudan 61 D2 14 24N 33 30E
Waiau r. New Zealand 73 B1 46 00S 167 30E
Waigeo i. Indonesia 60 E2 0 15S 130 45E
Waikato r. New Zealand 73 D3 37 30S 175 30E
Wairau r. New Zealand 73 C2 41 30S 174 00E
Waitaki r. New Zealand 73 C2 44 45S 170 30E
Wakatipu, Lake New Zealand 73 B1 45 06S 168 31E

Wakayama Japan 59 M1 34 12N 135 10E
Wakefield England 35 D2 53 42N 1 29W
Wakkanai Japan 59 N4 45 26N 141 43E
Walbury Hill England 38 C2 51 25N 1 35W
Wales country United Kingdom 36 D2 52 40N 3 30W
Wallasey England 34 B2 53 26N 3 03W
Walls Scotland 29 D3 60 14N 1 34W
Walsall England 37 F2 52 35N 1 58W
Waltham Forest England 38 D2 51 36N 0 00
Walton on the Naze England 39 F2 51 51N 1 16E
Walvis Bay tn. Namibia 67 B2 22 59S 14 31E
Wanaka, Lake New Zealand 73 B2 44 28S 169 09E
Wanganui New Zealand 73 D3 39 56S 175 03E
Wanganui r. New Zealand 73 D3 39 30S 175 00E
Wansbeck r. England 33 H3 55 10N 1 50W
Wantage England 38 C2 51 36N 1 25W
Ward Hill Scotland 29 B1 58 54N 3 20W
Ward's Stone hill England 34 C3 54 03N 2 38W
Wareham England 41 E3 50 41N 2 07W
Warley England 37 F2 52 30N 1 59W
Warminster England 38 B2 51 13N 2 12W
Warrenpoint tn. Northern Ireland 32 C2 54 06N 6 15W
Warrington England 34 C2 53 24N 2 37W
Warrington u.a. England 34 C2 53 23N 2 37W
Warsaw Poland 42 L6 52 15N 21 00E
Warwick England 37 F2 52 17N 1 34W
Warwickshire co. England 37 F2 52 15N 1 40W
Washington England 34 D3 54 54N 1 31W
Washington state USA 78 G5/H5 47 00N 120 00W
Washington D.C. USA 79 M4 38 55N 77 00W
Wash, The b. England 35 F1 52 55N 0 10E
Waterlooville England 38 C1 50 53N 1 02W
Water of Luce r. Scotland 32/33 E2 54 55N 4 55W
Watford England 38 D2 51 39N 0 24W
Wau Papua New Guinea 72 E5 7 22S 146 40E
Waveney r. England 39 F3 52 30N 1 30E
Weald, The geog. reg. England 39 E2 51 05N 0 25E
Wear r. England 34 C3 54 40N 2 05W
Weddell Sea Southern Ocean 86 71 00S 40 00W
Wei He r. China 59 B3 34 00N 106 00E
Welland r. England 38 D3 52 30N 0 40W
Wellingborough England 38 D3 52 19N 0 42W
Wellington England 41 D3 50 59N 3 15W
Wellington New Zealand 73 C2 41 17S 174 46E
Wells England 41 E4 51 13N 2 39W
Wells-next-the-Sea England 39 E3 52 58N 0 51E
Welshpool Wales 36 D2 52 40N 3 09W
Welwyn Garden City England 38 D2 51 48N 0 13W
Wenlock Edge hills England 37 E2 52 30N 2 45W
Wensum r. England 39 F3 52 45N 1 05E
Weser r. Germany 49 E5 52 45N 9 00E
West Berkshire u.a. England 38 C2 51 30N 1 17W
West Bromwich England 37 F2 52 31N 1 59W
Westbury England 38 B2 51 16N 2 11W
West Dunbartonshire u.a. Scotland 33 E3/4 56 03N 4 30W
Western Australia state Australia 72 25 00S 123 00E
Western Ghats mts. India 58 C2 15 30N 74 00E
Western Isles u.a. Scotland 30 B2/C3 57 30N 7 00W
WESTERN SAHARA 66 A5
West Friesian Islands Netherlands 49 C5 53 25N 5 15E
West Lothian u.a. Scotland 33 F3 55 50N 3 36W
West Midlands co. England 37 E2/F2 52 28N 1 40W
Weston-super-Mare England 38 B2 51 21N 2 59W
West Palm Beach tn. USA 79 L3 26 42N 80 05W
Westport New Zealand 73 C2 41 45S 171 36E
Westray i. Scotland 29 E4 59 18N 3 00W
Westray Firth sd. Scotland 29 B2/C2 59 15N 3 00W
West Rift Valley Africa 67 D4 0 00 30 00E
West Sussex co. England 38 D1 51 00N 0 25W
West Virginia state USA 79 L4 39 00N 81 00W
West Yorkshire co. England 34/35 D2 53 50N 1 30W
Wetherby England 35 D2 53 56N 1 23W
Weymouth England 41 E3 50 37N 2 25W
Whakatane New Zealand 73 D3 37 58S 176 59E
Whalsay i. Scotland 29 E3 60 22N 0 59W
Whangarei New Zealand 73 C3 35 43S 174 19E
Wharfe r. England 34 C3 54 10N 2 05W
Whernside sum. England 34 C3 54 14N 2 23W
Whitby England 35 E3 54 29N 0 37W
Whitchurch England 37 E2 52 58N 2 41W
Whiteadder Water r. Scotland/England 33 G3 55 50N 2 10W
Whitehaven England 34 B3 54 33N 3 35W
Whitehorse Canada 78 F7 60 41N 135 08W
White Nile r. Sudan 61 D2 11 00N 32 00E
White Sea Russia 42 P9 66 00N 37 30E
Whithorn Scotland 33 E2 54 44N 4 25W
Whitley Bay tn. England 33 H3 55 03N 1 25W
Whitney, Mount USA 79 H4 36 35N 118 17W
Whyalla Australia 72 D3 33 02S 137 35E
Wichita USA 79 K4 37 43N 97 20W
Wick Scotland 31 F3 58 26N 3 06W
Wicklow Republic of Ireland 32 A6 52 59N 6 03W
Widnes England 34 C2 53 22N 2 44W
Wiesbaden Germany 49 E4 50 05N 8 15E
Wigan England 34 C2 53 33N 2 38W
Wigston England 37 F2 52 36N 1 05W
Wigton England 34 B3 54 49N 3 09W
Wigtown Scotland 33 E2 54 52N 4 26W
Wigtown Bay Scotland 33 E2 54 46N 4 20W
Wilhelmshaven Germany 49 E5 53 32N 8 07E
Wilkes Land geog. reg. Antarctica 86 68 00S 105 00E
Wiltshire co. England 38 B2/C2 51 30N 2 00W
Wimborne Minster England 41 F3 50 48N 1 59W
Wincanton England 41 E4 51 04N 2 25W
Winchester England 38 C2 51 04N 1 19W
Windermere England 34 C3 54 23N 2 54W
Windermere l. England 34 C3 54 20N 2 57W
Windhoek Namibia 67 B2 22 34S 17 06E
Windsor England 38 D2 51 29N 0 38W
Windsor & Maidenhead u.a. England 38 D2 51 30N 0 45W

Winnipeg Canada 79 K5 49 53N 97 10W
Winnipeg, Lake Canada 78 K6 53 00N 97 00W
Winsford England 34 C2 53 11N 2 31W
Winterthur Switzerland 49 E2 47 30N 8 45E
Wisbech England 38 E3 52 40N 0 10E
Wisconsin state USA 79 K5 45 00N 90 00W
Wishaw Scotland 33 F3 55 47N 3 55W
Witham England 39 E2 51 48N 0 38E
Witham r. England 35 E2 53 05N 0 10W
Witney England 38 C2 51 48N 1 29W
Wittenberg Germany 49 G5 51 53N 12 39E
Woking England 38 D2 51 20N 0 34W
Wokingham England 38 D2 51 25N 0 51W
Wokingham u.a. England 38 D2 51 24N 0 51W
Wolfsburg Germany 49 F5 52 27N 10 49E
Wollongong Australia 72 F3 34 25S 150 53E
Wolverhampton England 37 E2 52 36N 2 08W
Wonsan North Korea 59 D3 39 07N 127 26E
Woodbridge England 39 F3 52 06N 1 19E
Wooler England 33 G3 55 33N 2 01W
Worcester England 37 E2 52 11N 2 13W
Worcestershire u.a. England 37 E2 52 13N 2 13W
Workington England 34 B3 54 39N 3 33W
Worksop England 37 F3 53 18N 1 07W
Worms Head Wales 36 C1 51 34N 4 20W
Worthing England 38 D1 50 48N 0 23W
Wrangel i. Russia 57 U5 61 30N 180 00
Wrath, Cape Scotland 31 D3 58 37N 5 01W
Wrexham Wales 36 D3 53 03N 3 00W
Wrexham u.a. Wales 36 D3 53 00N 3 00W
Wrocław Poland 42 K6 51 05N 17 00E
Wuhan China 59 C3 30 35N 114 19E
Wuppertal Germany 49 D4 51 15N 7 10E
Würzburg Germany 49 E3 49 48N 9 57E
Wye r. England/Wales 37 E1 51 40N 2 40W
Wymondham England 39 F3 52 34N 1 07E
Wyndham Australia 72 C4 15 28S 128 06E
Wyoming state USA 79 J5 43 00N 108 00W
Wyre r. England 34 C2 53 50N 2 50W

X
Xi r. China 60 C5 23 00N 112 00E
Xi'an China 59 B3 34 16N 108 54E
Xi Jiang r. China 59 C2 22 00N 111 00E
Xingu r. Brazil 84 D7 5 30S 52 40W
Xining China 59 B3 36 35N 101 55E
Xuzhou China 59 C3 34 17N 117 18E

Y
Yakutsk Russia 57 N4 62 10N 129 50E
Yamagata Japan 59 N2 38 16N 140 16E
Yamoussoukro Côte d'Ivoire 66 B3 6 50N 5 20W
Yangon Myanmar 58 E2 16 47N 96 10E
Yangtze r. see Jinsha Jiang (upper course), Chang Jiang (lower course)
Yaoundé Cameroon 66 D3 3 51N 11 31E
Yarlung Zangbo Jiang (Tsangpo) r. China 58 D3 30 00N 90 00E
Yaroslavl Russia 56 D3 57 34N 39 52E
Yarrow Water r. Scotland 33 F3 55 35N 3 05W
Yazd Iran 61 F4 31 54N 54 22E
Yekaterinburg Russia 56 G3 56 50N 60 30E
Yell i. Shetland Islands Scotland 29 D3 60 35N 1 10W
Yellowknife Canada 78 H7 62 30N 114 29W
Yellow Sea China 59 D3 35 30N 122 30E
Yell Sound Scotland 29 D3 60 30N 1 15W
YEMEN REPUBLIC 61 E2
Yenisey r. Russia 57 J4 64 00N 88 00E
Yeo r. England 41 E4 51 00N 2 45W
Yeovil England 41 E3 50 57N 2 39W
Yerevan Armenia 43 Q4 40 14N 44 31E
Yes Tor sum. England 40 C3 50 42N 4 00W
Yogyakarta Indonesia 60 C2 7 48S 110 24E
Yokkaichi Japan 59 M1 34 58N 136 38E
Yokohama Japan 59 M2 35 27N 139 38E
York England 35 D2 53 58N 1 05W
York u.a. England 35 D2 53 56N 1 02W
York, Cape Australia 72 E4 10 41S 142 32E
Yorkshire Wolds hills England 35 E3 54 00N 0 30W
York, Vale of England 35 D3 54 10N 1 20W
Ypres see Ipres
Yucatan Channel Caribbean Sea 79 L3 21 00N 85 00W
Yucatan Peninsula Mexico 79 L2/3 19 00N 89 00W
Yukon r. Canada/USA 78 D7 65 00N 155 00W
Yukon Territory Canada 78 F7 62 00N 135 00W

Z
Zagreb Croatia 42 K5 45 48N 15 58E
Zagros Mountains Iran 61 E4/F3 32 45N 48 50E
Zahedan Iran 61 G3 29 32N 60 54E
Zahlé Lebanon 43 P2 33 50N 35 55E
Zambezi r. Southern Africa 67 D3 17 00S 34 00E
ZAMBIA 67 C3
Zamboanga The Philippines 60 D3 6 55N 122 05E
Zanzibar Tanzania 67 D4 6 10S 39 12E
Zaporizhzhya Ukraine 43 P5 47 50N 35 10E
Zaragoza Spain 50 E4 41 39N 0 54W
Zaria Nigeria 66 C4 11 01N 7 44E
Zarqa Jordan 43 P2 32 04N 36 05E
Zaysan, Lake Kazakhstan 56 J2 48 00N 84 00E
Zealand i. Denmark 49 F6 55 00N 12 00E
Zeebrugge Belgium 49 B4 51 20N 3 13E
Zhambyl Kazakhstan 56 H2 42 50N 71 25E
Zhangjiakou China 59 C3 40 51N 114 59E
Zhangye China 59 B3 38.58N 100.30E
Zhanjiang China 59 C2 21 10N 110 20E
Zhengzhou China 59 C3 34 45N 113 38E
Zhytomyr Ukraine 42 M6 50 18N 28 40E
Zibo China 59 C3 36 51N 118 01E
Ziel, Mount Australia 72 D3 23 30S 132 24E
ZIMBABWE 67 C3
Zinder Niger 66 C4 13 46N 8 58E
Zonguldak Turkey 43 N4 41 26N 31 47E
Zürich Switzerland 49 E2 47 23N 8 33E
Zwickau Germany 49 G4 50 43N 12 30E